THE ENCYCLOPAEDIA OF LIARS AND DECEIVERS

The ENCYCLOPAEDIA *of* LIARS *and* DECEIVERS

ROELF BOLT

REAKTION BOOKS

Published by
REAKTION BOOKS LTD
33 Great Sutton Street
London EC1V 0DX, UK

www.reaktionbooks.co.uk

This book is a revised edition of
Leugenaars & vervalsers: Een kleine encyclopedie van misleiding
published in 2011 by Em. Querido's Uitgeverij BV, Amsterdam

First published by Reaktion Books in 2014

English-language translation by Andy Brown

This publication has been made possible with financial support from the Dutch Foundation for Literature

Printed and bound in Great Britain
by TJ International, Padstow, Cornwall

A catalogue record for this book is available from the British Library

ISBN 978 1 78023 271 3

CONTENTS

INTRODUCTION

ONE: Why?

For many years, everything on display in Room 46 of the Victoria & Albert Museum in London was fake. From the Roman mosaic floor – in reality made by the inmates of a modern women's prison – to the Baroque chandeliers that were younger than the visitors. Nothing was what it pretended to be. The fact that I made the effort to visit Room 46 some years ago suggests that, even then, I had an above average fascination for the art of deception.

I have often wracked my brains to try to unearth the cause of this curiosity. I remember that when I was about eight years old, my mother told me about Han Van Meegeren, and that I found it a strange and interesting story that I didn't fully understand. But did that lead to a genuine fascination? I doubt that very much, as there are plenty of convincing examples to prove the opposite. My mother told me about a woman she knew who saw angels in her back garden. Winged anthropoids appearing in a well-off neighbourhood are also strange, interesting and incomprehensible. Yet I never felt the urge to study them closely.

Perhaps my interest in heinous deeds is based on my own experience. I don't think that is very likely either. Deception is endemic to our society. We live in a world that favours achievers, and who can say that they have never bent the truth a little to create that impression? Next to my keyboard lies a leather pen case that I bought some 25 years ago and which has done me good service. In good light I can still make out a few words scratched into the back. 'Pariochs'? 'Ephors'? I can no longer decipher what I should have known back then but didn't consider important enough to learn. On the inside of the flap, concealed amid nonsensical signs designed to distract the attention of any observant invigilator, I can see the remains of formulae with the help of which I passed my Economic Science II exam. I have never been interested in economic science – I, II or whatever number it was. These are the first words I have written on the subject since that exam. As far as I know, economic science has not suffered from the fact that I pretended to possess knowledge that I did not have, but the qualification that I obtained partly as a result of that pretence has helped me to develop into a more or less useful member of society. Let the reader who is without sin in this respect cast the first stone. No, I don't think my fascination with deception has its origins in my own experience.

Whatever it was that made me go to Room 46, it was the first step in a journey of which this book is, for the moment, the last stop. At the exhibition, I thought I recognized a marble Madonna and Child by master sculptor and forger Alceo Dossena, and my companion took a picture of me with it. Back at my desk I studied with pleasure how I had studied the Dossena with pleasure. The grin and the twinkling eyes in the photograph made me realize that I had found something – oh dear! – which could be the object of that most futile, time-consuming, money-wasting and infuriating pastime: collecting for the sake of it.[1]

What in those early years consisted of little more than keeping the occasional newspaper cutting, evolved into gigabytes of articles and notes and a truckload of books, documentaries, films, court reports, photographs and a small number of cherished objects.

I am pleased to say that writing this book has finally answered the question 'why?' The *condition humaine*, that impossible to grasp phenomenon that has been driving us all to distraction for centuries, is too great a prey for me. But bring the question back to manageable proportions and this microscopic image will show us something of that universal, fascinating phenomenon: how sentient beings live together.

'Principally I hate and detest that animal called man, although I heartily love John, Peter, Thomas, and so forth', wrote Jonathan Swift in 1725 (Woolley, 2001). My viewpoint is the exact opposite: I am not a people-person, but I have a soft spot for 'that animal called man'. A people-person writes about the shortcomings of those around him: John does nothing but complain, Peter can only speak in vague terms while Thomas, who has almost no capacity at all to speak in the abstract, is in any case unable to think about himself.

This book does not offer an abstract theoretical treatment of the phenomenon of deception; instead, it comprises only individual cases. The reasoning for this is that individuals have an inherent and imperative habit of comparing themselves with others, whether they like it or not, and I hope to have been able to avoid many Johns, Peters and Thomases since I have been in a position to choose *a posteriori* from many stories. And I can allow a court of law, a journalist or history to dish out a corrective slap every now and again.

Swift's 'animal called man' is an interesting object. Evolution has endowed him with the capacity to abstract, which makes the species a kind of evolutionary freak. *Homo sapiens* is most likely the only species capable of preparing itself for many evolutionary battles and is therefore able to at least partially sidestep the process of natural selection. Survival of the fittest? Agriculture, baby food and spectacles took us beyond the evolutionary playing field long ago.

This capacity for abstraction makes the species the victim of an unexpected enemy: itself. It allows humans to imagine scenarios that most other species cannot even dream of. Humans can impose an endless variety of tortures upon each other, and this hell is not reserved only for others: *Homo sapiens* is probably the only species to possess sufficient powers of abstraction to commit self-destruction. In less serious cases, this leads to self-overestimation, jealousy and a loss of contact with reality.

Evolution provided man with the power of abstraction because *Homo sapiens* is a social species. As no one can survive alone, the capacity to manipulate others is an advantage. Lying is an excellent tool to achieve this, offering considerable gain for minimum effort. Just how important lying is can be illustrated by a simple example of someone who didn't do it. In September 2010 Sha Zukang, then Under-Secretary-General for Economic and Social Affairs at the United Nations, proposed a toast to UN Secretary-General Ban Ki-Moon during a gathering of high-ranking UN officials in Austria. Sha had already had a couple of drinks and forgot that he was expected to be economical with the truth. 'I know you never liked me, Mr Secretary-General', he said, as he raised his glass. 'Well, I never liked you, either' (*NRC Handelsblad*, September 2010). Colleagues tried to protect Sha from himself by relieving him of his microphone, but in vain. In a speech lasting ten to fifteen minutes the diplomat explained that he had actually never wanted to work for the UN. He was also not happy that the headquarters is in New York, because he doesn't like Americans. Poor Sha. The following morning, lying to keep everyone happy may have seemed a better option.

This important skill is visible at an early age. Research shows that in the eleven to sixteen age group 'adolescents with higher levels of social competence [are] generally better at deceiving than adolescents of lower social competence' (Feldman, 1999). This is an artificial distinction: deception itself is a social skill.[2] 'Childish innocence' offers no escape, because it doesn't exist. 'Babies can start to make moral judgments by the age of six months and may be born with the ability to tell good from bad hard-wired into their brains', says psychologist Paul Bloom (Chittenden, 2010). So what choice do they make? Children of two to three years old are not good at lying but they do use lies as a social tactic. 'By the time they are five or six they actually become very good', says psychologist and expert on lying Robert Feldman (Jarvis, 2010).

The power of abstraction, the ability to imagine alternative realities, is the cause of all the mischief to which this book is dedicated. One person might be convinced that the only thing stopping him having a wonderful life is his partner. Another is certain that he would have been able to cure AIDS if his secondary school had not refused to give him a certificate because it did not share his visionary ideas on chemistry. Yet another believes that he will not be recognized as a great artist until a century after his death.

Since my visit to Room 46 I have started to understand, I hope, liars and forgers a little more. This book takes a look at the *condition humaine*, seen through the lens of deception.[3] Man, clumsy as he is, is a wonderful creature gifted with opposable thumbs. He is also sufficiently endowed to be aware of the tragedy and hopelessness of his own fate. So it's just a matter of time: the husband fakes his own death (or that of his partner); the AIDS guru markets his miracle cure, a concoction of distilled turnip and plantain; the artist forges a Bacon or Hockney to demonstrate his superiority.

This close-up study has produced interesting results. A good example is a psychological experiment that the participants believe is about the quality of sunglasses. The 85 female guinea pigs are each given an authentic pair of Chloé sunglasses, which cost around $300. One group is told that the glasses are fake. They then have to perform a series of tasks, and it emerges that the women who think that they are wearing fake sunglasses cheat more often than those who have been told their sunglasses are authentic. Furthermore, the group with the 'fake' sunglasses believe that the other participants in the experiment are more likely to cheat than the women with the 'real' glasses do. On the basis of the results of the experiment and earlier studies, the researchers conclude that consciously using fake goods changes the user's view of the world. Those who walk around with a fake Dolce & Gabbana handbag over their shoulder experience conflicting feelings. On the one hand, there is the reason they use a fake in the first place (they want to be admired) while, on the other hand, using a fake makes them feel fake themselves. The authors of the study propose that using fake goods leads to a 'fake' self. These are consequences that someone who buys a fake bottle of Joop! perfume from a market trader on a fine summer's evening is most likely unaware of.

BEFORE I EXAMINE the different kinds of deception, a few words on those who are deceived. We tend to think of them as victims who deserve our sympathy, who have suffered harm at the hands of an artful conman or conwoman. Yet it is worth mentioning that not everyone can be deceived. If a deceiver succeeds, this is in most cases at least partly due to the victim, whose behaviour makes the deception easier: 'Stupidity, and its sibling Cupidity' often work in close harmony. This book contains various examples of scientists who believed that their experiments produced the results they expected, even while the actual results did not justify this conclusion. Anyone who asks their lover 'Do you love me?' is wasting their breath. The question implies a desire to hear the truth in the answer, a desire that the lover cannot fulfil if he or she does not love the hopeful poser of the question. The same applies to those who expect to be reborn or to go to some kind of Valhalla when their journey through this earthly vale of tears is over. These scientists, lovers and believers apparently cannot accept the fact that there comes a point when one must admit that this is all there is. To put it bluntly: anyone who can be led to believe they have struck gold has probably been looking for it.

TWO: Types and degrees, definitions and terminology

Lying and forgery are complexes of factual occurrences. Wearing a piece of clothing, opening a door, or the blowing of the wind have no moral connotations. They take place in the physical world, in which no researcher has ever found an ounce of morality. Nor has any researcher ever succeeded in finding a moral viewpoint capable of generating such a physical phenomenon.

Anyone who does not think will often be unable to keep these two worlds separate. Some of the reactions to Hurricane Katrina, which devastated the city of New Orleans at the end of August 2005, are good examples of 'not thinking'. Although Katrina was a purely physical, meteorological phenomenon, some confused souls saw it as 'judgement from God' exacted because New Orleans had five abortion clinics or because it was organizing a Gay Pride parade (Cooperman, 2005). One confused individual even saw the face of an aborted foetus in the satellite images of the storm a case of morality disrupting the way we see the physical world.

The physical and moral worlds are linked only through thought. That lying and forgery normally have negative moral connotations should come as no surprise. If in the physical world there were fewer people being deceived than were doing the deceiving, deception would no longer be worthwhile and would die out. General public opinion is, however, formed by the majority – those who are deceived – so lying and forgery are seen as bad things.

Yet deception does not necessarily carry negative moral connotations. No one would condemn members of the resistance who forged documents during the Nazi occupation of Europe, even though it not only violated regulations announced by the occupiers but also legislation put in place by their own pre-war governments. Nor is there any reason to morally condemn someone who deliberately writes poetic nonsense to expose the ignorance of literary critics, as in the ERN MALLEY case. This forger may have incurred the hatred of the critics, but he fulfilled an extremely useful social function by forcing narrow-minded 'experts' – literary or otherwise – to think about what they do and ask whether this could happen to them too. No right-thinking person would wish the perpetrators of such valuable work to be punished for their 'crimes'.

In this book, I try to avoid moral platitudes. An artist who forges paintings for money is treated the same as one who does it to make a point to their critics. And I can laugh equally heartily about someone who pretends to be someone he is not for material gain as someone who does it for a good practical joke.

There are, of course, exceptions. Anyone who buys a forged Corot is a fool. A few inquiries would have taught the potential buyer that Corot is perhaps the most forged artist ever. For a fraction of the price he paid for the forgery, he could have hired an expert who would have advised him not to buy it. Compare this with cancer patients who seek salvation at the 'clinic' of Patrick Van Eeghem, where the most important work is not performed by staff of flesh and blood but by 'divine guides'. Patients who allow themselves to be seduced by such nonsense are as hare-brained as the buyers of forged Corots, perhaps even more so, given what is at stake for them. Everyone knows that students of medicine have to learn a lot, but that this does not include the use of a divining rod and calling in angels to perform surgery. Institutions such as that of Van Eeghem – from a scientific perspective, the equivalent of a shabby fairground stall – should definitely be avoided.

The difference between the two examples lies in the types and degrees of hope and despair. There is a quantitative difference between the kleptomania of the Corot buyer and the fear of death of the cancer patient. Anyone who prudently decides not to buy a dubious Corot only to hear later that it was authentic, is entitled to sulk for a year or two, as far as I am concerned. And anyone who buys a Corot because of an unbridled compulsion to collect for the sake of it, and it proves to be a forgery, can do the same. But a cancer patient who makes a wrong choice may not even have a year or two. In other words, I would have a drink with the Corot forger. Van Eeghem, however, deserves a good hiding.

This 'moral neutrality with exceptions' does not mean that I devote no attention to motives or ethical frameworks. If that were the case, all that would remain would be a barren list of cases. This book is a look at us, the human race, from a perspective of which I have some knowledge. The bare facts alone are not very interesting. It is often the human elements, why we deceive each other and why we lie or commit forgery with such ineptitude – or such invention – that I hope make the names and facts in this encyclopaedia interesting.

Liars

It seems self-evident when attempting to define what makes a 'liar' or a 'forger' to resort to law. After all, definitions in law books have proved their worth in practice. Many of the cases included in this book describe practices that are not permitted by law, yet a president, South Africa's Thabo Mbeki, who claims that there is no link between HIV and AIDS, and denies his people medical care so that millions die, escapes punishment (see SOUTH AFRICAN SALAD).

As I said, there are countless examples of deception that have been useful rather than caused harm. Anyone who invents a historical character to show that an encyclopaedia is unreliable deserves praise, not punishment. There are also countless examples of improper behaviour that do not merit a mention in this book. If a couple who are drawing a benefit and officially live separately are discovered to be living together by some overzealous pen-pusher at the social services department, that is a pity for the lovers and nice for the taxpayer but is of no interest to me, as a chronicler of deception.

Laws bring order to society, but this book serves a completely different purpose and therefore requires a completely different definition. Inspired by law books, dictionaries and sages, I define 'liar' as follows:

> (1) A person, a group of people, an institution or an enterprise that (2) deliberately and knowingly (3) expresses something that is not true (4) for a purpose formulated or pursued by said person, group, institution or enterprise, (5) where the person, group, institution or enterprise does not belong to the excepted categories (see below), (6) and the person, group, institution or enterprise does not belong to the exceptions, including those cases in which the displayed action or the reaction to it is not of above average interest.

Three phrases in my definition – 'deliberately and knowingly', 'not belonging to the excepted categories' and 'does not belong to the exceptions' – need some elucidation here.

'Deliberately and knowingly' in criterion (2). Regarding this, 'deliberately', anyone who deceives without intending to deceive is spared here. A lunatic in a cocked hat made of newspaper who thinks he is Napoleon Bonaparte does not count. Such pathological actions are not considered deliberate and therefore have no place in this book.

I would like to make two comments, however. First, in the material I considered, it is not always possible to say for certain if the perpetrators really believed in their own delusions or only successfully pretended to. If there is reasonable doubt as to a well-considered expression of intention on the part of a liar or forger, I specify so explicitly (see, for example, MOTHER'S BOY). Second, 'deliberately' does not always require a conscious decision to take people for a ride. A scientist who continues to adhere to a theory despite overwhelming evidence to the contrary does not make a conscious decision to lie, but we should be able to expect a scientist of all people to assess his own ideas critically. If he fails to do this, he consciously takes the risk that the ideas he propagates no longer correspond to reality. And he is responsible for taking that risk.

In his twenties, zoologist J.L.R. Agassiz believed that all animal species on earth were created by God, an opinion shared by the large majority of his colleagues. By the time of his death at 66, Agassiz was about the only zoologist in the United States who still believed this theory; his colleagues had reviewed their standpoints on the basis of Darwin's *On the Origin of Species*.

The only reason a scientist in such a position cannot be seen as 'deliberately' obfuscating reality is that he does not even ask himself the question whether he is doing it deliberately. And he can be held accountable for that.

'Knowingly' indicates that, for example, anyone using a counterfeit banknote without being aware that it is a forgery, is not a deceiver. But here too, a certain degree of common sense can be expected. The average citizen who finds printer's ink on his fingers after putting a banknote in his wallet should ask questions. Anyone who does not ask questions when this would be expected of him is considered to be 'knowing'.

The line between ignorance and unacceptable ignorance is not fixed and depends on a variety of factors. Take the theory of evolution for example again. A zoologist or a milkman who did not believe the theory of evolution in 1858 cannot be accused of ignorance, as the theory was not formulated coherently and convincingly until a year later. If the milkman had still not accepted the theory in 1890, so be it – the corpus of scientific literature on evolution was still being built up and new ideas always need some time to become widely known. A zoologist, however, should have known better. Anyone – milkman or zoologist – who does not accept in 2012 that the theory of evolution is a correct scientific interpretation of the facts is being intentionally stupid. Such people are not just ignorant, they are deliberately ignorant. And they can be held accountable for that. An example of those who fall into this category are the advocates of 'intelligent design' (see PROFESSOR BEHE).

An explanation of criterion 5, 'not belonging to the excepted categories', is also required. It is a sad truth that in today's society, some professions so frequently give an intentionally inaccurate presentation of the facts that these lies can hardly now be qualified as such. We have actually come to expect that anything people in these categories say will regularly be far from the truth. So we rarely respond with indignation when they lie, or if we discover later that they have lied.

The categories of people not considered liars in the sense used in this book are defined next. *Persons, groups of people, institutions or enterprises that make political statements.* If every broken election promise and patently inaccurate presentation of the facts by a politician were to be included in this compilation, it would be much larger than it is now, and leave no space for other categories.

Politicians prefer not to take a position – if they do they can later be held to it and that can be difficult in the daily horse-trading that politicians have to engage in. The problem is however that politicians have to be elected and therefore have to win over voters, which they cannot do without taking positions. Political lies therefore ping-pong between saying what voters want to hear and saying nothing at all.[4]

If a politician is forced to take a position, he or she will choose the one that seems most opportune at that moment, irrespective whether it corresponds with reality. In January 1998, when U.S. president Bill Clinton found himself in trouble because of alleged extramarital shenanigans in the Oval Office with intern Monica Lewinsky, he declared under oath that he had not had a 'sexual relationship', 'sexual encounters' or 'sexual relations' with Lewinsky (Van Natta, 1998). 'I did not have sexual relations with that woman, Miss Lewinsky', he stated.[5]

Another example of political deception is election fraud. Antillean politician Claude Wathey (1926-1998) was a fervent practitioner of cheating in elections. For 40 years he acted as though the island of Sint Maarten were his own personal property. It is alleged that he once described himself as a 'benign dictator' and, as for all his fellow politicians, 'democracy' is simply an obstacle to be approached with pragmatism (Gollin, 1998). Wathey engaged in 'clientelism', a euphemism for corruption. At election time, trucks would drive back and forth, filled with refrigerators, air-conditioning equipment and vacuum cleaners, with which the islanders were encouraged to make the right choice. Once in power, Wathey would use the government apparatus for his own ends. He would also buy people's support by promising them a job in the civil service, an unemployment benefit or cancellation of their utility bills.

There are simpler – and cheaper – ways. Take the parliamentary elections in Egypt in December 2010. As in many dictatorships that like to keep up a grotesque veneer of respectability, the voters were allowed to drop a voting slip in a box. But it didn't matter which name they ticked; after the polling stations closed, the contents of the voting boxes disappeared straight into the recycled paper container. The following morning, the High Elections Commission announced that the ruling NDP had achieved a resounding victory, winning 97 per cent of the seats. The number of seats won by the opposition, the Muslim Brotherhood, had fallen to zero. Completely unnecessarily, the Commission announced that 'the elections as a whole were conducted properly and the results . . . reflect the will of the Egyptian electorate' (Shenker, 2010). The only practical problem with this method is that you need a spokesperson who can make such announcements without bursting into laughter. A variation on this form of fraud is inventing non-existent voters. This is how the President of Zimbabwe, Robert Mugabe (*b.* 1924), secures his election victories. An investigation in January 2011 showed that a relatively large number of voters were between 110 and 120 years old, very unlikely in a country where average life expectancy is 43. A total of no less than 27 per cent of registered voters proved to be no longer living, but they were still managing to vote.

Lying is such an inherent part of politics that it is difficult to speak of 'politicians who lie' since they are just 'politicians who are engaging in politics'.

With a few exceptions (politicians who have adopted extremely nefarious means like actual forgery, for example the Zinovjev Letter), I do not address lying by politicians. However, the fact that I have studied a substantial number of political forgeries says something about the ethics of the profession as a whole.

Persons, groups of people, institutions or enterprises that engage in espionage and/or counter-espionage. Once, while surfing the internet, I found myself on the website of the philosophy department of an American university. Some of the staff members were addressing what appeared to be a rather other-worldly question: are spies allowed to lie?[6] In practical terms this is the same as asking 'Are bakers allowed to bake?' Philosophy, however, has the prerogative of not always having to be practical.

Espionage and counter-espionage are all about obtaining information by deceit, trying to prevent the opposing party from obtaining information and providing false information. All of these activities by definition involve lying. With a few exceptions, I have not studied the activities of spies and counter-spies in this book.

Persons, groups of people, institutions or enterprises that engage in legal business transactions. Every businessman or woman who wishes to sell something will try and make potential buyers believe it is worth twice as much as it really is. Everyone knows, for example, the real estate agent's rhetoric of 'in original condition' or 'many authentic details', which means that if you connect more than two light bulbs the wiring will burst, sparking and crackling, out of the walls and the gas cooker is only of any use if you are contemplating suicide.

As with politics and espionage, lying is part and parcel of commerce. Again, with a few spectacular exceptions, I have not included trade practices in this book.

Persons, groups of people, institutions or enterprises that claim to propagate a religious or some other form of metaphysical standpoint. People who live according to a metaphysical or supernatural conviction have dubious beliefs which have never been corroborated by hard evidence. Catholics and protestants share a number of rather extravagant claims, including rising from the dead, walking on water, the odd appearance by an angel and a burning bush that doesn't burn up.

Here, too, if I were to look at every nonsensical claim from this quarter, this book would be much bigger than it is. And here, too, an inherent characteristic of such beliefs is a clear disregard for reality. In other words, our society accepts not only that which is proven to be true and that which is proven to be false, but also a third category: unproven statements that are made on the basis of a supernatural conviction that takes precedence over our natural convictions.

This sort of unsubstantiated propaganda is not included in this book either, because it is so clearly and easily recognizable as such. Matters of religion and other nebulous phenomena are listed only because of they relate to cases of blatant deception that go a step further than the usual dubious practices (for example, see RELICS).

Persons, groups of people, institutions or enterprises that achieve results in the field of sport. Nandrolone, clenbuterol, stanozolol, tetrahydrogestrinone, Beta-2 agonists, erythropoietin, probenicid, intralipid, bromantane... Anyone who wants to engage in sports at the highest level seems better off these days with an alchemist than a trainer. In recent decades, sporting events have been plagued by 'doping scandals'. Why these sagas are still referred to as 'scandals' is a mystery to me. No one expects any different and, although there is a lot of compulsory bleating on about measures, no one is shocked when they prove to have been evaded yet again. Since cyclist Tom Simpson collapsed and died while riding up Mont Ventoux in 1967 – felled by amphetamines – doping has been an inseparable part of sport.

At the Olympic Games in Montreal nine years later, it became clear just how great a part that is. The Games are usually nothing more than a question of odds: the larger the country, the greater the chance that it will produce excellent athletes, a better Olympic team and therefore win more medals. In Montreal, the United States won 34 gold medals while the German Democratic Republic (GDR, East Germany) – with only 8 per cent of the population of the U.S. – won 40. Of the 13 possible gold medals for swimming, the GDR won 11 and broke eight world records. Admittedly, East Germany did have a programme which tested schoolchildren for potential sporting ability at a young age and sent those with budding talent to a special sports academy. However, it is important to add that these young athletes – around 10,000 in total over a period of three decades – were subject to doping in the form of 'vitamin pills' from the age of about twelve.

Doping has won its spurs; sport without doping is unthinkable. If political pride alone is not incentive enough, there is the value of sponsorship and advertising contracts, broadcasting rights, merchandising and so forth. Together these are worth hundreds of billions of euros a year worldwide. An athlete, team or sponsor that allows results to depend on fair play runs a financial risk that can be limited by doping.

Users and inspectors play a game of cat and mouse. Sports associations have been praising the value of doping tests since the 1970s, but it is always possible to find a doctor (or a vet) who has come up with something new. The scale that doping has achieved became clear in the 1998 Tour de France. After a carer attached to a Belgian team was stopped at the French border carrying a cartload of banned pharmaceutical products, the race was unofficially renamed the 'Tour de Doping'.

Doping is not the only form of deception in sport. Competitions between two or more players can be fixed, so that gamblers can be certain of making a profit from betting on the result. This occurs, for example, in professional football, with not only players, but also trainers, referees and other officials being bribed. Since these are cases of consensual crime, sports associations rarely succeed in proving allegations of fixing. In 2011, after many years of suspicion, it was finally determined conclusively that match fixing occurred in Japan's national sport, sumo wrestling. Wrestlers were regularly paid to lose matches so that opponents could maintain their positions in the highest division of the sport and continue to enjoy the advantages, including tax relief. Prime minister Naoto Kan called it 'a serious betrayal of the people' (Straaten, 2011).

Results can also be affected by ad hoc cheating. During the 2008 Singapore Grand Prix, Formula 1 driver Nelson Piquet Jr flew out of a bend and crashed against a wall. This helped his Renault team-mate Fernando Alonso, who had a chance of winning the World Championship for drivers, to go on and win the race. At first no one suspected foul play. It was only in 2009, when Piquet was dismissed from the Renault team against his will and revealed that the 'accident' had been intentional, that Formula 1's monitoring organization, the Fédération Internationale de l'Automobile, set up an inquiry and imposed sanctions.

A third form of cheating in sport is bribing officials of sports associations. In 2010, for example, Lalit Modi, chairman of the Indian Premier League – a new cricket federation set up only two years previously – and Indian Minister of State for External Affairs, Shashi Tharoor, were forced to resign after allegations that they received and paid out hundreds of millions of euros to ensure that an Indian cricket club was issued with a licence to play in the League. In 2010, the international football association FIFA initiated an inquiry after reporters from the *Sunday Times* provided evidence that senior officials were prepared to accept bribes in exchange for voting for countries hoping to host the World Cup. One official told the reporters that he was only open for negotiations for the 2018 championships as he already had 'other obligations' for 2022 (*NRC Handelsblad*, 18 October 2010).

In this book, 'sport' refers not only to physical activities. Cheating in card games, for example, would fill a (very boring) book in itself. Marked cards, the clandestine use of computers to work out the odds of winning and, in casinos, complex forms of collaboration with other players or even the croupier: there is very little that has never been tried in practice.

Finally, 'does not belong to the exceptions' in criterion 6. The definition I have decided to use in this book covers very many liars who are completely uninteresting. A man who tells his wife that he has worked late so that he can spend a few hours with his mistress qualifies to be called a 'liar'. A man who is due to take his theory driving test and sends a substitute who the authorities cannot distinguish from the candidate himself, fulfils the definition of a 'forger'. But including cases like these would make this book virtually impossible to organize or to write and not particularly interesting to read. The countless forgers of credit cards are not included, for the same reason.

Forgers

A 'forger' is a liar who produces some kind of tangible good that helps him provide a basis for the expression of something that is not true referred to in criterion 3 (see page 14), or who expresses something that is not true as referred to in criterion 3, with the intention of establishing the authenticity of a tangible good produced by him.

Lying and forgery therefore go hand in hand. Pretenders to the throne will often produce a family tree based on their own imagination (which places them in the category of forgers), while vendors of fake Kandinskys will often tell of the exceptional circumstances in which they came into possession of the painting ('I just happened to run into his grandson at JFK, otherwise . . .'), which makes them liars. The difference between a fake and a forgery depends on the nature of the work produced. A new copy of a known painting by Francis Bacon is a forgery, while a completely new painting presented as a hitherto unknown work by Francis Bacon is a fake.

Specific terminology

Some areas of interest develop their own terminology for deception in their field. This is sometimes based on practice and sometimes on theory. An example of the first is numismatics, the study of money. Anyone who forges a banknote that was in circulation 200 years ago will do so for a different reason than someone who forges a note that is currently in use. To distinguish the two, numismatics has its own terminology. It reserves the use of forger for those who fall into the first category, who copy a coin, note or postage stamp that is no longer in circulation (for example, an ancient Greek coin). Those who forge coins, notes or stamps still in circulation are known as counterfeiters (Larson, 2004). For numismatists, forgers and counterfeiters are therefore opposites. In texts that are not specifically about numismatics, however, counterfeiting is seen as a kind of sub-category of forgery.

An example of specific terminology based on theory relates to scientific deception. In addressing this kind of deception, the 'gradations' expounded by Charles Babbage (1791–1871) in his *Reflections on the Decline of Science in England, and on Some of its Causes* (1830) are still widely used today. First there is 'cooking', which involves selecting data at meta level. If, for example, several experiments have been conducted on the issue at hand, only those that endorse the desired conclusion are referred to. Then there is 'trimming', manipulating data down so that it better matches the expected conclusion. Ironing out unexpected and undesired peaks or troughs in graphs are a good example of trimming. Third, there is the scientist's deadly sin of forging. This entails reporting on phenomena that have never been observed. Non-existent test subjects, readings from apparatus, or even complete experiments – all figments of the scientist's imagination.

Given the general and introductory nature of this book, where possible, I do not include specific terminology. When I do use it from time to time, it is intended only to provide a little *couleur locale*.

THREE: When and how much?

On being asked when counterfeiting of money was first invented, the author of a book on numismatic forgery replied: 'About five minutes after coins were invented.' (Larson, 2004) Human beings have an inherently problematic relationship with reality. Take, for example, a homeless woman who is cold and hungry. How is she to escape this situation? She might pretend that she is an exotic princess. A conflict arises between reality and self-interest. Self-interest wins and – at least for a time – the vagrant is delivered from her cares.

Deception – of oneself or of another – is an inseparable part of the human condition. In the words of American columnist H. L. Mencken: 'Lying is not only excusable; it is not only innocent, and instinctive; it is, above all, necessary and unavoidable' (Gilbert, 1988). In this respect, the reply by the author of the book on numismatic forgery ('About five minutes after coins were invented') is not as strange as it seems. Leaving aside romantic reflections on the noble savage, there has probably never been a form of human society without lying and deception.

A well-known, albeit factually inaccurate, view of human history can be found in the Biblical Book of Genesis. The original version of this text was probably written around 1000–500 BC and is based on earlier sources, which I will not examine here. What does this book tell us – not as a divine revelation but as an anthropological document? In Paradise, Eve is seduced into eating the fruit of the Tree of Knowledge by the serpent.[7] This is a clear-cut case of deception. Eve then uses a rather dubious argument to persuade Adam to commit the same misdemeanour. There are as yet only two people in the world, and one cannot resist the temptation to deceive the other.

A few generations later, with Paradise long forgotten, the art of bending the truth has evolved somewhat. Twin brothers Jacob and Esau are squabbling about their birthright. Jacob – the wimp – succeeds in persuading Esau – the macho – to exchange his birthright for a bowl of soup which he offers his brother at just the right moment.

Jacob then receives his father's blessing by appearing at the latter's deathbed dressed in goat's fur and pretending to be Esau, who is big and hairy. This is one of the oldest accounts of false identity.

People have been lying and deceiving each other since time immemorial. Only the ways they go about them change. Cultural developments led to new applications of age-old principles. Election fraud can only occur if there are elections, and taxes have to be imposed before they can be evaded. Some of these developments are so obvious that we hardly stop to think that things were ever different. If we think of forgery, we immediately think of forged paintings, though this variant, with a few exceptions, is no more than 500 years old. To forge the work of a painter, after all, you need to have some concept of what a 'painter' is. And this concept did not reach maturity until the Renaissance. Before then there were no painters in the artistic sense, only anonymous workers who painted for a living. What was imitation before the Renaissance became forgery after the Renaissance.

❋

CRIMINOLOGISTS SPEAK OF 'the dark figure of crime' to refer to the amount of unreported or undiscovered crime: official statistics on criminality, based on crimes reported to the police and then investigated by them, are an inaccurate reflection of all the violations and offences committed each year (Koffman, 1996). These statistics say something about the number of crimes that are known, not the number that take place. Just how serious this discrepancy is, depends on the nature of the crime. The difference between the actual and the reported numbers of bomb attacks and kidnappings is probably very small, especially as such actions are often intended to attract attention. At the other end of the spectrum, the number of reports of bicycles being stolen is most likely completely out of proportion with the actual number of bicycles stolen.

As far as lying and forgery are concerned, the 'dark figure' is most probably of negligible significance in one specific category: deceivers who set a trap for others for ideological reasons, either to harass them or just for the fun of it. Someone, like sculptor David Černý, who makes a work of art for the headquarters of the European Union and says that artists from all member states worked on it, can expect a pat on the back from approving European politicians. But the joke only really has any effect if the artist then reveals that he made up the names of the contributing artists. This sort of deception only works if the trick is revealed.

If a crime is to appear in the statistics, it first has to be recognized as a crime. In the case of most unlawful actions, this is not a problem. An owner sees that his bicycle has been stolen and reports it to the police, and the crime appears in the statistics. This has no consequences for the bicycle thief: the theft was still a success. Lying and forgery, however, are defined by presenting something as true that is not true: 'this painting is real' or 'this mysterious machine can cure you'. This means that criminal forms of lying and forgery differ from other forms of crime in one important respect: a successful lie is accepted as the truth, and a successful forgery is seen as real. The crimes are not unmasked as crimes. The victim does not know that a crime has been committed. In other words, it is the aim of many criminal lies and forgeries to become part of the dark figure of crime. And that makes it difficult to say anything meaningful about the scale of deceit. The comments that follow are therefore intended purely to examine the problem from different aspects.

The first comment relates to scientific fraud in the United States. In 2006, the country had almost 23 million scientists and engineers. The Office of Research Integrity (ORI), the body concerned with investigating scientific fraud, observed 107 cases of scientific misconduct between 1998 and 2007. That would appear to be good news: only one in almost 215,000 scientists is guilty of fraud!

However, many potential offenders have neither the motivation nor the opportunity to commit fraud. A laboratory assistant who simply does his job and closes the lab door when he goes home at five, and whose employment contract nor his happiness depend on the results of the research he is helping with, has no reason to commit fraud. I don't have the figures, but let us assume that this group accounts for half the scientists and engineers referred to above. That puts the odds up to a little over one in 100,000 stepping out of line. Surely that is not so bad either? As readers of this encyclopaedia will discover, science is by no means always willing to hang out its dirty washing in public. Long-term sick leave, early retirement in exchange for disbanding a university commission of inquiry . . . The reader should also bear in mind that the cases included here caused enough fuss to attract the attention of the media. No one knows how many more are solved behind closed doors. This may be a little optimistic, but let's assume that only half of the cases of fraud at universities become known beyond the campus. This pushes the number of offenders up again, to one in 50,000.

The most elusive figure is of course the percentage of fraudulent acts that actually come to light. This is difficult to investigate for a variety of reasons. Not many scientists would answer the question 'Have you ever committed fraud?' with a resounding 'Yes!', not even anonymously. The question is therefore often posed more cautiously, for example by asking: 'Have you ever experienced fraud in your immediate circle . . . ?' This method, however, has the fundamental problem that undiscovered hanky-panky remains undiscovered. A scientist can truthfully answer 'No' to the question, unaware that an immediate colleague is very practiced in the art of deception. *New Scientist* tried this approach in 1976. The survey suffered from other shortcomings: the sample was not representative and there were not enough responses for the data to be statistically reliable. Yet the results are difficult to ignore: a staggering 92 per cent of respondents said that they were aware of one or more cases of intentional falsification (Judson, 2004). There is clearly an enormous discrepancy between this result and the ORI's estimate of 107 cases of lying and forgery among nearly 23 million scientists. Let's take a conservative view and say that half of the cases of scientific fraud are never discovered. That pushes the number of offenders up again, from the original one in 215,000 to one in 25,000.

What we should not underestimate is how great an impact a forger can have. In *Numismatic Forgery*, Charles M. Larson calculates that, in the United States with a population of 280 million, some 2,800 people have the necessary skills and the intent to forge historic coins. This seems a negligible number. But consider what a single numismatic forger can do. He goes into a pawnshop and shakes a few antique coins out of an envelope, giving the pawnbroker the impression that he knows nothing about historic coins. There may be five or six coins, interesting but not spectacular. The pawnbroker offers $50 to $300 for them, and the forger accepts. He pulls the same trick at the next three or four pawnshops, perhaps totting up a dozen in a day. Then he gets on a plane, flies 1,000 km to another town, and goes through the same routine the next day, until he has put in a good week's work. Just think how many coins this man can put into circulation in a year.

Larson ends on a dry note: 'Picture the number of numismatic forgeries that could be introduced in the coin marketplace in a single year by just one professional forger. Now try to picture the effect of two dozen – or about half of what could be expected just for the city of Los Angeles. Now picture 2,800 of them. And you begin to get the picture' (Larson, 2004).

Those who deceive for ideological reasons or for fun may be the most fascinating, but they are in a minority. The lion's share do it for a much more obvious reason: money. It's not difficult for a scientist writing a grant application to use inflated language to describe an imminent breakthrough as a blessing for whole mankind. But anyone who sells imitation medicines or puts an expensive-looking label on cheap wine will have a more difficult time. Reading this book will hopefully make it clear that in this latter category, lumped together as 'fake goods', the market operates almost identically to its bona fide counterpart. Of course, other factors – like their specializations and production capabilities – play a part for individual forgers, but whether they focus collectively on microprocessors or bonbons is determined by the law of supply and demand.

As for the scale of this kind of forgery, the figures vary. In Great Britain alone, the annual turnover of fake designer goods is estimated at £10 billion. Around nine-tenths of this ends up in the hands of organized crime. Between 1998 and 2004, forgery in the European Union increased by 1,000 per cent. In 2008, the Organisation for Economic Co-operation and Development estimated economic losses caused by fake products worldwide at $100 to $200 billion a year. This excludes fake goods consumed in the country where they are produced and piracy through the internet (OECD, 2008). In 2008, almost 180 million fake products were seized in the territory of the European Union.[8] The 'forgery sector' can clearly afford to make such a loss and still turn a profit, otherwise those working in it would have long found something better to do.

Not all cases of faked goods deserve their own entry in this book, as so many of them are so similar. To give you an idea of what kinds of goods are commonly faked, here is a small selection: Fake T-shirts with the Formula 1 logo sold during Grand Prix races. Yonex badminton rackets. Handbags by Gucci, Louis Vuitton, Caroline Herrera, Hermès, Kelly and other top names. Melamine – which is of no value at all – added to pet food as a cheap substitute for high-protein ingredients (see also CRIMINAL MILKMEN). Approximately 90 per cent of fish food produced in China is comprised mainly of filler, including ground birds' feathers. Clothes by Nike, Adidas, Reebok, Lacoste, Yves Saint Laurent and Levi's. In 2007, 20 tons of fake Lipton tea was seized in a Belgian port, around half a million boxes of teabags. Also in 2007, 800,000 fake Oral-B toothbrushes were discovered.

To all these we can add Colgate toothpaste, containing anti-freeze, razor blades by Gillette and Bic, Red Bull energy drink, watches by Rolex, Cartier and so on, Head & Shoulders shampoo, Peugeot hub-caps, Nokia mobile telephones, printer ink cartridges of various brands, Marlboro cigarettes and Monte Cristo cigars, Swiss Army knives, Zippo lighters. And then there are drinks like Bénédictine, Dubonnet, Pernod, Cointreau and Dom Pérignon. In March 2003, a woman in Ireland died after drinking vodka that consisted mainly of methanol. Toys, including figures from the television series *Beyblade*, Barbie dolls, *Star Wars* figures (with dangerous lead levels in the paint), *Pokémon* watches, *Bob the Builder* dolls (so badly stitched that they fell apart spontaneously). Children's clothes, especially T-shirts and pyjamas, made of lightly inflammable or otherwise suspect materials. In May 2007, hundreds of children in Yangzhou (China) developed skin irritations after wearing cheap clothes. The clothes proved to be made from hospital waste. Hair curlers and dryers, of various makes, with unsafe wiring.

The scale of deception and forgery remains partly veiled in mystery, but this shows that it should not be underestimated.

FOUR: Why 150 cases in point?

The encyclopaedic section of this book contains not only liars and forgers. Neither could practice their hobby or profession without their victims. The victims of deception are sometimes mentioned in the entry about the deceiver, but sometimes they themselves are the focus of attention. That may be because they have been the victim of an anonymous deceiver or a series of deceivers not worth mentioning individually, or because it is their names and not those of the perpetrators that will be associated in perpetuity with the deception concerned.

An interesting category of entries are the doubtful cases: lies and forgeries that may be true and real, or items and stories that are considered authentic but which may be fake or fabricated. I have included a number of such cases by way of illustration (see for example JOHN OLSEN).

This book, even with the comprehensive list of sources, does not pretend to deal exhaustively with the subject. I have already given a number of reasons why it is incomplete; cases that fall into the excepted categories or which are exceptions are not included.

A second reason for its incompleteness is that this book deals with relatively few cases on which there is already a large corpus of literature. For this reason, I have not included well-known cases like Piltdown Man or the Turin Shroud. In recent years, scientific fraud and medical quackery have received quite a lot of publicity. This book therefore only contains cases from these 'disciplines' that are particularly interesting, notorious, striking or recent.

A third, practical reason for the limitations of this book is accessibility. I am convinced that the most famed cases of deception and forgery can be found in sources written in languages that I am able to read. However, there must be priceless examples of the deceiver's art to be found in books and newspapers published in Russian, Hebrew, Arabic and all the other languages of the world that I am unfamiliar with.

A fourth and final restriction is size. In researching this book, I studied some 1,400 cases of lying and forgery. I wrote entries for more than 900 of these, a grand total of around 600,000 words. However, economic considerations prevent the publication of a book of this nature: its size alone would price it out of the market. This edition therefore contains a representative selection of 150 cases.

FIVE: Unknown is unloved

The characters that appear in this book fall into three categories. First there are those who have found fame in a different guise than as a liar or forger. These people are liars, deceivers or victims, either within or outside of that guise. ALBERT EINSTEIN achieved fame as a physicist and tampered with scientific data at least once. There is often plenty of information available on this category of deceivers. If they have not been the subject of at least one hefty biography, newspapers and magazines will have written enough about their lives as scientists or writers – and often as deceivers.

Second, there are people who have become famous for being liars or forgers. Of these, HAN VAN MEEGEREN is perhaps the most well-known example. Even those who are not interested in the subject often recognize his name and know that he had ' something to do with art'. And here we see something of the arbitrary nature of fame in this category. Everyone knows why those in the first category, like Einstein and his predecessor, SIR ISAAC NEWTON, are famous. Anyone who contributes a greater understanding of the world we live in deserves our praise: well done, give them a big round of applause, possibly a Nobel Prize. But why is Van Meegeren famous? Compared with ELMYR DE HORY, Van Meegeren produced very little. But how many of those who know the name Van Meegeren have also heard of De Hory? Van Meegeren was extremely rich, but that was because he managed his money very carefully. Van Meegeren was a practiced forger, but an amateur compared to Vasters (see COLLECTING REINHOLD VASTERS) But has anyone ever heard of Vasters?

Famous deceivers are not as well-known as famous physicists or writers. But for anyone who is interested, there is enough information to be found on their lives and work: a good monograph or newspaper reports. The available information on people in this category is, of course, primarily related to their activities as deceivers or forgers.

Thirdly, there are those who do not find fame at all, either as liars or forgers, or as anything else. Their fame extends no further, and often significantly less, than the fifteen minutes that Andy Warhol allowed all of us. If they get into the newspapers, it is because they have done something clever, stupid or voluminous. I am often frustrated when I see an article which does not even take the trouble to state the age or profession of a defendant in court. This first and last report often describes the punishment demanded by the Public Prosecutor, adding that the judge is due to pass sentence 'in two weeks', after which the defendant disappears without trace into obscurity.

It is my intention to look at human activity from a specific perspective. Perhaps I should have spent several weeks searching for the date of birth of that one person sentenced in 1978, but I chose to spend the time searching for another one or two interesting cases. Consequently, this third category of deceivers may get something of a raw deal in this book in terms of their personal details, but not in terms of the attention I devoted to them, and hopefully not of the pleasure they give the reader.

Albert Einstein, older and wiser in 1947.

An
A *to* Z *of* 150 CASE STUDIES

❧ *A* ❧

ADOLF HITLER, SECRET AGENT

The Special Operations Executive was set up by Sir Winston Churchill in the summer of 1940 for the purpose of planting spies and saboteurs behind enemy lines. Creating false identities and documents was core to its mission. Based in Baker Street in London, an address made famous as the home of Sherlock Holmes, the members of the SOE were sometimes called the Baker Street Irregulars, after the gang of street urchins who assisted the famous detective.

In 2002, when some of the records in the SOE archives were unearthed from the archives and put on show, it became clear that the British can hardly do anything without a joke. Among the items was a false passport in the name of Adolf Hitler. According to this travel warrant, Hitler was a Jewish painter seeking to emigrate to Palestine.

ALBERT EINSTEIN COULDN'T FIGURE IT OUT

In 1915 Albert Einstein conducted experiments together with Dutch physicist Wander Johannes de Haas into the magnetic properties of iron. They predicted that the experiments would produce a gyromagnetic factor (which measures the direction and strength of magnetism) of 1, widely accepted as correct at the time. However, two series of experiments came up with factors of 1.45 and then of 1.02. So Einstein and De Haas kept quiet about the outcome of the first series, only publishing the second factor. Later, the gyromagnetic factor proved to be not 1, but 2.

THE ALPHA PROJECT AT THE MCLAB

Scientific research into paranormal phenomena sounds very acceptable in theory. After all, is there anything science cannot investigate? In theory it is acceptable to explore, for example, whether a planned polder in the Netherlands could ever spontaneously run dry after a mass appeal to St Christopher. But, of course, no scientist with a sense of reality would ever take this on.

Research into supernatural phenomena does, however, take place. This entry is about telepathy (extrasensory communication of thoughts or ideas), precognition (knowledge of an event before it occurs, in which the knowledge cannot be traced back to sensually perceived phenomena), psychokinesis (moving objects by mental effort alone) and ESP (extrasensory perception). We are here in the realm of spoon-benders, where many a charlatan earns their daily bread and where there is no place for science.

James S. McDonnell, co-founder of aerospace manufacturer McDonnell Douglas, believed that there was more between heaven and earth than just aeroplanes. In 1979 he donated $500,000 to Washington University in St Louis. The money was intended to set up a laboratory that studied paranormal phenomena. Initially it looked as though the donation would have to be declined, as not a single member of staff felt called upon to lead the lab. Finally, however, physicist Peter R. Philips agreed to take on the job and the donation was accepted.

The McDonnell Laboratory for Psychical Research, which was soon dubbed the McLab, placed an ad in the newspapers, looking for paranormally gifted young people who were willing to be tested. From the more than 300 responses, the researchers chose Steve Shaw and Michael Edwards, who were eighteen and seventeen years old respectively at the time.[1] The choice suggested that the selection procedure was not all it might have been: Shaw and Edwards were young magicians who had applied after consulting with James Randi (the stage name of Randall James Hamilton Zwinge, a professional magician on a mission to expose pseudoscientific nonsense, his Alpha Project).

Shaw and Edwards succeeded in fooling the researchers. The duo's tricks were mostly fairly simple. They would leave a window ajar before they went home and the next morning the lab would be 'mysteriously' strewn with bent cutlery. Clocks jumped around of their own volition and coffee grounds formed mysterious symbols. Often Shaw and Edwards did not even have to use their imagination because an experiment was badly set up. Asked to 'see' a picture in a sealed envelope, for instance, they were left alone with the envelope for several minutes. The envelopes were closed with staples. All they had to do was pry them open, look at the picture, insert the staples back into their original holes and bend them closed. In many of the experiments, Shaw and Edwards had to deliberately make mistakes so as not to get a perfect score, as that would have been too conspicuous. The fact that the researchers became more and more convinced of the duo's paranormal powers was of course not what Randi had in mind, and he repeatedly tried to show the McLab researchers the error of their ways. He spread the rumour that the 'gifted subjects' were frauds. He expressed (justified) criticism of a videotape showing their 'skills'. His efforts had some success, in that the researchers tightened up the measures they took to prevent deception. This made it more difficult for Shaw and Edwards to perform their tricks, but not impossible.

Randi's eventual confession and his recommendation that research into paranormal phenomena should be conducted in the presence of a good magician, however, were counterproductive. From then on, paranormal researchers considered magicians as unsuitable to work with, because they were by definition unsympathetic to the subject-matter.

ARSENIC QUEEN AUDREY HILLEY AND THE TWIN WHO NEVER WAS

Audrey Marie Hilley's fame is based on her prowess as a poisoner. She earned her place in this book, however, by taking on a series of false identities, including twin sisters, while on the run.

In 1975 Hilley's husband Frank died as the result of small doses of arsenic being added to his food and drink over a long period. The cause of death was determined as hepatitis and Frank's life insurance paid out more than $30,000. In 1978 Audrey Hilley took out life insurance for her 18-year-old daughter Carol who, a year later, started suffering from the same stomach pains as her father had. This time the doctors made the right diagnosis: arsenic poisoning.

The diagnosis led the authorities to exhume the bodies of Hilley's husband, her mother Lucille Frazier and her mother-in-law Carrie Hilley. All of the bodies contained abnormally high doses of arsenic, but this could be established as the cause of death only in the case of her late husband. Hilley was charged with the murders but, strangely enough, was released on bail. In November 1979 she disappeared without trace.

In 1980 Hilley, now calling herself Robbi Hannon, met John Homan. They married shortly afterwards and set up home in New Hampshire. From the perspective of a fugitive, Hilley's antics had so far been sensible. Her next step was, however, far from it. Now Robbi Homan, she told her new husband that she had to go to Texas for medical or family reasons (the sources differ on this point). A little later, Homan received a shocking call from Texas with the news that his wife was dead. He need not worry about her body, he was told, as she had donated it to medical science.

If Hilley had wanted to leave her partner, she then clearly changed her mind, for a few months later she turned up on Homan's doorstep, with blonde hair and 20 kilograms lighter. She introduced herself as Terri Hannon, Robbi's twin sister. The twins looked and acted very much alike and, having lost Robbi, Homan started a relationship with Terri. One of his friends, however, proved less gullible and informed the police. They soon guessed Terri Hannon's real identity and arrested her on 12 January 1983 in Brattleboro, Vermont. She was deported to Alabama, where she had committed her crimes. In June of the same year, Hilley was sentenced to life imprisonment plus twenty years, for the murder of her husband Frank and the attempted murder of her daughter Carol. John Homan, her hapless slave, moved to Alabama so that he could visit her in prison.

In February 1987 Hilley was given a three-day pass to meet Homan in a hotel, but she never kept her date. She spent four days drifting around, in cold and rainy weather. When she was found, she was incoherent and covered in mud. Despite being given immediate treatment, she died of hypothermia three or four hours later.

Hilley is buried in the Forest Lawn Gardens cemetery in Anniston, Alabama. She shares her grave with the man she murdered, her husband Frank.

ARTHUR ORTON, TICHBORNE CLAIMANT

On 5 January 1829, Roger Charles Doughty-Tichborne was born in Paris into an aristocratic British family. After a good upbringing and education Tichborne spent some time in the army. He entered into a relationship with his cousin Katherine Doughty, but her family did not allow them to become an engaged because of Roger's excessive drinking. Roger was so upset by this refusal that, like a true romantic, he embarked on a long journey. He crossed the Andes from Chile and, on 20 April 1854 in Rio de Janeiro, boarded the *Bella*, which was bound for Kingston, Jamaica. After leaving port, the ship was never seen again.

After the death of their father in 1862, in the absence of Roger, his younger brother Alfred inherited the title and the property. The mother of the two brothers, Harriette-Felicité, refused to resign herself to the death of her first born and placed advertisements in the world's press, asking for information on his whereabouts. In 1865 her persistence paid off: a butcher called Tomas Castro from the Australian town of Wagga Wagga claimed to actually be Roger Tichborne. So how did he explain his absence of more than ten years? Roger/Tomas claimed that after the *Bella* had overturned, he had managed to survive in a lifeboat and had been rescued by a ship bound for Melbourne. Once there, he had worked as a cattle rancher and butcher, adopting the name Tomas Castro from a man he had met in Chile. Under that name he had married the illiterate Mary Ann Bryant.

Harriette-Felicité asked the butcher to come to Europe. When they finally met on 10 January 1867 in Paris, she recognized her son, but her family thought she had taken leave of her senses. Castro was corpulent and looked nothing like Roger, who was very slimly built. He could not speak French, in which Roger had been fluent, and knew very little of Roger's past. Enquiries by the family in South America and Australia had meanwhile revealed a connection between Castro and a man called Arthur Orton (1834–1898). The wife of one of Castro's former employers in Australia then identified him as Orton. The family of the Chilean whose name he had supposedly adopted did not remember Roger Tichborne, but they did recall Arthur Orton.

When Harriette-Felicité Tichborne died of heart failure in 1868, the family saw the opportunity to take the matter to court. The case dragged on from May 1871 to March 1872, with 100 witnesses to support the claimant Castro and 250 witnesses on the side of the Tichborne family. It also revealed a hitherto unknown juicy titbit: before leaving in 1854 Roger Tichborne was worried that his cousin Katherine Doughty might be pregnant by him and had left a packet with instructions about 'what to do in this eventuality' (McWilliam, 2007). It must have been an unpleasant time for Katherine, who was by then Lady Radcliffe, after making a good marriage.

The case ended in an anticlimax when a Lord Bellew testified that, during their boarding school days, he had given Roger Tichborne a tattoo. In this respect at least, Orton proved to be without blemish.

Orton was charged with perjury. He had no money to defend himself but gathered enough funds to enlist the support of maverick Irish lawyer Edward Kenealy. Mainly thanks to Kenealy the case continued, running from April 1873 to February 1874, becoming the longest trial in English legal history at the time. Kenealy managed to arouse such hatred among the magistrates and the members of the jury that the final judgement against Orton can probably in no small measure be attributed to his lawyer.[2] Orton was given two consecutive sentences of seven years and Kenealy was disbarred.

In the years that followed, the former lawyer turned this to his advantage. As a defender of the common people, who to some extent identified with Orton, he managed to win a seat in Parliament in 1875 (Kenealy was no great success as an MP, either: the only bill he introduced that I know of was rejected with three votes in favour and 433 against).

On 11 October 1884 Orton was given provisional release. By then Kenealy had been dead for four years and, as Orton took no interest in his political heritage, he signed up with a theatrical agent. He performed in music halls and circuses and ventured on a tour of America, which he started as a lecturer and ended as a barman. Destitute, he returned to England. As his illiterate wife had deserted him while he was in prison, he was free to marry a singer called Lily Enever. For some time they tried to live on his fame, but without success.

In 1895, presumably for financial reasons, Orton signed a confession, published in the tabloid newspaper *The People*, admitting that he was not Roger Tichborne, but Arthur Orton. As soon as he got the fee, he retracted the confession and used the money to set up a tobacconist's shop. The business collapsed and it will come as no surprise that when he died on 1 April 1898, Orton was destitute.

In an act of generosity, the Tichborne family gave permission for Arthur to be buried with the name 'Sir Roger Tichborne' on his coffin. Perhaps they hoped this would rid them of the claimant once and for all. But their hopes proved fruitless. In 1912, when the next heir, Joseph Tichborne, was about to be married, Teresa, one of Arthur Orton's daughters, attempted to shoot him. The marriage eventually took place the following year, with Teresa safely behind bars for six months for sending threatening letters to Joseph and his mother.

ASHLEY TODD AND SOMETHING ODD

In 2008 the battle was raging between the campaign machines of U.S. Republican presidential candidate John McCain and his rival, Democrat Barack Obama. As usual in American political campaigns no means were considered too mean, as long as you didn't get caught. But Ashley Todd was one ardent campaigner that McCain could have done without.

The twenty-year-old volunteer claimed that she had been attacked and robbed in Pittsburgh near an ATM. An Obama supporter had taken offence at Todd's McCain bumper sticker and had assaulted her, scratching the letter 'B' for Barack into her cheek so that she would be a walking advertisement for the Democrats.

The police were not convinced by Todd's story: why would an Obama supporter scratch a letter B into her face, especially as the B was *in reverse*? It didn't make any sense. In the end Todd confessed: the truth was that she had done it herself, at home, in front of a mirror. If nothing else became clear from this confession, it did at least explain the reversed letter.

Todd was sentenced to nine months' probation and 50 hours of community service. She was also ordered to participate in a probation programme for first-time offenders. Maybe she got another B.

ASTROTURF – PLANTED OPINIONS

The term 'grassroots' is primarily used in politics when a policy comes up against great public resistance. Policy-makers are accused of being out of touch with grassroots opinions. Since these opinions can influence policy, it can be worthwhile to falsify them. In the United States, special bodies to disseminate fake grassroots opinions have experienced something of a boom. As they have no roots, they are likened to artificial grass, or 'astroturf'.

Creating astroturf bodies usually follows a similar path. Company A secretly finances an 'independent' foundation B which then calls in 'independent' expert C and concerned 'independent' citizens D, E, etc. It is the expert's task to refute the opinion company A wishes to debunk with a 'scientific' argument. The citizens are there to demonstrate their power as voters. Many astroturf bodies disguise their real aims by giving themselves a name that sounds the opposite to what they want to achieve.

For example, when software giant Microsoft was threatened with anti-monopoly legislation, an organization called Americans for Technology Leadership rushed to their aid. It distributed preprinted 'personal' letters to potential Microsoft supporters and asked them to send the letters to the government. This organization was partly, perhaps even fully, financed by Microsoft. An investigation by the Public Prosecutor in Utah revealed that at least two of the people who 'sent' the letter were in fact already dead at the time their letters were posted.

In 2000–2001 the state of California was suffering from an energy crisis. Although it was partly due to mismanagement, the crisis was mainly caused by the behaviour of energy companies which had deliberately limited the supply of energy to California, forcing the state to buy extra, more expensive, energy. After the crisis, governor Gray Davis tried to curb the power of the companies. In 2003, the American Taxpayers Alliance opposed Davis's policy and managed to have him removed from office, something that had happened only once before in American history (Davis was succeeded by Arnold Schwarzenegger). The American Taxpayers Alliance was fully financed by two large energy companies.

Astroturf opinions can also be disseminated in other ways. Today, many online editions of newspapers offer readers the opportunity to comment on articles. A journalist at *The Guardian* noticed that many comments on articles on global warming – denying the existence of the phenomenon – were almost identical. When the journalist tried to discover the real identity of one of the contributors, the latter refused to cooperate.

(For an interesting astroturf body, driven by religious rather than business interests, see the Discovery Institute's Center for Renewal of Science and Culture in PROFESSOR BEHE.)

B

BARONESS MURPHY'S CELLO SCROTUM

In an issue of the *British Medical Journal* in 1974, Dr Elaine Murphy (*b.* 1947) read a letter by a Dr P. Curtis on a medical phenomenon called 'guitar nipple', which could occur as a result of the continuous pressure of the upper edge of the guitar against the breast.

As Murphy (wrongly) assumed that Curtis had made a joke, she decided to take it one step further. In a letter to the *BMJ* she described a case of 'cello scrotum', caused by the body of the cello rubbing against the crotch. Because of her position – at that time she was a medical professor – Murphy decided to have the letter signed by her husband, who was not a physician. To their astonishment the letter was published.

For 30 years, the letter was occasionally quoted in articles, the last citation being in December 2008 – much to the amusement of the Murphys. But then they decided that the prank had gone on long enough. In January 2009 the *BMJ* published a letter from Baroness Murphy, who is now in the House of Lords, stating, 'Perhaps after 34 years it's time for us to confess that we invented cello scrotum.' The Baroness also pointed out that 'anyone who has ever watched a cello being played would realise the physical impossibility of our claim' (Murphy, 2009). Especially if the cellist were a woman.

BECCAH BEUSHAUSEN AND HER BABY DOLL

In April 2009 the anti-abortion movement in the United States thought it had found a new figurehead in the form of Beccah Beushausen, a social worker in a suburb of Chicago. On her blog, Beushausen, who presented herself as a Christian, revealed that she was expecting a daughter, April-Rose, who had a chromosomal defect and would probably not live longer than a few days, or perhaps even hours. The fact that Beushausen chose not to have an abortion led to widespread expressions of support. The message spread quickly through pro-life and conservative Christian websites and, before long, visitors thronged to Beushausen's website, and she received gifts and money through the post.

The child was born in June. A friend of Beushausen announced the good news on the blog: 'April is here! Praise Jesus!' (Usborne, 2009). There was a picture of the mother and her newborn daughter, wrapped in blankets. The blog had nearly 1 million visitors that day.

One of those visitors was Elizabeth Russell, a New York doll-maker. She recognized immediately that April-Rose was not a real child. Exposed as a fraud, Beushausen offered her apologies. She said that she had fabricated the story and made use of a doll to serve as April-Rose because she was 'dealing with unresolved pain' resulting from the loss of a baby boy some years previously (Usborne, 2009). It was unclear whether this 'unresolved pain' derived from a miscarriage or an abortion.

BERINGER'S TABLETS, THE LYING STONES

It is Beringer's misfortune that this case of forgery will not go down in history under the name of the forgers, but under that of the victim, although it is often referred to by the name of the forged items, the *Lügensteine* (Lying Stones).

Around 1724 Dr Johann Beringer (1667–1738), from Würzburg, decided to devote his attention to the young science of archaeology, which was at that time not yet very scientific and was described as interest in 'things dug from the Earth' (Jahn, 1963). On 31 May 1725 some young boys who knew about the doctor's interest gave Beringer a few pieces of limestone with strange markings. They looked like worms, and something that resembled rays of sunlight. Beringer decided to investigate further and, in the subsequent weeks and months, found many stones with images of animals on a mountain near Eibelstadt. Beringer realized that the animals could have been 'drawn' by natural causes but the images of the sun, moon and stars continued to puzzle him. Were they perhaps the remains of a heathen culture? The pieces fell into place when he found stones bearing the name of Jehovah. Beringer concluded that the stones were carved by God, which also explained the grooves and gouges on the other rocks.

Two of Beringer's university colleagues, J. Ignatz Roderick, professor of geography, algebra and analysis, and Georg von Eckhart,

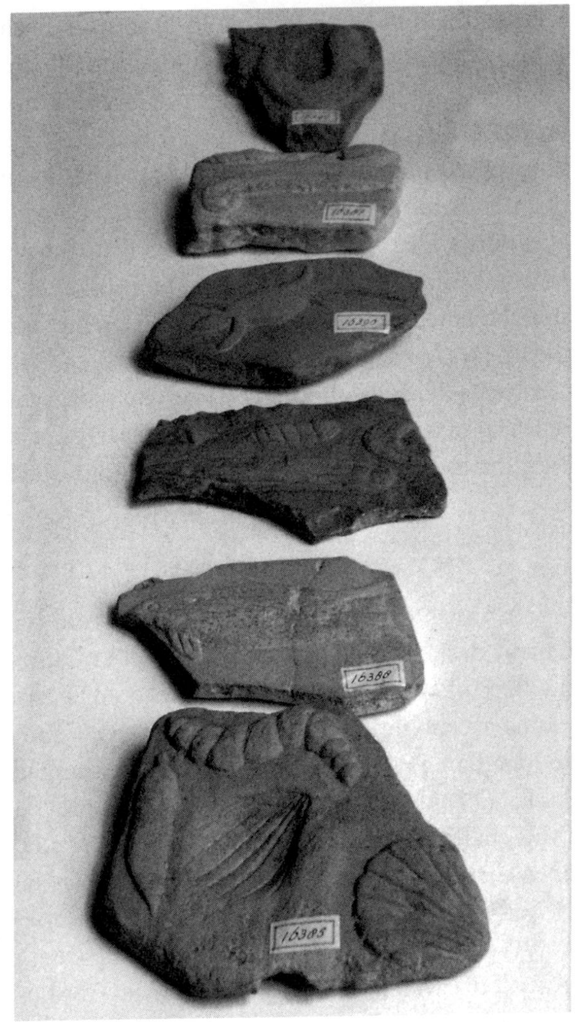

The 'Lying Stones', pieces of limestone carved into the shapes of various animals, apparently discovered in 1725.

privy councillor and university librarian, observed Beringer's belief in the authenticity of the stones with alarm. A year earlier, they had decided to teach Beringer a lesson because 'he was so arrogant', by faking a few fossils (Jahn, 1963). When Beringer continued to take his 'discoveries' seriously, they tried to show him the error of his ways by carving the name of God on some of the stones. This, unfortunately, did not have the desired effect.

When the two hoaxers heard that Beringer had called in an engraver to draw the stones with the intention of publishing a book about them, they decided to confess. However, Beringer was so convinced that he was in the right that he refused to believe them and accused them of being jealous. In 1726 he published *Lithographiae Wirceburgensis*, describing the markings on the stones. Shortly afterwards, he must have become suspicious, as he initiated legal proceedings on 13 April 1726 to 'save his honour' (Jahn, 1963). In an effort to preserve his reputation, he is also alleged to have bought as many copies of his book himself as possible (which explains why it is now so rare).

Only fragments of the trial records have survived and the outcome is unknown. We do know, however, that Georg von Eckhart stepped down and J. Ignatz Roderick left Würzburg, suggesting that the trial was a resounding victory for Beringer. In the remaining fourteen years of his life, Beringer wrote two more scientific works, both of which were well received. Yet his name will remain forever associated with the image of the fool who believed in the 'Lying Stones'.

BMW BIG BOY GOES BACK TO SCHOOL

Anoushirvan D. Fakhran, an immigrant from Iran, had the praiseworthy desire to be educated at the Paul VI Catholic High School in a suburb of Washington, DC. But how could he ensure that the school would accept him as a pupil? First of all, Fakhran changed his name to Jonathan Taylor Spielberg. (There is nothing illegal about that in itself, but Fakhran committed fraud when he stated on his application 'This change of name is not sought for any fraudulent purpose'.) He then changed his age: the rejuvenating 27-year-old wrote down that he was merely sixteen. He also gave the school the impression that he was the nephew of film director Steven Spielberg. He even drove a BMW coupé with the licence plate 'SPLBERG'. The hoax worked perfectly. Impressed by his surname, in September 1999 the school enrolled him in a class of teens. Staff allowed him to come and go as he pleased, and he was given less homework than his fellow pupils.

When his teachers started to become concerned about his bad grades, the school decided to contact his only known relative and called the DreamWorks studios. They were told that Steven Spielberg had no nephew living in Washington, DC.

Fakhran pleaded guilty to providing false information on the school's enrolment forms and forging his application for a change of name. He was given a conditional sentence of eleven months.

C

C. F. GOLDIE, TOWN PAINTER

In 1985 Karl Feodor Sim, a New Zealand shopkeeper, was convicted of forging the work of a fellow countryman, artist Charles F. Goldie (1870–1947). Sim was ordered to paint municipal buildings and toilets in the town of Foxton, where he was tried. After the court case, Sim legally changed his name to Carl Feodor Goldie, so that he could legitimately sign his paintings 'C. F. Goldie'. He no longer tries to pass his works off as authentic, and has the dubious honour of being New Zealand's first and so far only convicted art forger.

THE CAPTAIN OF KÖPENICK

On 16 October 1906 shoemaker Wilhelm Voigt (1849–1922) dressed himself in a second-hand Prussian officer's uniform and ordered a group of soldiers that he encountered near the local army barracks to follow him to the town of Köpenick, to the east of Berlin. As it did not occur to them to ignore the orders of a Prussian officer, they accompanied him to the railway station. On arrival in Köpenick, Voigt led the group to the city hall, where he arrested the mayor on suspicion of crooked bookkeeping and confiscated some 4,000 marks. No one doubted his authority – after all, *Deutschlands Ehr ist das Militär*!

Voigt did not enjoy his ill-gotten gains for long. At the end of October he was arrested and sentenced to four years in prison. A year later, however, he was pardoned by Kaiser Wilhelm II, who called him 'an amiable rogue' (Wietzorek, 2006). Voigt started to earn a living selling signed photographs and appearing in small theatres and variety shows. He wrote an autobiography, published in 1909 and later translated as *How I Became the Captain of Köpenick*, and toured the United States and Canada. A wax effigy of him appeared in Madame Tussauds in London. In 1910 he moved to Luxembourg and retired two years later. When German troops invaded on 2 August 1914, Voigt donned his uniform for the last time and the soldiers all sprang to attention.

Voigt's life inspired many a writer. In 1930 Wilhelm Schäfer published a novel about it, and the following year Carl Zuckmayer wrote a successful play that still tours in the English-speaking world under the title *The Captain of Köpenick*. Twenty-five years after his play appeared, Zuckmayer co-wrote the screenplay for a film of it together with director Helmut Käutner. The film starred Heinz Rühmann.

When Voigt died in 1922, impoverished by the inflation that followed the First World War, he was buried in the Notre Dame cemetery at the expense of the city of Luxembourg. His grave was neglected and was nearly cleared on several occasions. In 1961, however, the performers of Circus Sarasani from the German Democratic Republic paid to have the grave restored and fitted out with a new, albeit incorrectly dated, gravestone bearing the text 'Hauptmann von Koepenick' and 'Wilhelm Voigt, 1850–1922', together with the image of a Prussian helmet.

This was not the only honour conferred on Voigt. To my knowledge he is the only hoaxer to have his own statue – for being a hoaxer. In Köpenick, where he made his name, he still stands – cast in bronze – on the steps of the city hall where he arrested the mayor and took off with the city's cash.

CHARLEY PARKHURST, STAGECOACH QUEEN

Charlotte Darkey Parkhurst (1812–1879) allegedly escaped from an orphanage dressed as a boy. The disguise was a success, so she kept it up. As Charley Parkhurst she found a job as a stable boy in a small town in Massachusetts. She used to watch the stagecoach drivers closely and, recognizing her talent, the owner of the stables taught her how to drive two-in-hand, then four-in-hand and, later, six-in-hand teams of horses. Charley, who always wore gloves to disguise her small hands, became the most sought-after stagecoach driver on the East Coast, and many people hired coaches only on the condition that she took the reins.

Perhaps because someone discovered her identity, Charley headed west, settling in San Francisco in 1851. From the city she set out new routes through the state of California. During these years, she lost an eye, apparently after being kicked by a horse, earning her the nickname Cock-Eyed Charley.

In the 1860s Charley's talent, fearlessness and loyalty were so highly valued that she regularly worked for Wells Fargo. One evening during this period, she was so drunk that the wife of her boss Andy Jackson Clark told her seventeen-year-old son to put Charley to bed.

The boy came back, trembling, and told his mother that Charley was a woman. The family decided to keep her secret: 'Those good people, sensing Charley's humiliation if confronted with the fact that he was unmasked, never mentioned it to a soul until after Charley's death' (Sams, 1995).

At the end of the 1860s Charley retired from stagecoach driving and bought some land in Santa Cruz County, where she ran a ranch and stage station, and did seasonal work as a lumberjack.

She died of tongue cancer in 1879. The first obituaries were full of praise but, as news of her true biological sex became more widely known (as well as the fact that she had once given birth to a child), the mood of some of the newspapers changed. One unkind journalist working for a Rhode Island paper wrote: 'Charley Parkhurst died of a malignant disease. She could act and talk like a man, but when it came to imitating a man's reticence, nature herself revolted, and the lifelong effort to keep from speaking, except when she had something to say, resulted at last in death from cancer of the tongue' (Sams, 1995).

A CHRISTIAN MARTYR IN THE COLUMBINE MASSACRE

On 20 April 1999 Eric Harris and Dylan Klebold, both of whom were born in 1981, killed thirteen people at Columbine High School, Colorado, where they were themselves pupils, and then committed suicide. A wave of shock and horror passed around the world. Shortly after the incident, several stories emerged, many of which are still in circulation. The two killers were allegedly inspired to commit their awful crime by the deliberately shocking work of rock singer Marilyn Manson (pseudonym of Brian Hugh Warner). To stop the situation escalating, Manson was forced to cancel the rest of his American tour. It only became clear much later that the two boys were not fans of Manson's music at all.

A second myth developed around Cassie René Bernall (also born in 1981), a teenager who found God after a rebellious adolescence. According to the myth, one of the two killers put a gun to Bernall's head and asked her if she still believed in God. After she answered 'Yes', the boy shot her dead. The story contains all the ingredients of an American legend: a white, all-American teenager who converts after committing sin and is then killed. Dying for one's faith is seen as praiseworthy in the United States – as long as it is the Christian faith, of course.

In 2000 Bernall's mother Misty published a book, *She Said Yes: The Unlikely Martyrdom of Cassie Bernall*, which confirmed Bernall's status as a martyr. As with many similar examples of Catholic martyrdom, closer research showed that very few of the supposed facts underlying the account can be corroborated. An investigation by the FBI showed that there never was a dialogue between Bernall and one or both of the killers. The killers' question was actually put to Valeen Schnurr, who had not had a wild adolescence and did not die during the attack, and was therefore not eligible for martyrdom.

Facts and legends are incompatible. The Bernall family – along with many other American Christians – made a clear choice. The family's website still carries the text: 'Cassie Bernall, who was killed at Columbine High School on April 20, 1999, after professing her faith in God.'

CHRISTINE JOY MAGGIORE, AIDS DENIALIST

In 1992 in a routine check-up, U.S. citizen Christine Joy Maggiore (1956–2008), owner of an import clothing company, was found to be HIV-positive. In the years that followed she became one of the most prominent American AIDS denialists. She claimed that there was no link between HIV and AIDS and expounded her 'theory' in a book she self-published, *What if Everything You Thought You Knew about AIDS Was Wrong?*

Maggiore refused to take anti-retrovirals, had unsafe sex with her husband and breastfed her daughter Eliza Jane. On 17 May 2005 Eliza Jane died at the age of three and a half. Maggiore herself died at the end of December 2008. Her death certificate and the autopsy report on her daughter leave no doubt as to the cause of both their deaths.

CLAUDIUS PTOLEMY, NOT QUITE THE RHODES SCHOLAR

The universe that Ptolemy described in *Amalgest* (*c.* AD 150) remained intact for fifteen centuries until Copernicus presented his own version in 1543. In *Amalgest*, which wielded an enormous influence for an

Claudius Ptolemy.

incredible length of time, Ptolemy claimed that he had made all his astronomical observations himself. It was only in the nineteenth century that scientists started to feel that something was not quite right. Some of the observations seemed not to have been made in Alexandria, where Ptolemy lived, while others which would logically have been made in the city were not included. In 1977, in a book that is practically incomprehensible to anyone but an astronomer, Robert R. Newton presented his solution to this puzzle. *The Crime of Claudius Ptolemy* claims that all the observations and calculations in *Amalgest* would be correct if they had been made on the island of Rhodes and not in Alexandria. Newton shows that, rather than making the observations himself, Ptolemy had taken them all from the – now largely lost – work of Hipparchus of Rhodes, who lived three centuries earlier.

CLIFTON JAMES, THESPIAN, AND HIS NAZI FOLLOWERS

Meyrick Edward Clifton James (1898–1963) was born in Australia and grew up in Europe. From the age of sixteen he wanted to be an actor. His career was interrupted by the First World War, in which James was wounded while serving at the Front. After the war he continued building a career, but it never really took off. James became a stock actor, playing stereotypal roles with little depth. The 1920s and 1930s drifted by without event.

At the start of the Second World War, James joined up and was assigned to an office unit. He did not see active duty but, in the spring of 1944, when the preparations for D-Day were in full swing, James was offered the role of his life.

The Allies had long been disseminating incorrect information on the invasion in an attempt to mislead German intelligence. One of the officers involved in this operation was struck by the remarkable similarity between James and the commander of the Allied troops, Field-Marshal Montgomery (1887–1976). A plan was hatched to have James appear as Monty in all sorts of places to mislead the Germans about the impending invasion.

A few adjustments had to be made to achieve a passable physical match. James had lost most of one finger in the First World War, so a prosthetic was fitted. The actor prepared for his role by spending time with the General Staff so that he could study Monty's speech and mannerisms. Despite the physical resemblance, the two were complete opposites in terms of character. The Field-Marshal was an ascetic who didn't smoke or drink and was hard on himself and others. James was a libertine, who chain-smoked and drank like a fish.

In May 1944 James played his role with verve, appearing in strategic locations including Algiers and Gibraltar. As expected, his presence in Gibraltar was immediately reported by Major Ignacio Molina Pérez, a Spanish spy working for the Germans. This information reinforced the German High Command's belief that the invasion would take place in southern France and not in Normandy.

James reaped little benefit from his contribution to the Allied victory. The British Army simply ignored his efforts, not releasing the documents relating to the operation until 2010. After the war, James resumed his acting career. In 1954 he wrote a book about his wartime role, *I Was Monty's Double*, which was made into a film in 1958. The film starred M. E. Clifton James, playing Montgomery – and playing M. E. Clifton James playing Montgomery.

CLUELESS KRUGEL COPS OUT

Ex-policeman Danie Krugel claimed to have invented something that – if it worked – would guarantee him a Nobel Prize: if he had a strand of a missing person's hair (or some other source of DNA), he could pinpoint their location, wherever they were in the world. Unfortunately Krugel was not willing to explain how his invention worked. The only (non-) explanation he would give was that it had something to do with 'quantum physics', a matter of 'complex and secret science techniques' and a 'secret energy source' driving a 'matter orientation system machine' (Goldacre, 2007).

Krugel alleged to have had many successes. This in itself is not impossible, although it had little to do with the invention. Krugel used to be part of a police unit that traced missing children. It is not inconceivable that he used his professional abilities for his own ends and attributed the results to his magic box.

A distasteful example of Krugel's performance could be seen in *Carte Blanche*, a series broadcast by the South African TV company M-Net. At the end of the 1980s, two South Africans called Gert van Rooyen and Joye Haarhoff kidnapped six schoolgirls. None of the girls have ever been found. In an episode entitled 'Fingerprint of Fate', Krugel promised to locate the bodies. With no concern for the feelings it might unleash, the girls' families were asked to provide hairs from the missing children. After they had been kept in suspense for several weeks, Krugel came up with nothing at all.

COLLECTING REINHOLD VASTERS

Reinhold Vasters (1827–1909) was the 'nearly perfect forger'. His skill and knowledge of the art of the Renaissance were unequalled. Vasters, who worked in precious metals, made no errors of style, used no wrong materials, and ensured that there were no nineteenth-century influences in his work at all. It was only due to an alert curator at the Victoria & Albert Museum in London that Vasters was finally

A pendant of enamelled gold and pearls by Reinhold Vasters, c. 1860.

exposed, 69 years after his death. And that's when art historians started gnashing their teeth. Twentieth-century views on Renaissance art proved to be based partly on objects dating not from sixteenth-century Italy but from nineteenth-century Germany – from Vasters's studio in Aachen, to be precise. In the words of one curator, 'The problem is, he created so much he begins to distort perceptions of what Renaissance art should be' (Kessler, 1987).

Vasters registered his mark as a master goldsmith at Aachen in 1853. Although he had little experience, he was hired later in the same year to work on restoring the treasures of the city's cathedral. During his life he became renowned for his own creations, objects based on Renaissance artistic styles but which he sold as contemporary pieces. In secret, however, he was going much further. His forgeries were sold through Viennese art dealer Frédéric Spitzer (1815–1890), who had opened a salon in Paris in 1852. Spitzer's death also meant the end of Vasters's career as a forger. This may have been a good indication of his natural caution. His collaboration with Spitzer lasted for 37 years, during which time nothing at all leaked out about his illegal activities. So why, at the age of 63, run the risk of being exposed by working with another art dealer? Three years after Spitzer's death, his art collection was auctioned and the last wave of Vasters's forgeries flooded onto the market. By that time, Vasters had retired. But by selling an object from his own collection of authentic art now and again, he was able to ensure that he was in an excellent position financially.

Although financial gain was probably Vasters's main incentive, he must have enjoyed his career as a forger. His Rospigliosi Cup was attributed to one of the leading goldsmiths and sculptors of the Italian Renaissance, Benvenuto Cellini. The Metropolitan Museum of Art in New York proudly displayed its precious acquisition for 70 years.

After Vasters died, his papers were sold. In 1919 they were donated to the Victoria & Albert Museum, a fitting home for the records of a respected Victorian craftsman. The papers contained drawings of many treasures of the Renaissance era, which in itself was not strange. Vasters was believed to have made the drawings to study such pieces or perhaps to inspire him in the creation of his own contemporary works.

In the twentieth century art historians diligently studied hundreds of Vasters's forgeries without recognizing them as such. If Vasters had not wished to be exposed, he should have destroyed his papers. The fact that he failed to do so suggests that he had a character trait in common with many forgers – he wanted to be recognized as an equal to past masters, such as Cellini.

In 1978 Charles Truman, an assistant curator of the Ceramics department at the Victoria & Albert Museum, came across a package containing more than 1,000 drawings and notes by Vasters. Truman looked at the drawings in the same way that so many before him had done: 'Oh, look, here are the jewels from the Louvre, and isn't this bowl now in the British Museum?'

But when Truman tried to explain details in the drawings and deciphered some of the technical notes in the margins, the truth gradually dawned on him. The drawings were not of Renaissance art works, it was the other way around: objects supposedly from the Renaissance had been made by using the drawings. Truman didn't jump to any conclusions, but waited until 1980 to go public with his findings. The name Reinhold Vasters, a name that no one had connected with forgery until then, suddenly struck fear into the hearts of curators around the world. Using Truman's data, they set to work to check their collections. The Metropolitan alone discovered 40 pieces from the master forger's hand.

The revelations meant that the history of Renaissance art had to be rewritten. If Vasters had not revealed his secret, the prevailing interpretation would have been accepted as the truth. It makes you wonder how many forgers of Vasters's calibre have never been detected, and in how many different disciplines.

COMMON NAMES TO CONJURE WITH IN THE NEW CHINA

How childishly easy forgery can be. Liu Hui, active as a surgeon and vice-dean of Tsinghua University Medical School in Beijing in 2006, had an impressive-sounding curriculum vitae with a list of publications as long as your arm. The only problem was that Liu had added publications by another doctor with exactly the same name. Lu Jun, a former professor at Beijing's University of Chemical Technology, was recently caught doing the same thing.

COUNTERFEIT MEDICINES

Medicines are expensive and always in demand. So it is hardly surprising that there is a lively trade in fake ones. An investment of €1,000 in the trade in heroin, for example, generates a turnover of €3,000, leaving a profit of €2,000. The same investment in fake medicines brings in €30,000 – a substantial profit of €29,000. According to the World Health Organization, trade in counterfeit drugs now generates more than $30 billion a year in revenue. Estimates of the deaths caused by fakes are very vague but run 'from tens of thousands a year to 200,000 or more' (McNeil Jr, 2007).

What kinds of drugs are counterfeited? Malaria medicines are an old favourite. A study in Southeast Asia in 2007 showed that 53 per cent of available pills were fakes. Simple counterfeits contained chalk, starch or flour. More advanced versions contained paracetamol, which does not kill the malaria parasites but does lower the fever, fooling patients into thinking the medicine is working. Other favourites are antibiotics, AIDS drugs, tuberculosis tablets and meningitis vaccines.

For the most part, counterfeit drugs are copies of existing drugs. In May 2006, for instance, police at London's Heathrow Airport discovered 385 kg of counterfeit medicines bearing the labels of leading brands like Novartis, AstraZeneca, Pfizer and Proctor & Gamble. Eighteen months later, a consignment of half a million Plavix (a blood-thinning drug) pills were intercepted. The main ingredient proved to be cement.

Counterfeiters have mainly been active in Asia and Africa. In November 2002, a study showed that up to 20 per cent of all medicines in South Africa was fake.

The counterfeiters are interested only in making money. That is why they are sensitive to trends and produce medicines that do well on the market. In the recent past they have therefore focused mainly on Viagra (Pfizer's anti-impotence drug) and Tamiflu (a bird-flu drug produced by Roche).

Who are these counterfeiters and how do they sell their goods? Here, again, China can be identified as the main producer, followed closely by Russia. In China there was even a prominent figure involved. From 1998, Zheng Xiaoyu was for several years in control of the department that approved medicines in China. His unofficial policy was clear: anyone who manufactured rubbish for export received approval. His reign came to an end in 2005, however, when a medicine he had approved killed dozens of Chinese patients, including many children.

The journey from the Chinese factory to the consumer's medicine cabinet is long, and in many cases passes through the United Arab Emirates (UAE), and the city of Dubai in particular. Dubai is the junction between Europe, Africa and Asia. To encourage trade, the UAE has set up free trade zones, around twenty of which are now in operation. They act as transit depots for goods. Since the goods do not officially enter the country, no duties have to be paid and checks are minimal – ideal circumstances for concealing their origins. A real-life example shows how this works: RxNorth, once one of the biggest online pharmacies in the United States, used to get a large proportion of its drugs from China. From mainland China, the medicines were transported to Hong Kong. They were then forwarded to the UAE. The next stop was the Bahamas, where clients' orders were packaged and addressed. As a final smokescreen, the packages were sent to the UK, from where they were finally dispatched to the customer in the United States.

The counterfeiting of medicines is an 'almost-perfect crime', in the words of Maureen Kirkman, head of scientific and regulatory affairs at South Africa's Pharmaceutical Manufacturer's Association. 'The counterfeiting industry is like the Mafia: the rewards are big', Kirkman says. 'Either the patient dies or doesn't know they have taken counterfeit drugs' (Padayachee, 2002). Because of the substantial interests at stake, trade in counterfeit medicines is hard to combat. A few simple guidelines, however, would be enough to at least limit it a little. In Europe and North America, for instance, it is still common for charities working in developing countries and wishing to respect their autonomy to give them money to buy the medicines they need. However, these countries generally have neither the laboratories nor the necessary know-how to distinguish fake drugs from real ones. Donating reliable European or American medicines instead of money would be a step in the right direction. Paternalistic behaviour can sometimes be justified.

It is not only developing countries and internet buyers that are the victims of counterfeit drugs. The quality of imitations (and especially the packaging) has recently reached such a high standard that bona fide suppliers also get taken in. Over the past decade in Britain, for example, the NHS has issued around ten warnings after counterfeit medicines have ended up in conventional pharmacies.

CRIMINAL MILKMEN

From March to September 2008, China saw a sharp rise in the number of children with kidney problems. The authorities very probably knew in July that the problems were being caused by contaminated milk but, with the country hosting the Summer Olympics in August, they kept quiet. Public health clearly did not weigh up against this large-scale exercise in public relations. Revealing the truth would be an embarrassing business, especially as the toxic products mainly came from the state-owned dairy company Sanlu, sponsor of the Olympic Games and supplier to the Olympic village.

The facts were not made public until mid-September. It turned out that somewhere in the supply line to Sanlu, the milk had been diluted with water. It remained unclear if it was the farmers who had first committed the fraud to make an illicit profit, or others further down the line. Either way, Sanlu was stuck with watered-down milk with a nutritional value much lower than required. The company came up with a devious solution. The nutritional value of milk depends on the protein content, which is measured by counting the number of nitrogen molecules. Sanlu realized that if they increased the nitrogen content, the watered-down milk would pass the test. So they added melamine, a nitrogen-rich material used for synthetic resin and plastic hardeners. Over a period of several months, some of the milk had been processed into more than 1,500 tons of milk powder, which doctors paid by Sanlu recommended in the media as ideal food for babies and infants.

As a result, between March and September 2008 some 300,000 infants became ill, many seriously. Children who had been perfectly healthy one week suddenly turned out to have half a dozen kidney stones a week later. The official number of deaths was six but must have been higher, though how many is anyone's guess. Research in 2010 showed that around 40,000 victims suffered permanent kidney damage.

China responded by mobilizing all the power at the disposal of a totalitarian state. A swift investigation of the dairy industry revealed melamine contamination at another 21 companies. In January 2009, 21 company executives went on trial. Later that same year, the first two sentences were passed: Zhang Yujun and Geng Jinping – who together sold 1,500 tons of tainted milk powder – were executed by firing squad. To the anger of many, former Sanlu general manager Tian Wenhua escaped the firing squad and was 'merely' sentenced to life in prison.

The brand name Sanlu ceased to exist but the affair cast a long shadow. In February 2010 milk products contaminated with melamine were discovered again. They were probably old Sanlu products removed from the shelves in 2008 and repacked by manufacturers. After all, it would be a shame to waste them, wouldn't it?

In the aftermath of the scandal the Chinese government responded with the incongruity so typical of totalitarian regimes. In December 2009 Zhao Lianhai, the father of one of the sick infants, was arrested while demonstrating with other parents and, nearly a year later, sentenced to two and a half years in prison for 'disturbing the peace' (*De Volkskrant*, 2010).

In April 2011 the Chinese government announced that it would be shutting down 553 of the country's 1,176 dairy companies in an attempt to clean up the industry.

D

D-DAY DECEPTION DIDN'T END BACK THEN

It was a great honour: in 2009 Howard Manoian (*b. c.* 1925) was awarded the Légion d'Honneur for bravery by the French state. And with good reason. On 6 June 1944, D-Day, he was an American paratrooper with the famous 82nd Airborne Division and landed in the town of Sainte-Mère-Église:

> One planeload jumped and landed in the square by the church and of course the Germans were already up and they were firing as they [the paratroopers] came down . . . Half of them were killed or wounded immediately. That was the first time I saw a person dead face to face. (BBC, 2009)

Manoian fought his way to Paris. During the push German bullets wounded him in one hand and both legs. When German planes targeted the hospital where he was recovering, he was injured once again. This all made Manoian a hero in Sainte-Mère-Église, where a plaque was even erected in his honour. The 85-year-old veteran fully deserved his Légion d'Honneur.

On the day of the award, 6 June 2009, exactly 65 years after D-Day, the *Boston Herald* announced that Manoian's stories were largely fabricated. Yes, he did land in Normandy, though not by parachute but on a supply ship that moored at the Utah landing zone long after a beachhead had been established there. Manoian did not belong to the 82nd Airborne Division but to the 33rd Chemical Decontamination Company. As no chemical weapons were used in the fighting in 1944 and 1945, the Company had little to do. And yes,

Manoian had been injured, eleven days after D-Day. On 17 June 1944 he broke a finger – due to his own clumsiness.

DANIEL GOLDREYER, ART RESTORER ON A ROLL

In 1986 a man called Gerard Jan van Bladeren walked into the Stedelijk Museum in Amsterdam and repeatedly slashed Barnett Newman's painting *Who's Afraid of Red, Yellow and Blue* with a Stanley knife. The City of Amsterdam contracted Daniel Goldreyer in New York to restore the painting for a fee of 800,000 guilders. It took Goldreyer four years to complete the job, but he claimed that he had closely followed Newman's own style. Using a thin brush, he had applied thousands and thousands of dots of paint in the large field of red covering most of the canvas (which measured 245 × 543 cm in total). The work had hardly been back in Amsterdam when there was a wave of criticism about the quality of the restoration. An investigation by the Netherlands Forensic Institute eventually concluded that Goldreyer had painted over the whole field of red with non-removable paint using a roller. A legal tug-of-war followed, which cost the municipality of Amsterdam some €680,000. Goldreyer filed a suit for defamation of character and claimed $125 million in damages. In the end, the City of Amsterdam paid him $100,000, after which Goldreyer abandoned his legal fight. And *Who's Afraid of Red, Yellow and Blue* was carried away to the Stedelijk's unvisited storerooms.

DEREK ATKINS, THE VERY FISHY MARINER

Committing fraud ran in Derek Atkins's blood. He not only captained the fishing vessel *Zuiderzee* without holding a captain's licence, but also fiddled the logbooks and exceeded his fishing quotas. Furthermore, Atkins changed his name while he was on the sex offenders' register and tricked a woman he had led to believe he wanted a relationship with out of several thousand pounds sterling.

When Atkins had run up fines of up to £1 million for some twenty charges of flouting fishing regulations, the Marine and Fisheries Agency received a letter from Atkins's girlfriend asking them to halt prosecution proceedings against her partner as he had died of a heart attack.

Soon afterwards, *Fishing News* published an obituary, which spoke highly of Atkins's qualities: 'People found him to be a gentleman at sea with a great sense of humour who would always help anyone. He was a quiet family man and will be deeply missed by his family and friends' (Bamford, 2009).

An inspector at the Marine and Fisheries Agency became suspicious and asked the police to look into the matter. Handwriting analysis showed that the letter from his partner had been written by Atkins himself. He was found not much later, alive and kicking. The obituary proved to be his own work, too.

In February 2009 the judge, who described Atkins as a 'lying, cunning and calculated fraudster', sentenced him to 30 months in prison (*Daily Mail*, 2009).

DISMEMBERING *MICHELLE REMEMBERS*

Michelle Pazder (née Smith) was a trendsetter. Her book *Michelle Remembers* (1980, written with her therapist and later husband, the Canadian psychiatrist Lawrence Pazder) told stories of ritual abuse, causing a hype that made headlines for a decade. It probably started with a *folie à deux*, though the question is who was the craziest.

Michelle Smith, a receptionist, suffered from depression and started therapy with Lawrence Pazder. Pazder must have missed the lectures on transference and counter-transference and on professional ethics when he was at college, because love blossomed between the therapist and his patient. During many sessions with Michelle, forgotten memories of her early life in Victoria, British Columbia, resurfaced while she was under hypnosis. They were recollections of the kind that a bona fide therapist would soon have dismissed as fictitious. Michelle recalled that her mother, Virginia Proby, had forced her to take part in satanic rituals. In the years 1955–6, according to her forgotten memories, Michelle's life was like a horror film. The five-year-old was forced to endure a wide range of atrocities, including the sacrifice of small babies and other ritual murders, the mutilation of snakes and kittens, drinking blood, poisoning and acts of sexual perversion. There was no evidence at all for any of these allegations. Any elements of her story that were verifiable proved to be incorrect. Michelle claimed that she had not been brought up religiously, while witnesses said that she had attended church with her parents regularly every Sunday for many years. Torture was highly unlikely as former neighbours said that the walls of the houses were so thin that it could never have passed unnoticed. Michelle had been poisoned twice: once she drank turpentine and on another occasion she ate shoe polish, but both on her own initiative. Her parents had rushed her to the accident and emergency department.

Michelle Remembers became a bestseller thanks to American fundamentalist Christians, who seized on the concocted memories to prove that Satan is among us. Ritual abuse became a worldwide hype and immediately caused untold damage. The child protection authorities in Rochdale, England, believed the nonsense and sixteen children were removed from their homes. Paediatricians in England's northeast region of Teesside discovered no fewer than 121 cases of ritual abuse in a very short period. In the Dutch village of Oude Pekela, family doctors Fred Jonker and his wife Ietje Jonker-Bakker sounded the alarm after a mother had discovered that her young son had anal injuries, most likely the result of quasi-sexual experimentation with a friend of the same age. The Jonkers stoked up the mass hysteria until there were 215 cases of satanic child rape in the village. In Oude Pekela, the Prince of Darkness delegated his dastardly deeds to even more scary assistants – clowns! The affair at Dutch crèche De Bolderkar was another low point in this tragic saga. The staff at the crèche discovered that parents were committing incestuous paedophilia en masse. They gathered this information by allowing the children to play with anatomically correct dolls. Although the method is known to be suggestive and notoriously unreliable, fourteen children were taken from their homes. A number of parents admitted their guilt, but the police had used banned interrogation techniques and, eventually, no one was charged.

It is impossible to even guess at the damage caused by the hysteria. Twenty-two years later, in April 2010, the legal successor to De Bolderkar paid 'appropriate financial compensation' to a woman who had been taken away from her parents at the age of four because her father had allegedly abused her. The case had been dismissed (Haenen, 2010).

DOLLAR DUPLICITY, NORTH KOREAN STYLE

It all started with an observant bank teller at the Bangko Sentral ng Pilipinas. In December 1989 he was handed a U.S. $100 banknote, which didn't 'feel' right to the touch. He was puzzled since all the control equipment indicated that the bill was real. The note made its way to Japan, to Yoshihide Matsumura, a currency expert whose machines for detecting fake bills are among the most advanced in the business. Matsumura was impressed by the quality of the banknote. The paper was identical to that of real $100 bills – 75 per cent American cotton, 25 per cent linen – and manufactured using the right machinery (a Fourdrinier machine). Equally remarkable was that the notes were produced on an intaglio press, while forged notes are almost all printed using an offset press. Intaglio presses are so expensive and heavy that normally only governments own them for printing banknotes.

Matsumura passed the banknote on to the U.S. Secret Service, where it was assigned code C-14342. After a careful investigation, the bill turned out to have three flaws. But, the Service concluded the flaws might have been deliberately added by the forgers so that they could distinguish their own products from the real thing.

The Secret Service thought it had found a clue to where the fakes came from when bills from the same series turned up in Lebanon's Bekka Valley. The Hezbollah movement, which was active in the area, was financed by Iran. And shortly before his fall, the Shah had taken delivery of two intaglio printing presses. This promising trail, however, came to a dead end.

When rumours about the 'supernote' started spreading at the beginning of the 1990s, it was not only governments that were concerned. Gunmen who took schoolchildren hostage in the Russian city of Rostov on the Don in December 1993 demanded a ransom of $10 million in $100 bills – along with a sophisticated machine to weed out the fakes.

In 1996 the U.S. government changed the design and safety features of the $100 bill. But this had little effect as the existing bills were only withdrawn from circulation in phases. This meant that the counterfeiters could continue to use the fakes until they were able to copy the new bill. The new version of the fake bills first turned up in London in 1998, and was given the code C-21555.

Slowly but surely the Secret Service gathered clues for a new suspect. Japan traced the supernotes to Yoshimi Tanaka, a Red Army terrorist who had disappeared inside North Korea in the 1970s. In Northern Ireland an estimated $28 million worth of supernotes were also in circulation. This trail led to the Official IRA, a faction of the

Irish Republican Army, which opposed peace talks. It was discovered that an Official IRA leader, Seán Garland, had made four trips to Moscow, where he had visited the North Korean embassy.

North Korea was a logical candidate as producer of the supernote. Good counterfeit money is a cheap way to finance terrorist organizations that are trying to destabilize the capitalist world, one of the ambitions of dictator Kim Jongil (who has since died, in 2011). However, this was not the main reason. In an attempt to bring Kim Jongil to his knees, especially in negotiations on North Korea's nuclear facilities, the West had been trying for years to bring down North Korea's economy. It had imposed trade embargos and the country was unable to borrow money on international markets.

Western secret services have known for many years that North Korea makes money from illegal trade. It produces counterfeit cigarettes, for example (Marlboro is a popular brand), that are estimated to generate more than $700 million in gross revenue every year. North Korea also manufactures and exports hard drugs like heroin and crystal methamphetamine on a large scale and it is the place to go for counterfeit pharmaceuticals and weapons. In the mid-1990s the secret services realized that, even with these extra sources of income, North Korea should have been bankrupt. And that was clearly not the case. On the contrary, Kim Jongil doggedly continued to expand his arsenal, and 70 per cent of the necessary components were imported and paid for with dollars.

The U.S. Secret Service and its counterparts focused their attention on Office 39. This organization runs cigarette and drug factories and organizes criminal activities abroad. Some 130 people work in its headquarters, a plain, barracks-like building on Changgwant Street in Pyongyang. The secret services reckoned that if North Korea was producing the supernote, Office 39 was running the operation.

So they deployed all the weapons of the espionage armoury: satellite photos, bribery, defectors . . . , and no doubt the odd case of threat and blackmail. This led them to discover that there were three dollar-printing plants in North Korea. One was under the control of the North Korean army reconnaissance corps. The second produced counterfeit dollars for the Communist Party Central Committee. The third, housed at 62 Printing House in Pyongsung, printed fake bills for Kim Jongil. Estimates varied, but the plants were believed to produce between $500 million and $1 billion a year in supernotes.

At the beginning of this century, there was a new development. Until then, most supernotes had turned up outside the United States, which was to be expected, since two-thirds of all dollar bills circulate overseas. From around 2000, however, North Korea tried to export huge quantities of supernotes to the home of the dollar. In 2003, the U.S. responded by changing the design of the $100 bill again. But history repeated itself: North Korea was able to use the old counterfeit bill until the new one was ready. In March 2005 the FBI managed to get hold of two new samples. When they were given to a Secret Service agent to have them tested, the agent called a few days later and said: 'Why'd you give me these? They're real!' (Rose, 2009).

An interesting question is why President George W. Bush's administration did not take any action. Normally, it had few qualms about dropping bombs on someone else's territory. But Bush's policy was clearly not to alienate Kim Jongil any further, presumably so as not to jeopardize the talks on restricting the latter's nuclear arsenal.

Either way, by 2007 Kim Jongil's plans were clear. That year North Korea imported a huge quantity of Fourdrinier paper, enough to print several billions of dollars.

DROWN! BATHTUB TIPS FOR STAYING MAGNETIC

The life of Dr Ruth B. Drown (1891–1965) is a perfect illustration of how difficult it is to combat deception. Drown learned the art of quackery from Albert Abrams, who was being exposed as a fraudster in America around the time Drown's career took off. Like Abrams, Drown used an electrical circuit that was completed when the patient was connected to her devices. Like Abrams, Drown sold weird contraptions for a lot of money, in her case the Drown Radio-vision Instrument, the Drown Therapeutic Instrument and the Drown Homo-vibra Ray Instrument. And like Abrams, Drown made incorrect diagnoses, causing distress to many innocent victims.

Drown's 'achievement' was that of adding a few odd twists of her own to Abrams's crazy notions. The 'Drown Atlas of Radio Therapy', for example, offered guidelines for dangerous manoeuvres, like emptying a bathtub:

> Any patient who is weak and depleted should never take shower baths and stand in the water over the drain, because

> the patient's magnetism is washed down with the water through the drain, leaving him depleted.
>
> Also, a weak patient, after having had a tub bath, should leave the tub and have someone else drain the water and clean the tub. If it is necessary to do this himself, he should leave the tub and put on a robe before starting to drain the tub. Too many people sit in the tub and drain the water while finishing the bath, and their own magnetism is sucked away through the drain pipes to the ground, leaving the patient with that much less reserve. (Smith, 1968)

Drown also discovered a hitherto unknown cause of cancer: jazz music. The disease could fortunately be reversed by listening to more soothing music.

Drown claimed that her Radio-vision Instrument would make x-rays a thing of the past. A photograph made with the instrument in London revealed a blood clot and cancer in a patient in Connecticut, 5,500 km away.

In 1951 Drown was found guilty of 'introducing a misbranded device into interstate commerce', after the court ruled that her therapeutic instruments were not therapeutic at all.[3] The trial took place after a complaint from Marguerite Rice, who Drown treated in 1948 for a lump in her breast. Sadly, Rice died just before the trial was due to start. Drown was fined $1,000 and stopped dispatching her machines to other states, but otherwise persisted with her quackery.

In May 1963 the California State Department of Public Health deployed an undercover agent to gather evidence against Drown. The agent gave Drown blood samples from 'her three children' to analyse. The blood actually came from a turkey, a sheep and a pig. She also bought a Drown Therapeutic Instrument for $588. Drown was sensible enough to pass away before the trial in 1967, but her two colleagues, Cynthia Chatfield and Margaret Lunness, came up before the judge. During the trial, photos made by the Drown Radio-vision Instrument were shown to be photographic plates that had been momentarily exposed to light. An expert also dismantled a Drown Therapeutic Instrument, showing that the nine switches on the instrument, all of which had settings from 1 to 10, were totally ineffective: the power in the circuit was the same irrespective how they were set.

Lunness was placed on probation for three years, while Chatfield was sent to prison.

E

EBAY'S ALTERNATIVE REALITY

For anyone who wants to be safeguarded from counterfeit goods there is an easy-to-remember rule of thumb: don't buy anything on eBay. A few figures should suffice to illustrate eBay's unreliability. Between 60 and 90 per cent of sports memorabilia put up for sale on eBay is fake (see NEW SIGNINGS). If you want an Egyptian amulet or a flint arrowhead, you should also steer clear of eBay: 'less than five per cent' of the archaeological artefacts put up for sale on the site are authentic (Ammelrooy, 2009). The same applies if you are looking for a piece of design furniture (see FURNITURE FAKERS).

eBay and all the companies it has bought up offer the reliable citizen an easy way to dispose of a redundant cradle or a wedding dress that has been worn only once. But the site is also a godsend for forgers. It enables them to reach a large audience in images and text at almost no cost to themselves. By using the right keywords forgers can be almost certain that their goods will come to the attention of potential victims. Contact through a fraudulent internet identity enables the forger to decide whether, from his point of view, the buyer can be trusted.

One thing that works in the forgers' favour is that eBay does not 'police' the transactions on its site very effectively. Legal rulings are by no means consistent, with eBay getting off scot-free in some cases and not in others. In July 2008, for instance, the company was ordered to pay €38.8 million in damages to LVMH, a consortium of Paris-based handbag manufacturers and perfumers, including leading brands Louis Vuitton and Christian Dior, for not adequately policing the sale of counterfeit goods on its sites. In 2009, however, cosmetics company L'Oréal and Swiss watch manufacturer Rolex lost a case against eBay. The court did not deny that fake products of both brands were sold on eBay, but it concluded that the online auction site was taking sufficient steps to restrict the sale of counterfeit items.

I am not so sure. eBay is reported to have some 15,000 employees worldwide. Every day 2 million new items are put up for auction or sale. Suppose none of these employees are engaged in secretarial work, management, catering, programming or other activities, this means that each one will check some 133 advertisements every day. I would imagine that few eBay employees would be capable of that.

eBay offers a small advantage to those who hold history dear. Since the arrival of the auction site, dealers in archaeological artefacts, especially in Iraq and Iran, no longer make the effort to sell smuggled objects. The sale of counterfeits on eBay proves just as lucrative and they don't risk being punished for it.

ELMYR DE HORY AND THE ART OF LIVING WELL

Elmyr de Hory (1906–1976) preferred a good story to historical fact. Since the main source of information about his life is his own autobiography, the facts all have to be taken with a pinch of salt.

De Hory claimed (with no evidence to back this up at all) to be the son of an ambassador of the Austro-Hungarian monarchy and a lady from a banking family. What is certain is that he left his home town of Budapest in the mid-1920s and ended up in Paris, where he studied art under Fernand Léger and others. If his claims are to be believed, he was close friends with Picasso and Matisse, whose work he would later forge on a grand scale.

During the Second World War, because of his suspected Jewish origins and his homosexuality, De Hory was sent to a concentration camp. He managed to escape and returned to Paris, where the tried to earn a living from his paintings.

After the war De Hory discovered forgery, selling his works throughout Europe and, after 1947, in the United States. While in America on a three-month tourist visa, he decided to stay on when it expired. For many years, his life became like a road movie with farcical elements, including a long series of pseudonyms, an expired passport, paintings hurriedly sketched on hotel-room walls, a flight to Mexico after being exposed as a forger, and a melodramatic suicide attempt.

In the mid-1950s De Hory lived in Miami in an uneasy *ménage à trois* with Fernand Legros and Réal Lessard, who sold his forgeries for him. When De Hory discovered that his two partners were keeping most of the proceeds for themselves, tensions between them rose until, in 1959, De Hory returned to Europe. Their paths crossed again in Paris and they reached an agreement. De Hory moved into a luxury villa on Ibiza, built specially for him, and was paid a 'salary' of $400 a month. Legros and Lessard would visit every now and again to pick up his paintings, but did not interfere with him in any other way. It soon became clear to De Hory that little had changed. His $400 a month was peanuts compared to what Legros spent on houses, cars and paying off the families of the young boys he loved so much.

In 1966 the curtain fell when a Texan oil magnate discovered that 56 paintings he had bought from Legros and Lessard were forgeries. De Hory evaded the police for two years but in 1968 turned himself in and ended up in front of a Spanish judge. That he was given only a remarkably short prison sentence of two months was due to the fact that none of his victims were prepared to make statements and that there was no proof that he had produced any of his forgeries on Spanish territory. After completing his sentence he returned to Ibiza.

By now De Hory was enjoying a certain notoriety and his autobiography was ghostwritten by Clifford Irving (see GHOSTING AN AUTOBIOGRAPHY). In 1974 De Hory and Irving worked together on the film *F for Fake*, directed by Orson Welles. The film is a must for anyone interested in De Hory.

On 11 December 1976 De Hory learned that the Spanish and French governments had reached agreement on his extradition to France. The same day, he died from an overdose of sleeping tablets.

Irving estimated that De Hory produced around 1,000 works of art, which sold for some $60 million. His forgeries are now commanding such high prices at auction that forgers are forging his forgeries.

EMIL ABDERHALDEN AND HIS UNREPEATABLE EXPERIMENTS

In 1909 the Swiss biochemist and physiologist Emil Abderhalden (1877–1950) published an article on *Abwehrfermente* (defensive enzymes). He claimed that the body produces these enzymes when confronted with foreign proteins and came up with a practical application based on them: a pregnancy test. In 1912 he published a book, also entitled *Abwehrfermente*. His findings were confirmed by many laboratories, and when the fourth edition of the book was published

Dr Emil Abderhalden.

in 1914, Abderhalden was able to refer to 451 publications on the phenomenon. Besides pregnancy tests, the *Abwehrfermente* were used to diagnose cancer, infectious diseases such as syphilis, and psychiatric diseases like schizophrenia.

German-Jewish biochemist Leonor Michaelis (1875–1949) tried to prove that defensive enzymes did not exist, but his was a voice in the wilderness. When Michaelis published his argument in 1914, it marked the end of his career in Germany.

In the 1920s and 1930s Abderhalden steadily continued to publish on his beloved *Fermente*. During the Nazi regime Josef Mengele applied the theory in experiments in which he deliberately infected Auschwitz inmates of various races.

After Abderhalden's death, his son Rudolf took up the torch. Interest in the *Abwehrfermente* gradually waned and, after the 1960s, nothing more was heard of them.

We will never know whether Abderhalden deliberately committed fraud from as early as 1909. However, the experience of Hans Brockmann, who worked for him for a short period of time in the 1930s, speaks volumes. When an experiment worked the first time but not the second, Abderhalden asked Brockmann why he had repeated it at all, as it had worked well the first time. Brockmann saw Abderhalden for the half-baked scientist he was and left immediately.

ERICH VON DÄNIKEN'S ALIEN BELIEFS

Swiss-born Erich von Däniken – the best-known representative of a group of pseudoscientists who claim that there is evidence of extra-terrestrial beings having visited earth – started his career as a petty criminal.[4] In the 1960s he served several jail sentences for embezzlement. In 1968 he wrote the book that would establish his reputation, for good or ill, *Chariots of the Gods? Unsolved Mysteries of the Past*. The book is by no means original. It is based on *Le Matin des Magiciens* by Robert Charroux, published by the science-fiction magazine *Planète* in the early 1960s, which in turn can be traced back to fiction written by H. P. Lovecraft (1890–1937) in the last ten or twelve years of his life. Everything that Däniken has written since has essentially rehashed the 'hypothesis' launched in this first book: that numerous ancient artefacts offer conclusive proof of alien intervention in human history. In simple terms, the pyramids in Egypt are too complex to have been built by human civilization over 4,000 years ago, and must therefore have been constructed with the assistance of extraterrestrial intelligence. To provide 'evidence' for his theory, Däniken appears to have worked his way systematically through the UNESCO World Heritage list: Stonehenge, Easter Island, even the Nazca lines in Peru, which are either drawings by alien visitors or runways for flying saucers. All in all, Däniken's theory shows little respect for our ancestors, claiming that they could not have produced these wonderful artefacts without the help of aliens. Just how nonsensical this hypothesis is has been proved often enough. The adventurer Thor Heyerdahl (1914–2002) – despite his other theories often proving inaccurate – showed as early as 1958 that the statues on Easter Island could have been made by the islanders themselves, while a team led by archaeologist Anthony F. Aveni (1938) showed in 2000 that it is relatively easy to create figures in the Nazca desert.

The theory of evolution is lost on Däniken. Here, too, he believes that the Earth could not have managed on its own: man owes his existence only to the fact that extraterrestrial beings came to our planet and interfered with DNA.

Chariots of the Gods remains a bestseller and a source of inspiration for many crackpot theorists. Other than that, however, Däniken's influence is quite limited. The Ancient Astronaut Society has only 10,000 members worldwide, while the Mystery Park that Däniken opened in Interlaken in 2003, a mishmash of pyramids and space-age constructions, went bankrupt in 2006.

ERN MALLEY, AUSTRALIA'S BELOVED BOGUS POET

Ernest Lalor Malley may well be the most celebrated poet in Australian history: many people know at least some lines of his poetry and he is quoted regularly. Perhaps this says something about Australian poetry, because not only did Malley write just sixteen poems, none of which made any sense at all, he was a complete fabrication.[5] He was cooked up by two young but conservative Australian poets, James Phillip McAuley (1917–1976) and Harold Frederick Stewart (1916–1995). They were irritated by the modernist poetry in the Australian magazine *Angry Penguins* and decided to teach its editor, Max Harris (1921–1995) – whom they considered pretentious – a lesson. Their aim was 'to exaggerate to the point of imbecility characteristics of the poetry esteemed by Harris' (Porter, 1993). McAuley and Stewart, who were both in the Army, wrote the complete works of the fictitious poet in a single afternoon while hanging round the barracks, making good use of all the sources at their disposal:

> Swamps, marshes, borrow-pits and other
> Areas of stagnant water serve
> As breeding grounds . . . (Winder, 1993)

Evocative as it sounds, this opening to one of Malley's poems is no more than a chopped-up sentence from a U.S. military report on mosquitoes.

Posing as an equally fictitious sister, Ethel Malley, the pair sent the works of Malley, who had allegedly died prematurely from a thyroid disease in July 1943, to Max Harris. Along with an introduction he wrote himself, Harris published the poems under the title 'The Darkening Ecliptic' in the autumn 1943 issue of *Angry Penguins*. According to the magazine Malley was a poet on a par with W. H. Auden and Dylan Thomas. On 25 June 1944 the *Sunday Sun* published a statement by McAuley and Stewart, describing in colourful detail how they had written the poems by lifting words and phrases at random from the *Oxford English Dictionary*, the collected works of Shakespeare and the *Oxford Dictionary of Quotations*. Harris tried to salvage what was left of his dignity by claiming that the two had nonetheless subconsciously written beautiful poetry.

As for Malley, he is an indelible part of Australian cultural life. It must have been strange for McAuley, Stewart and Harris to know that their authentic cultural achievements will forever remain overshadowed by those of a poet who never existed.

F

FAKE PILGRIMAGE

In May 2012 the Italian police wound up a drugs gang, seizing 30 kg of cocaine and making 33 arrests. The cocaine had been carried from Colombia by fake monks and nuns travelling to Europe via Africa 'on a pilgrimage'. But the God they worshipped was Mammon, as they had no qualms about hollowing out Bibles and prayer books to carry their illicit goods.

The link between the supplier and the client was the South American doorman of a convent in Milan. The doorman had family ties with a Colombian drugs cartel and contacts in the 'Ndrangheta, the South Italian mafia.

FATSO FARNAM, THE FARE-DODGING FOODIE FRAUDSTER

On Monday 30 June 2008 a taxi in Wauwatosa, a suburb of Milwaukee, Wisconsin, took a fare to the Mayfair shopping mall. At 122 kg and only 5 ft 10 in., the passenger, apparently in his early fifties, was far too heavy for his height. The taxi driver was therefore probably not surprised when the man grimaced and clutched his chest while getting out of the cab. But when the man then collapsed to the ground the driver made a quick decision: better to lose the price of one fare than all that endless hassle with the police. He drove off, leaving the man groaning on the sidewalk.

Once the taxi was out of sight, Robert P. Farnam stood up, dusted off his clothes and went into the mall to look for a restaurant. At Applebee's he tucked into a sirloin steak, salad, mashed potatoes, a soft drink, a strawberry smoothie and a brownie. As he walked to the cash desk to pay the $22.66 bill, his face creased in pain and he collapsed.

The staff at Applebee's called the emergency number and, shortly afterwards, a crisis team from the Wauwatosa Fire Department arrived. They laid Farnam on a stretcher and whisked him off to the Wisconsin Heart Hospital, lights flashing and sirens blaring. But Farnam's welcome there was not too friendly. Dr William T. Kumprey had seen him far too often in the preceding months and had had enough of his antics. He told him that if he saw him just once more, he would call the police. Farnam, who was clearly not too bright, then let slip that he had been admitted to Froedtert Hospital earlier that same day, after eating a hearty meal and faking a heart attack to avoid paying for it. The doctor immediately called the police.

Farnam was no stranger to the cops. He had already been arrested five times in 2008 after pretending to be dying in restaurants or when getting out of taxis, and proved to have been regularly apprehended for the same curious crime in previous years. He was on probation and had been ordered to stay away from a number of restaurants, though Applebee's was not on the list. Farnam was charged with fraud and given a strong warning that he should stop faking heart attacks.

Farnam clearly paid heed to the warning. A few weeks later he was arrested again in a restaurant, Gyros Corner West, located in another Milwaukee suburb. This time he had pretended to lose consciousness due to a diabetic hypo.

THE FILM FESTIVAL THAT NEVER WAS

Turkish film director Özgür Doğan scored a hit with his feature film *İki Dil Bir Bavul* (*On the Way to School*), which premiered in October 2009. The film won nine awards in a period of only a few months. In February 2010 the director received a letter that the film had won an award for the best music at the Ankara film festival in December 2009. This honour was a complete surprise, especially as the film has no music.

The envelope also contained a visiting card from the 'Ministry of Public Works'. When Doğan called the number on the card, he got someone on the line who did not work at a ministry and who knew nothing about the award.

The Ankara film festival, which allegedly took place in December 2009, proved to be fictitious. The organizers disappeared without trace, as did the €12,000 grant that the Turkish Ministry of Culture had awarded to the festival.

FINDING THE PAST WITH HERR PROFESSOR PROTSCH

Professor Reiner Protsch (*b.* 1939) was not a run-of-the-mill academic. He had a liking for Cuban cigars, Porsches and gold watches, and used to brag about his apartments in New York, Florida and California, where he would hang out with film star Arnold Schwarzenegger and tennis legend Steffi Graf.

In the early 1960s, after studying in California, Protsch returned to his native Germany. He then made three very important finds. Hahnhöfersand Man, dated at 36,300 years old, was the world's oldest German. Binshof-Speyer Woman, 21,300 years old, had remarkably well-preserved teeth. Paderborn-Sande Man was apparently 27,400 years old. Scientific careers have been built on less. He had also become a professor at Frankfurt University.

In 2001 Thomas Terberger of Greifswald University became suspicious about Protsch's work. As a standard precaution he had the professor's finds re-dated at Oxford University. The results were astounding. Hahnhöfersand Man proved to be only 7,500 years old, Binshof-Speyer Woman was just 3,090, while Paderborn-Sande Man drew his last breath a mere 250 years ago.

The University of Frankfurt, where Protsch worked, set up a commission of inquiry which unearthed many more irregularities. According to his colleagues, Protsch did not know how to work the carbon-dating machine that was the department's pride and joy. He had offered to sell the university's collection of 278 chimpanzee skulls to an American collector for $70,000. He had also shredded piles of documents from the university's archives dating from the Second World War, some of which referred to 'experiments' by Josef Mengele. Further investigation showed that the aristocratic Prussian name Von Zieten, which Protsch liked to use as an appendage to his last name, had nothing to do with his family. Protsch turned out to be the son of Wilhelm Protsch, an ardent Nazi and Party stalwart. It is possible that Protsch destroyed the documents to protect his father's reputation.

On 18 February 2005 the University of Frankfurt reported that Protsch had been forced to retire. In July of the same year, he was charged with forgery, fraud and embezzlement. In June 2009, after a series of trials, Protsch was finally sentenced to eighteen months behind bars.

THE FIRST HUMAN CLONE

After the successful cloning of frogs in the 1960s, it seemed only a matter of time before the first cloned human being would make an appearance. And it was not only scientists who were fascinated with the idea; it also captured the public imagination and became a popular cultural theme. One of the best-known examples is perhaps Ira Levin's 1976 novel *The Boys from Brazil*, filmed in 1978.

On Friday 3 March 1978 the *New York Post* carried the remarkable headline on its front page: 'Baby born without a mother, he's the first human clone' (Culliton, 1978). The article was based on a book by journalist David Rorvik, *In His Image, The Cloning of a Man*. The book described how, in 1973, Rorvik had been approached by an American millionaire referred to only as Max. Then in his sixties, Max wanted to leave behind a clone of himself and hired Rorvik to put together a team that could make his wish a reality. After Rorvik had rustled up a group of willing scientists, including a geneticist who used the alias Darwin, the team moved to a secret location in a country 'beyond Hawaii' (i.e. outside the jurisdiction of the United States). They obtained ova by telling the female donors that they were taking part in an anti-infertility programme. Using the ova and genetic material from Max, Darwin set to work. When an ovum had divided to form more than 64 cells, it was implanted in the surrogate mother, known as Sparrow. In December 1976 a healthy child was born.

If this story had been written by a gutter-press reporter and published in a tabloid, no one would probably have paid it any attention. But Rorvik was no run-of-the-mill hack. He was a serious journalist and author of several books, including *Brave New Baby*, about the dangers of genetic technology. Furthermore, *In His Image, The Cloning of a Man* was published by J. B. Lippincott & Co., a far from frivolous publisher specializing in medical literature. This may explain why scientists felt the need to respond when they were approached by the media. Nearly all of them denounced the book as a hoax. Some claimed that if Darwin really existed, he would be shouting about his achievement from the rooftops: it would probably have earned him a Nobel Prize, and certainly eternal fame. Most of them pointed out that it could not be true, as science was simply not yet sufficiently advanced to achieve such a feat.

One problem in proving the book's authenticity was that Rorvik was very shy of publicity. Rumour had it that he was holed up in a cabin in Montana. Even Lippincott rarely spoke to him in person; all his business affairs were dealt with by his lawyer. A second problem was that Max had given Rorvik permission to publish his story on condition that the identities of all those involved were kept strictly secret, with the exception of Rorvik himself. The simplest solution, to get hold of Max and his clone and test their DNA – was therefore out of the question.

The case would perhaps have remained unsolved if, in the same year that the book was published, British biologist J. Derek Blomhall had not filed a lawsuit for defamation. Blomhall claimed that the cloning method described by Rorvik was based on work that he had performed on rabbits. Blomhall's work and name had been used in the book without permission and Blomhall demanded $7 million compensation. Despite the case dragging on for three years, it never came to a substantive treatment of the facts. The judge first wanted to determine whether the book was fact or fiction. The parties failed to reach agreement on how this question should be answered, while Max insisted on complicated conditions to protect his identity.

Early in 1981 the judge had had enough of the wrangling. He ruled that Lippincott/Rorvik had produced no evidence for the authenticity of the work and described the book as 'a fraud and a hoax' (Broad, 1981). From a scientific point of view, this was not a satisfactory outcome. The court did not consider it proven that the book was real and assumed that it was not, but did not prove that it was *not* real. Such rulings are grist to the mill of conspiracy theorists. Although this one was simply based on a summary of the facts, it was clear that Lippincott/Rorvik could never win the case. Lippincott paid Blomhall an out-of-court settlement suspected to be several hundred thousand dollars, while Rorvik continued to insist that the book told the truth.

The best that outsiders could come up with by way of explanation was that Rorvik published the book to stimulate a discussion on what was acceptable in terms of cloning and what was not.

A FISHY PRISON HOAX

In August 1872 Carl (aka Karl) Theodore Staiger, director of the Brisbane Museum, visited the penal colony Gayndah Station on the west coast of Australia. The inmates decided to play a prank on him. In the morning, Staiger got a curious-looking fish for breakfast that was unknown to him. The inmates told him that the fish had not been observed anywhere else, only recently near Gayndah. Staiger expressed his disappointment that he had only been able to see the fish cooked and not alive. Shrugging their shoulders, the inmates said there was little hope of that because it sometimes took a month between successful catches. Staiger made the best of the situation, got someone to make a few sketches of the fish from different angles, and ate it with gusto.

Staiger sent the drawings and a short description of the fish to the biologist Count Francis de Castelnau (1810–1880). A couple of years later Castelnau published a short article in the *Proceedings of the Linnean Society of New South Wales*, entitled 'On a New Ganoid Fish from Queensland'. After examining the sketch of the roughly 18-inch-long fish, Castelnau concluded that, considering its depressed spatuli-form snout, it was closely allied to *Atractosteus spatula*. However, there were also differences and, based on the drawing, Castelnau provisionally named the fish *Ompax spatuloides*.

In the years that followed, some ichthyologists seriously doubted the existence of *Ompax spatuloides*, whereas others entered the fish in their guidebooks because the possibility of finding ganoid fish in the waters of Queensland had been confirmed by a number of eminent naturalists (Whitley, 1933).

It took more than half a century for the truth about the *Ompax* to come out – almost six decades in which no other specimen of the fish was ever caught. On 6 August 1930 a newspaper in Sydney, *The Bulletin*, published an article by an author hiding behind the pseudonym 'Waranbini'. The author remembered with pleasure that morning in 1872, when Staiger was served a fish consisting of the head of a lungfish, the body of a mullet and the tail of an eel (the Staiger sketch shows a head that almost certainly belongs to a needlefish or a platypus: Waranbini probably made a mistake here). For many years the inmates of Gayndah Station had derived great pleasure from *Ompax spatuloides*. Whenever a marine mystery was captured, they remarked, 'It must be an Ompax!' (Whitley, 1933).

Gilbert P. Whitley of the Australian Museum in Sydney read Waranbini's story and wrote an article in the *American Naturalist* dismissing *Ompax spatuloides* as a myth once and for all.

FORGERS DONATE WORKS TO STOCKHOLM'S MOMA

On 7 November 1993 the Museum of Modern Art in Stockholm was the scene of a major art theft: the thieves sawed a hole in the roof and made off with a sculpture and seven paintings by Pablo Picasso and Georges Braque. The stolen works were valued at some €63 million.

A week later, the mood turned to jubilation when the paintings turned up on the museum steps. The police assumed that the thieves had become nervous and had brought the works back. But closer inspection offered a different scenario. 'They smell of paint', said the museum's security chief. 'They are dry but are no older than a week'.

The forgeries, complete with signatures, were most likely produced by otherwise innocent students of the art academy in Stockholm. The museum could not, however, appreciate the humour. 'This is a bad joke', said director Björn Springfeldt (Harper, 1993).

A FORGER OF FORGED ART

Andy Behrman arrived in New York in his late teenage years, and soon became embroiled in a world of fashion, drugs, sex and gossip.

At the end of the 1980s he was taken on as a salesman by Mark Kostabi, an artist with a very unusual method of 'painting'.

Kostabi was a talented graphic artist who built up a career in New York in the early 1980s. His ideas on art soon became ideas for their own sake, gimmicks that many an art critic considered vulgar. Nevertheless, his work was undeniably 'in' and was used, for example, for the cover of *Use Your Illusion*, an album by rock band Guns N' Roses. In 1988 Kostabi opened a studio where he himself did hardly anything at all. 'Ideas people' conceived ideas for paintings and submitted them to a 'committee'. If the idea was approved, the work was produced by 'painters'. A second committee then decided whether it should bear Kostabi's signature. If so, he signed it – a second or two's work.

The painters at his studio were paid $10 an hour, while Kostabi himself earned at least $50,000 for each work. He defended himself by saying that this was how it worked in Rembrandt's time too. At the same time, he was quoted as saying: 'Anyone who buys my paintings is a total fool. But the more I spit in their faces, the more they beg me to sell them another painting' (Greig, 1993).

The question is, of course, whether a Kostabi is a Kostabi. The fact that he signed the paintings says little. Normally, if a painter signs a painting it means that it is his work that he produced it. But now Kostabi himself was no longer responsible for whether the work should be signed or not, but had delegated this decision to a committee, this no longer applied.

These considerations became important in 1992, when Behrman started what could be called 'forging forgeries'. Together with one of the painters in the factory, Beate von Ploetz, Behrman put some 30 paintings he had signed with Kostabi's name up for sale.

When Behrman's extra earnings were discovered Kostabi accused him of 'forgery', but art critic Hilton Kramer hit the nail on the head, noting drily: 'The difference between a real Kostabi and a fake Kostabi is such that to date no method has been found of distinguishing between them' (Greig, 1993).

This excellent critical comment was of little help to Behrman. Kostabi's lawyers had called for him to be sentenced to five years in prison and a fine of $250,000, so the ultimate ruling of only five months behind bars and five months' house arrest must have come as a relief. Beate von Ploetz was acquitted, as it was simply impossible to determine whether she had produced 'real forged' or 'forged forged' Kostabis.

In 2002 Behrman published his autobiography, *Electroboy*, in which he talked about bipolar disorder, electroconvulsive therapy, mixed with a lot of sex, drugs and gossip. It showed that Behrman loves media attention as much as his former boss.

ST FRANCESCO FORGIONE AND HIS BOTTLED STIGMATA

Francesco Forgione (1887–1968) entered a monastery at the age of sixteen and was ordained as a priest in 1910. He seemed to have trouble with the vows of chastity (he had sexual intercourse twice a week) and of poverty (he was suspected of embezzling funds). Forgione's greatest 'achievement', however, was the stigmata that appeared on his hands and feet. Despite his activities being investigated in 1920 and him being banned from celebrating Mass for many years, Forgione was beatified by Pope John Paul II in 1999 and canonized in 2002.[6] The miracle required to achieve this status was Forgione's bilocation: he could be in two places at the same time.

In 2007 Italian historian Sergio Luzzatto published evidence for the allegation, which had already been made sometime earlier, that Forgione had produced his stigmata himself using chemicals. The proof included a handwritten letter from the priest in which he requested a pharmacist for carbolic acid 'in strict secrecy' (Popham, 2007).

The biography of Padre Pio, as Forgione is known, on the Vatican's website mentions only in passing the 'spiritual sufferings' that are the best-known fact about his life. The evidence that Forgione was a fraud has no consequences for his status as a saint. Popes are infallible and do not admit their mistakes.

Almost 40 years after Forgione's death, an absurd ecclesiastical circus was set in motion. His corpse was exhumed and the skull was fitted with a facial mask made by the company that supplies Madame Tussauds. The body, which incidentally showed no signs at all of stigmata, was put on public display in a glass cabinet reminiscent of Snow White's. All in all a respectable end for such a fraudulent trickster.

The veneration of this fornicating, embezzling and cheating monk was yet to reach its bizarre pinnacle, however. Plans were revealed in 2009 to erect a statue of Padre Pio – 60 m high – in southern Italy. The statue was to be coated with special photovoltaic paint that would trap the sun's heat, generating solar energy that could be used to illuminate it at night. This would make it the world's first 'ecological religious icon' (Squires, 2009).

FRENCH: THE LINGUA FRANCA OF EVERYONE ELSE

Born in France in 1818, Vrain-Denis Lucas was brought up in the country. He had little education, but did have an insatiable interest in history. In 1852 he left for Paris, hoping to find a job in a library or a bookshop, but he had no success because he could not read the classical languages. Instead, he went to work for a man called Letterlier, who kept genealogical records. His customers were mainly nouveaux riches wishing nothing more than to have their names related to illustrious names from the past. Lucas soon got the hang of the business and forged fifteen antique signatures to prove that the Marquis du Prat was a descendant of a prominent chancellor and cardinal.

Within no time, Lucas started using his skills to produce 'rediscovered' signatures of prominent historical figures. He presumably did this initially on a small scale until 1861, when he came into contact with the famous mathematician Michel Chasles (1793–1880). Chasles proved to be a keen customer and one incredible manuscript after another came to light. The documents testified to a glorious victory for French science: an exchange of letters between Blaise Pascal (1623–1662) and Sir Isaac Newton (1643–1727) showed that the former in reality had discovered the laws of physics with which Newton was later to make his name with his *Principia*. By accepting these documents as authentic, Chasles appeared to have lost his customary shrewdness. Not only is it very unlikely that Pascal and Newton ever corresponded with each other (given that Pascal died three years before Newton had even graduated at Cambridge), it is also unthinkable that they would have done so in French, for Latin was then the language of science. The documents that Lucas supplied contained one discrepancy after the other. The correspondence showed that Lucas possessed a wide knowledge of facts, but lacked sufficient intelligence to order them in any systematic way.

Letters from an aged Galileo Galilei (1564–1642) refer to him observing planets, while Galileo was completely blind in his latter years. King Dagobert I (*c.* 603–639) addressed his correspondence to 'Saint' Eligius (*c.* 590–*c.* 660), yet the latter was of course not canonized until after his death. Furthermore all correspondents – including Julius Caesar, Cleopatra, Martin Luther, Pythagoras and Mary Magdalene – were writers of excellent French!

Lucas also supplied Chasles with old books which he bought cheap at book markets and then forged stamps and marks, for example the *ex libris* of François Rabelais (1493–1555), to make them appear valuable.

Lucas' work ethic was remarkable. He would sit in a library in Paris every day, writing frantically like (as the judge later said) 'a Benedictine monk' (Rosenblum, 1998). In a period of eight years he supplied Chasles with an astounding 27,000 forgeries by 600 authors. All went well until 8 July 1867, when Chasles proudly presented a number of letters to the French Academy of Sciences. His colleagues became suspicious and, in the years that followed, he found himself facing increasing opposition. But it was not until 1869, when it was proved conclusively that the handwriting in letters from Galileo was not Galileo's, that the scales fell from everyone's eyes.

Lucas was arrested on 9 September 1869. The money he had earned had probably been spent by his mistress while he sat in the libraries. On 24 February 1870 he was sentenced to two years' imprisonment, a fine and payment of the costs of the trial. Nothing is known of what became of him after his release.

FRIEDERICH LICHTENBERGER AND THE MEDUSA WATER

In 1858 the San Francisco-based newspaper *Alta California* published a letter from a Friederich Lichtenberger, which was interesting from a scientific point of view. Lichtenberger, a doctor, described how he had seen an unfortunate gold prospector, Ernest Flucterspiegel, turn to stone. While looking for gold, Flucterspiegel found a geode, a hollow in a rock, and drank about half a pint of the fluid he found in it. After returning to the prospectors' camp, Flucterspiegel complained of pains in his 'epigastric' and 'left hypochondriac' regions.

He was dead within a short time, stiff and petrified. When Lichtenberger dissected the corpse with an axe, he discovered that Flucterspiegel's heart 'strongly resembled a piece of red jasper' (Rose, 2005). As it turns out, the story was a fabrication invented by the paper's editors to reel in readers.

FUDGE-FACTORING THE UNIVERSE

Scientists sometimes use the 'fudge factor' if empirical facts do not accord with a theory, or vice versa, while there are no discernible errors in either. Call it a little white lie.

In the hands of an unscrupulous scientist, the fudge factor can be used to disguise bad research or incorrect calculations. In the hands of a good scientist it often proves, with hindsight, to fill a gap in a theory that is later closed by new insights.

Perhaps the most famous application of the fudge factor was by Albert Einstein in his general theory of relativity, published in 1916. Einstein later called this his 'greatest blunder'[7] (Goldsmith, 1997). While working on his general theory of relativity, Einstein noted that his calculations implied that the universe was expanding or contracting. That was incompatible with the prevailing view of a static universe: galaxies could rise and fall, but the universe itself was believed to be immutable. Einstein solved the problem by adding an element to his theory: the cosmological constant. This was a kind of reverse gravity that held the limits of the universe neatly in place. Ten years later the American astronomer Edwin Hubble (1889–1953) discovered that the universe is not constant, but is expanding – just as Einstein's theory predicted before he applied the fudge factor. This apparent gap in his theory, which Einstein filled with the cosmological constant, was later closed definitively with the help of new scientific insights.

FURNITURE FAKERS GO VIRAL

Faking designer furniture dates back to the 1960s, when replicas of Harry Bertoia's Diamond Chair (1952) and Eero Saarinen's Tulip Chair (1956) were first produced. This generally occurred on a small scale, with the items often being sold in shops. Antiques dealers would be open about them being fake (this is less often the case these days because there is greater attention for fakes and the internet offers a safer alternative) or would tell a prospective buyer that he had 'just acquired something that is not yet on the market'.

The advent of the internet has been a godsend for 'furniture fakers', offering them a new market. Consequently, in the early twenty-first century, trade in fake designer furniture has increased alarmingly. Among the classics available as fakes are Pierre Paulin's Tongue Chair from 1967, Arne Jacobsen's Egg and Swan chairs from the late 1950s, the Lounge Chair (1956) and La Chaise (1948) by Charles and Ray Eames, the Panton by Verner Panton from 1967, Isamu Noguchi's coffee table from 1944, various items by Le Corbusier, Mies van der Rohe's Barcelona chair from 1929, Eileen Gray's side table from 1927, Eero Aarnio's Pastil Chair from 1967 and George Nelson's wooden bench from 1946.

These items can be found in many a museum, which is convenient for potential buyers, and even more so for potential 'imitators'. Producers of fake furniture only rarely make distinctive errors. Willy Van Der Meeren sideboards, for example, can be recognized as fakes only because the side panels are attached with rivets rather than screws.

Generally speaking, there are two ways in which potential buyers can identify fake furniture. First, it looks too good. An authentic early Eames Lounge Chair is half a century old and anyone lucky enough to own one will have spent many hours sitting in it. And that leaves its mark. Cupboards, tables, chairs: everything wears in its own way and the traces (or, in the case of fakes, the absence of them) can only be identified after careful study. Producers of fake copies are of course also aware of this and sometimes try to make their brand-new replicas look old or claim that the unsullied item has 'recently been restored'.

The second sign of a fake is that the price is too good to be true. For many years, finding a Maurice Calka polyester Boomerang Desk was like looking for a needle in a haystack but, in the early years of this century, a suspiciously large number suddenly appeared from nowhere – on eBay. Although these desks will easily fetch €30,000, they were available on eBay for one-third of that price. The low price is one of the standard tricks in the furniture faker's arsenal. Another is to get potential buyers to think that they have discovered this chance in a million themselves. A picture of a lamp worth only a few pounds might show a couple of Jacobsen chairs in the background. An enquiry from an interested party will receive a reply saying, 'No problem, the chairs are for sale, too.'

Today, fake designer furniture is mostly made in the mecca of the fake industry, China, and in a few other Asian countries. Intellectual property rights apply just as much there as in the West, but without effective controls they mean nothing.

G

GAZA CITY ZOO'S AMAZING ZEBRAS

Only ten of the 400 animals in a zoo in Gaza City survived the Israeli offensive against Hamas at the end of 2008 and the start of 2009. The rest died during the air raids, or later of starvation. In the autumn of 2009, looking for a new attraction, the zoo employed a professional painter to give two white donkeys a makeover of zebra stripes using hair dye. Sad as it may sound, the innocent impostors are a favourite with the children, who have never seen a real zebra and are therefore none the wiser.

A GENUINE LETTER FROM BEYOND THE GRAVE

Have you ever wanted to know who your real friends are? In 2007 Amir Vehabović, who lives in Bosnia, was so curious that he devoted a lot of time and effort to find out once and for all. He bribed a coroner to issue a fake death certificate and then found a company of funeral directors willing to organize the ceremony and inter an empty coffin.

On the day of his funeral, Vehabović hid behind a gravestone offering him a clear view of his open grave. He waited to observe just how many of the 46 people he had invited would congregate to see him launched into eternity. Some time passed. And then the pall-bearers came into view carrying the coffin. They in turn were followed by . . . his mother. And that was all; no one else had so much as bothered to turn up.

Not much time passed before the 45 absentee guests received the following missive from Vehabović.

> To all my dear 'friends',
>
> Some of you I have known since early school days, others I have only forged a relationship with in the last few years. Until my 'funeral', I considered all of you close friends. So it was with shock and, I admit, sadness and anger that I realized not one of you managed to find the time to come and say goodbye to me when you heard I was to be buried. I would have understood if just some of you came, bearing flowers or words of apology from others who could not make it. But no. Not a single one of you turned up to pay your last respects. I lived for our friendships. They meant as much to me as life itself. But how easy it was for you all to forget the pledges of undying friendship I heard on so many occasions. How different our ideas of friendship seem to be. I paid a lot of money to get a fake death certificate and to bribe undertakers to handle an empty coffin. I thought my funeral would be a good joke – the kind of prank we have all played on one another over the years. Now I have just one last message for you: my 'funeral' might have been staged, but you might as well consider me dead, because I will not be seeing any of you again. (Vehabović, 2007)

GET BETTER PRAYERS

Cardiologist Mitchell W. Krucoff studies the effects of prayer on the recovery of heart patients. The fact that he makes the results seem better in America's popular media than is justified on the basis of scientific publications suggests that he has a religious background.

In 2001 Krucoff published the results of a study that had tested four 'noetic' therapies: stress relaxation, imagery, touch and prayer. The account of the study makes amusing reading, although the money could have been better spent on something useful. Krucoff made the study into a veritable ecumenical event. The Unity School of Christianity held a 30-day-long 24-hour vigil in a chapel. In Nepal, 150 monks hummed the 'mantra of the deity that wears a leaf robe'. Jews placed printed prayers in the Western Wall and fundamentalist Christians went for 'daily prayers and motivation by Holy Spirit'. Baptists and Roman Catholics joined in to complete the scene.

In the months following publication of the study, Krucoff talked up the results. In one TV programme he claimed: 'In the group randomly assigned to prayer therapy, there was a 50 per cent reduction in all complications and a 100 per cent reduction in major complications' (Grant, 2007). Well, I'm not so sure about that. The percentage of deaths in the different groups showed that the use of imagery or stress-relaxation therapy was not to be recommended: 13.3 per cent of the patients had died six months after the start of the study. Touch therapy was less dangerous: only 6.7 per cent of the patients did not make it. Prayer seemed relatively harmless, with only 3.3 per cent of patients giving up the ghost. How Krucoff reconciled this result for the prayer group with 'a 100 per cent reduction in major complications' is a mystery to me; in my book, dying is a pretty major complication. Krucoff bragged that the power of prayer was the best form of noetic therapy, and he was right: other noetic therapies caused even more casualties. What he did not tell the media, however, was that the mortality rate in the control group – the 'standard therapy group' which had not received 'noetic' therapy – was zero per cent. For the truth you need to consult an article by Krucoff in *American Heart Journal*, hardly standard reading for the average American. In that article, Krucoff had to come clean, admitting that 'All mortality occurred in noetic therapy groups. By six months . . . mortality differences suggest a statistical trend favouring the standard therapy group' (Krucoff, 2001).

In 2005 Krucoff published the results of a large follow-up study. The 'noetic' therapies had been narrowed down to two: prayer versus MIT (music, imagery and touch). Once again there was a big difference between the scientific article and Krucoff's bragging in the press. The article made clear that it did not make any difference whether someone was prayed for. However, Krucoff implied that parts of the study justified a new follow-up study. His intention was obvious: to keep on undertaking trials until he happened to get a statistically significant result in favour of prayer.

Maybe Krucoff should study the work of his colleague Herbert Benson. Benson undertook a similar study, which lasted for several years and involved patients from six hospitals. The intercessors included Teresian Carmelites and members of the prayer organization Silent Unity.[8] To all their prayers they added the phrase 'for a successful surgery with a quick, healthy recovery and no complications' (Benson, 2006). The patients were divided into three groups: one that received prayer but did not know it, one that did not receive prayer but did not know it, and a third that received prayer and knew it. Complications occurred in 51 per cent of the first group of patients, in 52 per cent of the second group and in 59 per cent of the third group. So whether patients received prayer or not made no difference, if they did not know. But as soon as they knew that they had received prayer, there was a higher incidence of complications. Benson assumed that the certainty that they were being prayed for might well give patients unrealistically high expectations of recovery, which could actually lead to more complications.

GHOST ARMY: 23RD HEADQUARTERS SPECIAL TROOPS

Military deceit is as old as the Trojan Horse. It was also used in the Second World War. Field Marshal Erwin Rommel, for instance, had his tanks brought in by train prior to a battle. Wagon after wagon arrived, an impressive sight, news of which invariably reached the enemy through informants. The wagons were, however, partly filled with wooden frames shaped like tanks which, when covered in canvas, could not be distinguished from the real thing. When his troops passed through a city in convoy, Rommel also made them look more numerous by having the first vehicles through to then double back outside the city and join up behind the last one through. In North Africa, British forces used wooden dummies of soldiers laid flat on the ground. They could be pulled upright using a system of cables and pulleys to make the enemy shoot at them. This enabled the British to pinpoint the position of German artillery accurately without running risks, with the added bonus that the enemy wasted their ammunition.

When Germany declared war on the USA on 11 December 1941, four days after Japan's sneak attack on Pearl Harbor, American commanders knew that, as the U.S. was certainly not strong, it would have to be clever. The day after Pearl Harbor, the citizens of Washington, DC, saw heavy artillery set up on the roof of the White House. It was a fine symbol of resistance, but that is all it was: the artillery was fake, made of wood and painted black. The U.S. military, although expanding, was then far below the strength required to take the lead in a global war.[9]

In 1942 and 1943 the 23rd Headquarters Special Troops was formed. Its members were carefully selected: candidates had to have an IQ of at least 119 and a talent or skill that was useful for deception. Decorators, fashion designers, writers and actors may not be the first choice for a hardened warrior putting together a fighting unit, but 23rd Headquarters Special Troops had plenty of them.[10]

After the invasion of Europe, the Special Troops had to use cunning and guile to create the impression that the Allied forces were bigger than they really were. With only 1,100 men, they had to pretend they were a division (14,000–17,000 men) – or even two!

The first detachments went ashore in Normandy on D-Day, 6 June 1944. A few miles away from the actual landing points, they cleverly set up a number of floodlights so that, at night, it looked like a harbour, luring the Luftwaffe away from the real landing points, which were sheathed in darkness. By the end of June all 1,100 men were on French soil and the group could start performing its trickery. The 'Ghost Army', as the men had come to call the unit, had a wide variety of tricks at its disposal. There were dummies, including inflatable replicas of tanks, planes and artillery. They used recently invented wire recorders to project the sounds of tanks, artillery, soldiers laughter and so on.[11] They could create an imaginary infrastructure, like the non-existent harbour. They could imitate other units: if the generals wanted the enemy to believe that the 13th Army Corps was located at a certain position, the men of the Ghost Army would stitch that Corps' insignia onto their uniforms, spray its codes onto their vehicles and leak sufficient valid information to convince the local German spy that they were indeed the 13th. Finally, they used radio deception: members of the group would hold radio conversations which they knew the Germans would listen to, giving false information about orders and troop positions.

The Ghost Army was especially employed to discourage German attacks by giving the enemy the impression that they were facing a large army. And it did this successfully, repeatedly forcing German army units to mark time when they had the numerical superiority to have decimated the Ghost Army without much trouble.[12] The men of the Ghost Army showed great creativity. They used half-tracks to make tread marks in the snow that ended under camouflaging. To

German reconnaissance planes this looked as though tanks were hidden there, causing the enemy to choose a different route. A battery of inflatable cannons had the same effect.

The Ghost Army carried out 21 assignments (55, including assignments which were part of operations by other military units). This colourful group played a role in the Battle for Brest, the Battle of the Bulge, the Battle of Metz and the attempted crossings of the Mosel and the Rhine. According to a reasonable estimate, their efforts – two of whom lost their lives in combat and fifteen were wounded – prevented the deaths of 40,000 Allied soldiers.

For many veterans of the Ghost Army, post-war life was bitter. On the basis of their deeds these men qualified for many a medal, but the American ministry of war never acknowledged the unit's existence and did not therefore bestow any military honours on its members. This silence must be seen in the context of the times. After all, something that worked against the Germans in 1945 could also work against the Russians ten years later.

In the mid-1990s, parts of the archives about the 23rd Headquarters Special Troops were made public. The obligation to observe secrecy no longer applied, much to the relief of veterans who could finally tell their grandchildren what they did in the war.

GHOSTING AN AUTOBIOGRAPHY, CLIFFORD IRVING STYLE

In 1970 Clifford Irving was a reasonably successful American fiction writer who lived a happy life with his wife and children (and the occasional mistress) on Ibiza. However, he suffered from writer's block, a problem he shared with his writer friend Richard Suskind. One day, while they were talking about an article on the eccentric billionaire Howard Hughes (1901–1976), the conversation took a sudden turn. The struggle for power at the top of Hughes's business empire led Irving to suspect that Hughes was ill, or no longer alive. Besides a small group of aides, no one had seen Hughes during the past fifteen years. The two friends fantasized about writing Hughes's 'autobiography'. According to Irving this involved little risk. In the 1960s the recluse had lost $137 million in a court case just because he had refused to appear in person. So what were the odds that he would show his face to denounce a fake autobiography?

The first preparations were hardly taken seriously, as if it were a joke. Based on Hughes's handwriting – printed in a magazine article – Irving forged a letter in which Hughes contracted him as his biographer. This caused a stir at publisher McGraw-Hill. The handwriting was declared authentic and the negotiations started. According to Irving, Hughes demanded an advance of $1 million, of which Irving would get 10 per cent. McGraw-Hill offered $500,000, which it later raised to $750,000, back then the highest advance ever paid for a book. When McGraw-Hill's lawyers demanded a contract signed by Hughes in the presence of a notary, it looked as though the joke would end there. But McGraw-Hill ignored the advice and settled for a statement signed by Irving.

Irving and Suskind read interviews with Hughes and the memoirs of people close to him. They studied court cases in which he had been involved and plundered the substantial *Time-Life* archives. For a whole year Irving 'interviewed' Hughes in exotic locations like Puerto Rico, Mexico and Nassau. Irving told of blindfold car rides and mysterious factotums from Hughes's household. He genuinely visited these locations, if only to be able to produce the airline tickets and answer questions about the places. Women accompanied him on extramarital adventures.

The interviews (which McGraw-Hill was not allowed to listen to, at the insistence of the eccentric Hughes) were typed out by Irving and Suskind. These 'transcriptions' – in actual fact original material – formed the basis of the book. Hughes told stories of his time as a film director and playboy, of his adventures in aviation, and of his career as a real estate tycoon in Las Vegas. He recalled sexual escapades with many an actress and gossiped about actors and politicians. Irving and Suskind mostly named people who were no longer alive, in line with their motto 'Libel the dead!'. After all, the dead cannot take legal action. Hughes made surprising disclosures. Who had ever known that he had been a good friend of Ernest Hemingway and that he had made reconnaissance flights over occupied Europe in the Second World War?

Irving took care of the finances. Using a false passport, his wife Edith opened a bank account in Zurich under the name of Helga R. Hughes, where the cheques that McGraw-Hill made out to H. R. Hughes were cashed. Most of the money was then deposited in yet another bank account under yet another name – Irving and Suskind took account of the possibility that the hoax would be discovered and that they would have to pay the money back. But so far, everything was going according to plan. Experts who saw the manuscript concluded that they were reading the words of the one and only real Howard Hughes. Osborn Associates, a firm of handwriting experts, declared that his corrections and scribbled notes were authentic. On 7 December 1971 McGraw-Hill announced that it would be publishing the autobiography of Howard Hughes in March 1972. A representative of Hughes's organization responded that no such book existed, but this claim was easy to dispute. Managers at Hughes's empire hadn't seen or heard from their boss in fifteen years either. Nevertheless, the publisher started to get nervous and submitted Irving to a lie-detector test. The results were not decisive. It also emerged that the H. R. Hughes cashing the cheques in Zurich was a woman. Irving got himself out of that by admitting that his wife was acting as an assistant to Hughes; surely they didn't think that the recluse would travel to Zurich himself?

The end came a little closer when, during a TV broadcast on 7 January 1972, a panel of seven journalists spoke to someone on the telephone claiming to be Howard Hughes, who said he did not know Irving. As inventive as ever, Irving had an explanation for this, too: the voice on the telephone, he said, was not Hughes. To Irving's advantage, the man on the phone was asked seven questions to confirm his identity. The mentally ill Hughes answered five of the seven questions incorrectly.[13]

Someone who got very nervous about Hughes's forthcoming 'autobiography' was American president Richard Nixon (1913–1994). He correctly suspected that the book devoted attention to 'loans' that Nixon and his brother had received from Hughes and was afraid that the Democrats would use the information in the next election. Nixon, never averse to dirty tricks, decided to find out, and called in a number of shady figures to install listening devices at the Democratic National Committee's headquarters at the Watergate complex in Washington, DC. When one of Nixon's myrmidons got caught, the Watergate scandal was born.

Irving and his cronies were finally brought down by Swiss bankers. When the banks had incontrovertible evidence that Helga R. Hughes was in reality Edith Irving, they requested her extradition so that she could be prosecuted for fraud. To protect the least guilty person in the hoax, Irving and Suskind made a full confession to the U.S. Public Prosecutor in the vain hope that Edith would not have to face charges.

On 16 June 1972 Clifford Irving was sentenced to two and a half years in prison, of which he served seventeen months. Dick Suskind was sentenced to six months and served five. Edith Irving was given two years in prison, 22 months of which were suspended. After her release she was tried in Switzerland and sentenced to two years, of which she served more than a year.

The advance (which had to be paid back), unpaid tax on earnings, and lawyer's fees left Irving with a debt of around $1.5 million. Edith, who had learned from the papers who had accompanied her husband to various exotic places, sued for divorce.

Irving wrote a book about the affair, *The Hoax*. When it was turned into a film in 2006, with Richard Gere in the leading role, Irving demanded that his name be removed from the movie credits, saying on his own website: 'I didn't want anyone to believe that I had contributed to such a historically cockeyed story where the main character, almost by coincidence, happens to bear my name.'

In 1999 a small collectors' edition of Howard Hughes's 'autobiography' was published and in March 2008, 36 years after the planned date of publication, it was issued as a regular edition.

GRABBING BONBONS BY THE TRUCKLOAD

December is a busy month for bonbon producer Ferrero Rocher. And, of course, there is always someone who wants a piece of the pie. In November 2008 a refrigerated truck arrived in Paris from Turkey, where it unloaded its cargo at a wholesaler's. Shortly afterwards, the load was seized by the police. It proved to be 33,000 boxes of different kinds of Ferrero Rocher products – around 10 tons of chocolates. The bonbons were tested and discovered to be harmless but of inferior quality. The government inspectors ordered the whole consignment to be destroyed.

GREAT QUOTES FROM A PLUMBER

In the mid-1950s Cyril Henry Hoskins (1910–1981) started peddling a manuscript called *The Third Eye*, apparently written by a Tibetan monk called Dr Tuesday Lobsang Rampa. When London publisher Secker & Warburg received the manuscript, they asked Buddhism expert Agehananda Bharati to assess it. He later recorded his response:

> I was suspicious before I opened the wrapper: the 'third eye' smacked of Blavatskyan and post-Blavatskyan hogwash. The first two pages convinced me the writer was not a Tibetan, the next ten that he had never been either in Tibet or India, and that he knew absolutely nothing about Buddhism of any form, Tibetan or other. The cat was out of the bag very soon, when the 'Lama', reflecting on some cataclysmic situation in his invented past, mused, 'for we know there is a God.' A Buddhist makes many statements of a puzzling order at times, and he may utter many contradictions; but this statement he will not make, unless perhaps – I am trying hard to find a possible exception – he is a nominal Nisei Buddhist in Seattle, Washington, who somehow gets into Sunday school at age eleven and doesn't really know what he is talking about. (Bharati, 1974)

The book, according to its foreword 'Written in the Year of the Wood Sheep' by Lobsang Rampa, is a succession of one lunacy after another. After having his 'third eye' opened through a form of trepanation, Rampa acquired a much clearer view of the world and experienced a series of wonderful adventures. He flew with the help of kites but, if that was too much of a bother, he would travel using his astral body. He also regularly practised levitation, and all under the approving eye of the Dalai Lama in person.

Despite the criticism by Bharati and others, Secker & Warburg decided to take a gamble. And the gamble was a success, in commercial terms. By the end of 1957, a year after it was published, *The Third Eye* had sold 45,000 copies and been translated into twelve languages. If Hoskins needed any encouragement, this was it. The lama-cum-plumber from Plympton, Devonshire, gave his imagination free reign in another eighteen books. Although they were all consigned to the dustbin by anyone with any real knowledge of Tibet, including explorer, mountaineer and former adviser to the Dalai Lama, Heinrich Harrer, it did not impair their commercial success.

Hoskins was an extreme fantasist who actually lived out his own fantasies. He shaved his head, grew a beard and called himself a super-Buddhist. His determination is worthy of admiration. When doubts arose about the authenticity of Dr Tuesday Lobsang Rampa, journalists started to investigate. A British tabloid eventually disclosed the true identity of the pseudo-lama in 1958.[14] Hoskins's boundless imagination came up with a quotable answer to the question about how a plumber from Devon, who could not speak Tibetan and had never been further east than Dover, could be a Tibetan monk. The explanation is provided in his third book, *The Rampa Story*. One day, Cyril Henry Hoskins (body and spirit) climbed into a tree to photograph an owl. He fell to the ground and lost consciousness. When he came round again, he saw Dr Tuesday Lobsang Rampa approaching him (spirit only: Rampa had broken the link with his body). Rampa's spirit cut the link between Hoskins's body and spirit and then linked his own spirit to Hoskins's body. It was as easy as falling off a log, so to speak.

Hoskins's oeuvre was brim full of fantastic fantasies. He met the Abominable Snowman, flew to Venus in a UFO with two Venusians called the Tall One and the Broad One, and met his own mummy (body only), while his book *Living with the Lama* was dictated to him by his Siamese cat, Mrs Fifi Greywhiskers. Hoskins's ideas are kept alive today by his followers, who are unknown in number but who do lack their guru's imagination. They disseminate dull expositions of Hoskins's work via the internet on issues like drug use and homosexuality.

THE GULF IN THE WAR EVIDENCE

During March–May 2003, in the build-up to the Second Gulf War, the United States and Great Britain launched a PR offensive to sell the invasion of Iraq to their citizens. From around September 2002, putting a stop to the production of weapons of mass destruction by Saddam Hussein's regime was increasingly presented as an argument. In other words, Hussein was building a nuclear bomb and that was too dangerous for the rest of the world. The governments of George W. Bush and Tony Blair claimed to have evidence for this allegation but on security grounds refused to go into it in detail.

On 20 March 2003 a large military force consisting mainly of American and British troops invaded Iraq. Shortly after, the evidence for Iraq's nuclear weapons fell into the hands of Mohamed ElBaradei, Director-General of the International Atomic Energy Agency. ElBaradei was shocked at what he saw, as the evidence was completely unsound.

The first piece of evidence was that Iraq had bought 60,000 aluminium tubes which – according to the intelligence agencies – would be used for the production of nuclear weapons. ElBaradei deemed it 'highly unlikely' that these tubes could be used to produce nuclear material (Fidler, 2003). The key piece of evidence was a series of letters dating from 1999–2001 between Iraq and Niger concerning Iraq's purchase of uranium oxide (yellow cake), which is essential for the production of nuclear weapons. This correspondence turned out to consist of a number of simple forgeries that contained 'laughable and childlike errors' (Grey, 2003). One letter, supposedly from Niger's President Mamadou Tandja, bore a signature that did not resemble his at all. Another letter was dated as having been sent on 10 October 2000 by Niger's Minister of Foreign Affairs, Allele Elhadj Habibou. Habibou had, however, already resigned in 1989, eleven years earlier. According to the stamp showing the date of receipt, this letter was received in Iraq in September 2000, a month before it had been sent.

It soon became clear that the letters came from Niger's Embassy in Rome. An underpaid diplomat had sold the forgeries to Italian intelligence for a few thousand dollars, which had passed the information on to the CIA and British Intelligence. Is it really possible that these agencies took these amateur forgeries for real? It is not impossible: espionage is the work of real people and intelligence agencies have blundered before. The CIA, however, had sound reasons for doubting the information. In February 2002 the American diplomat Joseph Wilson had already concluded after investigation that Niger could not have sold uranium oxide to Iraq. Niger's two uranium mines were run by Cogema, a French state company. The extraction and transport of uranium oxide were closely monitored by the International Atomic Energy Agency and not a single barrel of uranium oxide had gone missing in the 40 years that the mines had been in operation.

This suggests a second possibility: the intelligence agencies did not believe the correspondence to be real. Intelligence agencies have no scruples about forging documents (see for example WHY A

LETTER SANK THE LABOUR PARTY). It is not inconceivable that the CIA considered it a stroke of good luck when they received this fictitious correspondence: instead of having to produce something themselves, the Italians had supplied them with a ready-made product.

GWEN HARWOOD, HOUSEWIFE AND POETESS

Gwen Harwood (1920–1995) felt that she was not taken seriously in the male-dominated world of literary editors in the Australia of the 1950s and therefore published her poetry almost exclusively under male pen names. In 1960 she dreamed up a nom de plume – Walter Lehmann, described as a poet originally from Europe and now an 'apple orchardist in the Huon Valley in Tasmania, and husband and father' (Atherton, 2002). The poetry that Harwood produced under this pseudonym was honest, ambitious work – that is, with the exception of two epistolary sonnets.

Harwood had become annoyed by the magazine *Bulletin*, whose editor Donald Horne, in her view, published mediocre poetry. She decided to expose Horne's lack of literary appreciation. In 1961 *Bulletin* received two sonnets from 'Walter Lehmann'. The subject of the sonnets concerned the well-known love tragedy of Pierre Abélard and Héloïse d'Argenteuil that occurred in early twelfth-century France. This pair of intense, seemingly religious poems were both published. Harwood then let it be known that the two sonnets were also acrostics. The first letter of each of the lines of 'Eloisa to Abelard' spelled out 'So Long Bulletin', while 'Abelard to Eloisa' produced an even clearer message: 'Fuck All Editors'.

Harwood claimed that 'those who couldn't tell poetry from a bunyip's arse might well be laughed at' (Atherton, 2002). Whether her hoax had a wider (and for Harwood much desired) effect is doubtful. Harwood complained that even the newspaper reports about her did nothing but confirm just how widespread were negative assumptions concerning women, with one paper even using the belittling headline 'Tasmanian Housewife in Hoax of the Year' (Atherton, 2002).

H

HAMBURG'S TERRACOTTA WARRIORS

In 2007 the exhibition *The First Emperor – China's Terracotta Army* attracted enormous numbers of visitors to the British Museum in London. Consequently, the director of the Museum of Ethnology in Hamburg was delighted to hear that, for a sizeable fee, he could acquire his own terracotta warriors on loan from the Centre of Chinese Arts and Culture (CCAC) in Leipzig (or, more precisely, the affiliated Qin Terrakotta-Armee Ausstellungs-GmbH). There were only eight warriors (and two horses) compared to the 120 in London, but it was better than nothing. On 25 November 2007 the exhibition *Macht im Tod* (Power in Death) opened at the museum. Less than two weeks later, angry representatives of the Chinese government were hammering at the door. China was aware of no terracotta warriors being lent anywhere but to the British Museum, so the statues on display in Hamburg had to be fakes. The museum had to offer the 10,000 people who had visited the museum their money back. The CCAC defended itself with a classic forgers' argument, claiming: 'There was never a word about originals in the Hamburg contract' (Connolly, 2007).

HAN VAN MEEGEREN, THE VERMEER FORGER WHO FOOLED THE NAZIS

Ever since his childhood in the Netherlands, Han van Meegeren (1889–1947) had a penchant for drawing. His art teacher at secondary school, Bartus Korteling, aroused his interest in the Dutch masters of the seventeenth century and taught Han the old techniques. His father, however, did not encourage his talent for art and, in 1907, Han fled to Delft – the city of Vermeer – on the pretext of going to study architecture at the Institute of Technology. For Van Meegeren 1911 was an important year: he met his first wife, his first child was born and he won a gold medal from the Institute of Technology for his drawing of a church interior. This medal gave Van Meegeren the courage to tell his father that he had dropped out as an architecture student. His dishonest disposition also emerged at this time: he sold the prize-winning original of the church interior and made a copy of it when a second prospective buyer showed an interest.

Van Meegeren received his degree from the Royal Academy of Art in The Hague in 1914, and in 1916 and 1922 he held exhibitions which were well received. In 1923 he left his wife for the actress Jo Oerlemans (who he married in 1929); halfway through his thirties, he realized that he was no longer a 'promising young man'. His career as an artist was at a dead end. That year, he made his first two forgeries, *The Laughing Cavalier* and *The Happy Smoker*, both in the style of Frans Hals.[15] The first work was bought by an auction house for 50,000 guilders, but was some months later detected as a forgery on technical grounds. This was good training for Van Meegeren. Between 1923 and 1931 he forged paintings by Gerard Terborch (1617–1681), Pieter de Hoogh (1629–1684) and Dirck van Barburen (*c.* 1595–1624). Together with restorer and forger Theo van Wijnbergen, Van Meegeren frequently spent time in Britain, apparently to 'paint portraits'. Considering Van Meegeren's high income in those years, it is more likely that he was selling forgeries there.

In 1932 Van Meegeren moved to the Côte d'Azur. Before leaving he took a first shot at his 'big project': forging the work of Johannes Vermeer (1631–1675). In the same year a 'Vermeer' entitled *Man and Woman at a Spinet* surfaced. With a few exceptions, the critics were not convinced by the painting. Between 1932 and 1945 Van Meegeren produced another ten paintings by Vermeer. His greatest Vermeer forgery, *The Disciples at Emmaus*, surfaced in 1937. After the previous

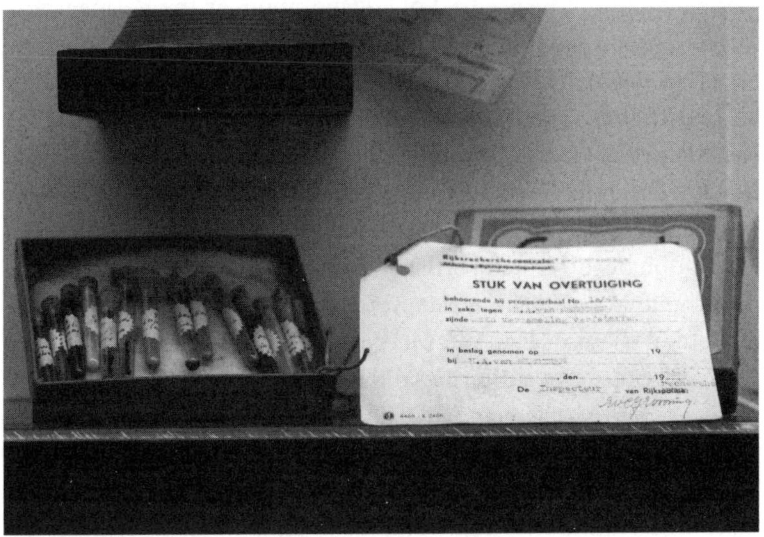

Evidence against Han van Meegeren, a collection of pigments.

discovery of the authentic *Christ in the House of Martha and Mary*, which dates from an undocumented period of Vermeer's life, Dutch art expert Abraham Bredius had predicted that other religious works by Vermeer would probably be discovered. Although Van Meegeren was probably unaware of Bredius's prediction, *The Disciples at Emmaus* came at just the right moment. It was snapped up by a consortium of art lovers for 520,000 guilders.

Living a life of luxury, Van Meegeren – already a chain-smoker – became addicted to alcohol, morphine and late nights. This had a noticeable effect on the quality of his later forgeries. The fact that these increasingly mediocre Vermeers were still bought in the Netherlands was largely due to patriotism clouding the collectors' judgment. In the early 1940s, it was considered better to buy an 'inferior' Vermeer to keep it in the Netherlands than to see it disappear to Germany. What is more, each new Vermeer was compared to the existing collection, an ever increasing share of which consisted of Van Meegeren's forgeries.

After the liberation of Europe, a Vermeer was found in the art collection of Reichsmarschall Hermann Göring. The painting, *Christ and the Adulteress*, was traced back to Van Meegeren, who was arrested on 29 May 1945 on suspicion of collaborating with the enemy. On 12 June, most probably suffering from withdrawal symptoms due to the lack of alcohol and drugs, Van Meegeren made a statement. He claimed that he could not be accused of collaboration, as the Vermeer was forged. This turned him into a folk hero overnight: he had fooled the Nazis! In reality he was not ill-disposed towards the Nazis. One of his best friends was Martien Beversluis, a poet and member of the Nederlandsche SS. A book produced by Van Meegeren, *Teekeningen 1*, contained texts by Beversluis and was imbued with fascist symbolism. Adolf Hitler's private library contained a copy with a handwritten inscription by the grateful artist: '*Dem geliebten Führer in dankbarer Anerkennung gewidmet von Han van Meegeren*' (To my beloved Führer in grateful tribute – Han van Meegeren) (Morris, 2009).

Since the legal authorities did not believe that such a mediocre painter as Van Meegeren could paint a Vermeer, he proposed that he paint a new one under police supervision, on condition that he would be supplied with the right materials, including Bols Genever and morphine. And so the twelfth and final Van Meegeren Vermeer, *The Young Christ Teaching in the Temple*, came into being.

In the meantime, a few buyers tried to get their money back. But Van Meegeren had made arrangements to secure his assets – which were considerable. In 1945 he owned 67 houses and rumours were circulating about boxes of money being buried in a garden in the Dutch town of Laren. Later Van Meegeren would testify that his forgeries had brought in 7,167,000 guilders, of which he had received 5,460,000. A large part of his capital had been transferred to his wife Jo Oerlemans, from whom he was later divorced. In 1945, due to lack of assets, Van Meegeren was declared bankrupt.

In 1946 a committee of experts examined the suspect Vermeers and reported back in 1947, during the trial against Van Meegeren. They concluded that there were at least nine technical reasons to assume that the works were not by Vermeer.

During his examination by the president of the court, Mr Boll, Van Meegeren gave an insight into the inner life of the forger:

> BOLL: Do you still admit that you painted all these fakes?
> VAN MEEGEREN: Yes, Mr President.
> BOLL: And also that you sold them, at a very high price?
> VAN MEEGEREN: I had no alternative. If I sold them at a low price it would have been obvious in advance that they were false. (Kreuger, 2004)

Van Meegeren was sentenced to one year in prison, less the time already spent in custody. He was not to serve his time. His body worn out and partially paralysed, the painter was admitted to the Valeriuskliniek in Amsterdam on 26 November 1947. There, in what would be his final month, he received visits from Jo and from Cootje Henning, the last in a long list of mistresses. On 29 December he had a heart attack, and he died the following day.

In 2010 film director Johan Nijenhuis announced that he intended to make a film of Van Meegeren's life, to be called *De Vervalser* (The Forger).

THE HAND-CRANK BANK

Back in 1812 Charles Redheffer claimed to have built a perpetual motion machine in his home in Philadelphia, and started making money by charging visitors to view it in action. The state government was so impressed that they sent a team of commissioners to inspect the machine. When they arrived, the visitors found the room containing the machine was locked (Redheffer said this was to protect it from damage), so they had to study it through a window. They suspected that it was a fake, but had no proof.

Redheffer slipped away and resurfaced in New York, where he charged people money to view the machine. One of the visitors was the renowned American engineer Robert Fulton, who had built the first steamboat. Fulton studied the machine and discovered a hidden cord of catgut that disappeared through a hole in the ceiling. On the floor above, he found an elderly man patiently turning a hand crank. Realizing they had been tricked, indignant visitors destroyed the machine.

HARVARD'S 'PRINCE OF CHARLATANS'

Jean Louis Rodolphe Agassiz (1807–1873) received a first-class education in Heidelberg, Munich and Paris. In Paris he studied under Georges Cuvier (1769–1832), who strongly influenced his thinking. In the 1840s Agassiz devoted himself to categorizing human races. He concluded that there were three races (white, black, Eskimo), each with their own climatic zone (temperate, hot, cold). In line with his Roman Catholic faith, which teaches that all humans descend from Adam and Eve, Agassiz claimed that these races were variations within *Homo sapiens*.

Agassiz was not the only one to concern himself with this subject. At that time, there was a battle between monogenism, of which Agassiz was an advocate, and polygenism, which saw the differences between human beings as variations not within the species but between separate species, with only the white race qualifying as *Homo sapiens*. Generally speaking, monogenism had the upper hand.

Agassiz determined his position on rational grounds, as a scientist should. However, shortly after leaving his native Switzerland and setting foot in the United States in 1846, his gut feeling made him abandon monogenism. This turnabout came when he saw African-Americans for the first time in his life. He expressed his feelings in a letter to his mother:

Louis Agassiz *c.* 1865.

> I experienced pity at the sight of this degraded and degenerate race, and their lot inspired compassion in me in thinking that they are really men . . . In seeing their black faces with their thick lips and grimacing teeth, the wool on their head, their bent knees, their elongated hands, their large curved nails, and especially the livid color of the palm of their hands, I could not take my eyes off their faces in order to tell them to stay far away. And when they advanced that hideous hand towards my plate in order to serve me, I wished I were able to depart in order to eat a piece of bread elsewhere, rather than dine with such service. What unhappiness for the white race – to have tied their existence so closely with that of negroes in certain countries! God preserve us from such a contact! (Gould, 1996)

This emotional reaction led Agassiz to conclude that black and white people could not be variations within one species; the distance he had perceived between the two was too great. In the years that followed, as he disseminated his new beliefs during lectures, he was welcomed enthusiastically by American advocates of polygenism. These scientists were severely outnumbered, but having Agassiz in their camp gave the theory more prestige than it deserved. He must have been aware by then that polygenism served a specific goal. Once you start talking about separate 'species' of human beings, it is obvious that *Homo sapiens* – who is after all supposed to think – will put them in some sort of order. And, of course, the so-called 'negroid' species was ranked lower than the white species: an excellent argument in favour of slavery. Although the northern American states had abolished slavery, in the South it was still widespread. Halfway through the nineteenth century the pro-slavery movement took on a more aggressive form, and Agassiz was content to see his theory being deployed in the battle.

In 1850 and 1851 Agassiz expounded his theory in articles in the *Christian Examiner*. He described the characteristics of the negro, which included submissive, obsequious and imitative behaviour. Accused of facilitating the preservation of slavery, Agassiz denied all responsibility. He argued that he was a scientist; what politicians did with his findings had nothing to do with him.

There were a number of problems with the theory. With a few exceptions, it is impossible for two individuals of different species to reproduce. If black and white people were separate species, how did Agassiz then explain the racially mixed population in America? His answer was shameful, from both a scientific and a humanitarian point of view. He explained that many housemaids were multiracial. These women and girls would seduce the slave owner's sons. The boys were attracted to the white part of the women, while the black part encouraged loose sexual morals. This obviously made no sense at all, if only because Agassiz did not explain where the first multiracial girls themselves came from; his 'answer' did not answer the question. In humanitarian terms, it was reprehensible. Agassiz must have been aware that many racially mixed people were the result of female slaves being raped by slave owners, their sons and their white employees. Unable to give a scientific explanation, Agassiz resorted to rhetoric:

> The production of half-breeds is as much a sin against nature, as incest in a civilized community is a sin against purity of character . . . The idea of amalgamation is most

> repugnant to my feelings, I hold it to be a perversion of every natural sentiment. (Gould, 1996)

However, there was also a theological problem with Agassiz's theory, which he solved with yet another original ruse. He explained that there had not been only one creation, but several: one for each species of human. Believers were hesitant: did that mean that the Bible is incorrect? The Bible is the literal truth, Agassiz insisted, but it describes only one creation, because the author of Genesis just happened to live in the area where it occurred and had no knowledge of other creations.

In 1847 Agassiz was appointed professor of zoology and geology at Harvard University. When Darwin's *On the Origin of Species* was published in 1859, it was a major blow to his credibility. Never had a theory answered so many scientific questions so elegantly and concisely. Agassiz's reputation suffered when he proved incapable of defending his multiple-creation theory against the new doctrine.

In the latter years of his professorship, Agassiz's students deserted in droves. One reason was his incessant plagiarism. Whether it was the work of students or of other staff members, Agassiz was of the opinion that – as the head of the faculty – he possessed the intellectual property rights to everything produced within the faculty. And so, the man who had been called the prince of naturalists in his younger years was given a new nickname towards the end of his life: 'The Prince of Charlatans'.

HEINRICH SCHLIEMANN AND THE TREASURE TROVE OF TROY

The German archaeologist Heinrich Schliemann (1822–1890) was a notorious liar. After a visit to the United States, for example, he claimed to have dined with President Millard Fillmore, although no record of the event can be found. On another occasion he penned an indisputably spurious 'eyewitness account' of the San Francisco Fire of 1851.

As an amateur archaeologist Schliemann only had one goal: to prove that Homer's *Iliad* and *Odyssey* were based on truth. Digging at the location where he thought Homer's city of Troy must lie, he discovered the Treasure of Priam, a large collection of artefacts including

Heinrich Schliemann.

jewellery, which Schliemann claimed had been worn by Helen of Troy. This convinced him that Homer's account was reliable and that he himself had been right.

Later investigation, including examination of documents left by Schliemann, showed that his reports on the excavations were completely fabricated. In addition, some critics have argued that the artefacts were put together and/or supplied by dealers with whom Schliemann had close ties, and that he himself had buried Priam's treasure in order to dig it up again.

HELENE HEGEMANN, A REAL LITERARY MIXER-UPPER

In January 2010 German publisher Ullstein presented the debut novel of seventeen-year-old Helene Hegemann, *Axolotl Roadkill*. The book was about a teenage girl's life of sex, drugs and self-discovery. It was a bestseller, shifting 100,000 copies in the first few weeks, and was nominated for a prestigious prize at the Leipzig Book Fair.

In mid-February 2010 it emerged that not all the text in *Axolotl Roadkill* had been written by Hegemann. Around twenty unaccredited quotes had been taken from a book called *Strobo*, a compilation of texts from a weblog by someone using the pen name 'Airen'. The blogger used a pseudonym because he worked at a firm of consultants, which might not have appreciated one of its employees describing a life of excessive drug use and wild sex with partners of both sexes. *Strobo* was not a success, with sales stagnating at around 100 copies. It was also claimed that *Axolotl Roadkill* contained a further twenty quotations from other sources.

Not wishing to see the profitable title disappearing from its list, Ullstein thought up a clever trick. This was not plagiarism, they claimed, but 'intertextual mixing'. Hegemann herself claimed that she was 'a member of a different generation of writers which is used to adapting and using the abundance of information available online for its own creative purposes' (Paterson, 2010). She did not explain exactly what is 'creative' about omitting quotation marks and a source reference. To add to the confusion, she added, 'I went everywhere I could find inspiration. There is no such thing as originality anyway, there is just authenticity' (Paterson, 2010). It was a nice idea, 'intertextual mixing', but not very convincing. The publisher clearly realized that, too: in the fourth edition, it finally included a list of references.

THE HOLY LANCE – THE ONE AND THE MANY

The *Lancea Longini* 'relic' – there are a number of them – refers back to the Gospel of St John, which describes the crucifixion of Jesus. The Roman soldiers were about to break Christ's legs to accelerate his death (without the support of the legs, the chest compresses and suffocation occurs more quickly), 'but one of the soldiers with a spear pierced his side and forthwith came there out blood and water.' This proved to the soldiers that Jesus was already dead.

One mention, in one verse, in one book of the Bible. After that, silence for half a millennium. Not a single cleric or ruler claimed to possess the lance that had pierced Christ's side. There were no references to its existence. But when the alleged weapon suddenly reappeared in the sixth century – when Christendom was in the ascendant – that all changed very quickly. Today, it is misleading to talk of the Holy Lance in the singular since there are several versions to choose from. Some are linked to the name Longinus, supposedly the Roman soldier who owned the weapon at the time of the Crucifixion (although his name only became known 500 years later). Others are luxury models, with the point forged from one of the nails used to fix Christ to the cross. There is a 'German' lance in Vienna and a suspected copy in Kraków, Poland. Then there is the 'Echmiadzin lance', and the 'Roman lance' in St Peter's Basilica in the Vatican. And the lance of Rudolf van Rheinfelden, the lance of St Olaf of Norway and the lance of the King of Hungary.

There is a fascinating story about how one of the spearheads was found (the one from the 'Holy Lance of Rome') on 15 June 1098, during the First Crusade. It was discovered by Peter Bartholomew, a profligate monk fuelled by alcohol. He said that the spirit of St Andrew the Apostle had told him that the Holy Lance was below the floor of a cathedral in Antioch. The floor was dug up but no one found anything until Bartholomew jumped into the hole and, a few seconds later, triumphantly held up a spearhead. As it seemed very reasonable to suspect that that he had concealed the spearhead in his clothing, not everyone believed it was authentic. Consequently, in early 1099, the indignant finder announced that he was prepared to undergo ordeal by fire to allow God to prove the verity of his story. On 8 April 1099, Good Friday, Bartholomew walked along a narrow path with burning logs stacked on either side, carrying the spearhead for protection. But God clearly doesn't take too well to deceivers: Bartholomew suffered terrible burns and died twelve days later in excruciating pain.

A striking number of fables have grown up around the Holy Lance. Kaiser Wilhelm II is alleged to have carried the lance during a victory march that passed under the Arc de Triomphe in Paris in 1914. In 1938 it was presented to German chancellor Adolf Hitler with the words: 'Mein Führer! The Spear of Destiny' (Adelson, 1966). At the end of the Second World War, an Allied commander is alleged to have asked: 'Where is the Holy Lance? If the Russians find it they shall rule Europe' (Adelson, 1966). All very fascinating, but all completely untrue.[16] The lance has also left its mark on popular culture. In an episode of *Tomb Raider: Chronicles*, a computer game from 2000, heroine Lara Croft goes in search of the Holy Lance, which is on board a German submarine sunk by the Russians.

HONEST ABE'S FORGED SPEECHES

Many American politicians – Democrats as well as Republicans – have tried to bask in Abraham Lincoln's reflected glory. In 1992, during his final speech to the Republican Party, Ronald Reagan, U.S. president from 1980 to 1989, quoted a number of statements by Lincoln that were intended as warnings against anti-liberal tendencies in the economy. 'You cannot help small men by tearing down big men', Reagan said, supposedly in Lincoln's words. And 'You cannot help the poor by destroying the rich' (Ferguson, 2007).The *New York Times* was delighted to point out immediately that the words were not spoken by Lincoln but written by a Baptist preacher in 1916. Reagan's speechwriters took them from a book called *The Toastmaster's Treasure Chest* (1979), in which the quotations were wrongfully attributed to Lincoln.

Fifteen years later, defeated presidential candidate Al Gore, a Democrat, made the same mistake. In his book *Assault on Reason* Gore quoted from Lincoln extensively to show that, back in 1864, Lincoln had foreseen the advent of President George W. Bush:

> I see in the near future a crisis approaching that unnerves me and causes me to tremble for the safety of my country. As a result of the war, corporations have been enthroned and an era of corruption in high places will follow, and the money power of the country will endeavour to prolong its reign by working upon the prejudices of the people until all wealth is aggregated in a few hands and the Republic is destroyed. (Ferguson, 2007)

As Andrew Ferguson argued in the *Washington Post* in June 2007, this quotation is remarkable for a number of reasons. First, Lincoln was not the kind of man to tremble in public. Second, the anti-capitalist tone is inconsistent with the fact that Lincoln himself made his fortune through his support for the American railroads. The quotation was a fabrication, from the first word to the last. A Lincoln historian reported as early as 1999 that he had traced the passage back to 1880, when it first appeared and had been denounced by Lincoln's son. So how did the quotation end up in Gore's book? He most probably came across it reading anti-Bush blogs, where it was a favourite of liberal bloggers.

HOW THE NUMBERS ADD UP IN HOMEOPATHY

A litre of tap water costs about 11 pence. An average homeopathic medicine costs about £11 per 100 millilitres. That means that the value of a litre of tap water increases from 11 pence to £110, simply by putting it into a small bottle and giving it an interesting sounding name and attractive packaging. That is an increase in value by 1,000: something even a heroin dealer would envy.

Homeopathy, devised by Samuel Hahnemann (1755–1843), is nonsense for two reasons. First, it is based on an incorrect principle, and second, it is incompatible with chemical reality.

The incorrect principle is that of *similia similibus curentur*, or 'like cures like'. If you have a cold, your eyes and nose run. Since onions also cause our eyes to run, homeopathy recommends treatment with onions. I can illustrate just how bizarre this principle is with the following example. I have a cold and am coughing a lot. Since coughing is also caused by chain smoking, I can cure myself homeopathically by lighting up a Gauloise.

Smoking cigarettes to cure yourself has one undeniable advantage over homeopathy. Nicotine and tar are at least active components, which is more than can be said for the ingredients of homeopathic medicines, which are prepared by diluting the substance to be administered many times. The strength of the solution is indicated with a number, followed by an x (ten) or c (hundred). For instance, we have 10 millilitres of substance y, which we dilute by a factor of 3c. The 10 millilitres of y are dissolved in a litre of water (the first round of dilution by a factor of 100). This litre of water is then dissolved in 100 litres of water (second round by a factor of 100). This 100 litres of water is dissolved in 10,000 litres of water (third round by a factor of 100). A little mathematics shows that the dilutions used in homeopathy are ludicrous. With a solution of 30c the poor patient has to ingest no less than 1,060 molecules of the liquid to swallow a single molecule of the active substance. To ingest the active substance, you would therefore need to drink a glass of the solution 30 billion times the circumference of the Earth (all sample calculations come from Meuleman, 1998).

I found the following pearl in the information provided by a homeopathic doctor known to me but who shall remain nameless:

> These substances are processed according to a prescribed procedure, after which they are diluted in progressive stages. While being diluted they are also shaken vigorously. This is known as potentiation. During this process the toxicity of the substance decreases while its healing power increases. Therefore the more the solution is diluted, the greater its potency. The medicines I use are potentiated in this way. That means that nothing of the original substance remains. They are then so potent that they only have to be taken very occasionally.

Homeopaths live in cloud cuckoo land and talk complete twaddle. If I go to a homeopath with my cough, he will probably prescribe me Oscillococcinum (like all quacks, homeopaths like to use complicated sounding names). Oscillococcinum has a solution of 200C. To ingest a single molecule of the active ingredient, I would have to drink 10,400 molecules of the solution. Ingesting sufficient quantities of the substance would mean drinking a glass of the solution four times larger than the known universe.

The real tragedy of homeopathy is of course the money wasted on it. In the Netherlands alone, this is around €100,000,000 annually, a huge amount of money that could have been put to real use. Everyone is of course completely free to spend what they have as they see fit, but the fact that some insurance companies cover homeopathic treatment is downright scandalous.

There is some light on the horizon. Homeopathy is becoming marginalized. In 2008, some 16.9 per cent of family doctors prescribed homeopathic medicines. Twenty years previously that was still 40 per cent. Hopefully this trend will continue and, in twenty years' time, we will finally, after two centuries, see the end of this nonsense.

HUBERT-JOSEPH HENRY AND THE DREYFUS AFFAIR

Major Hubert-Joseph Henry (1846–1898) worked in the statistics section of the Deuxième Bureau, the French secret service. The section was a cover for the counterespionage department. In October 1894 the department arrested Captain Alfred Dreyfus (1859–1935) on suspicion of espionage. The suspicions were based not on the very scant evidence against Dreyfus, but on the anti-Semitic tendencies of some of the department's leaders. After an extremely slipshod trial late in 1894, Dreyfus was sentenced to life imprisonment in a South American penal colony, Devil's Island, off French Guiana.

In 1896, in the knowledge that Dreyfus' supporters might demand a retrial, Major Henry started producing documents to prove that Dreyfus was guilty – documents that would pass the scrutiny of a fair and trustworthy investigator. To help him, he called in forger Moise Lehman (also spelled Lehmann, but primarily known as Lemercier-Picard).

Major Henry's forgeries were exposed in 1898. Lemercier-Picard was found hanging from a window handle in his hotel room. The official conclusion was suicide, though some believed he had been 'suicided', that is, murdered (Strong, 1898). Major Henry, in temporary custody, cut his own throat with a razor. On 18 September 1899 Dreyfus was given a full pardon.

J

JESUS DROPS A LINE

Once upon a time King Abgar v of Osroene (in the current border region between Syria and Turkey) was suffering from an incurable sickness and decided to write to Jesus, who was then touring and preaching the new faith of Christianity in Palestine. In his letter Abgar acknowledged Jesus's authority as the son of God and invited him to his royal palace in Edessa. Jesus sent a reply, which said, in brief, that he was unfortunately too busy but would delegate his power to one of his Seventy Apostles, Thaddeus, who indeed visited the king shortly afterwards.

This story is related in the *Historia ecclesiastica* by Eusebius of Caesarea (265–339). Eusebius also provided evidence of its authenticity: he had found the letter from Jesus in the government archives in Edessa and had studied its content. The story Eusebius discovered held a prominent place in the Christian faith for some 150 years until it was assigned to the dustbin of fictional history at the end of the fifth century.

Who forged the letter? It could have been Eusebius himself, but since his other writings are so dull, it is unlikely that he had the imagination for such a deception. King Abgar died before Jesus had become widely known, according to Christian chronology, so he too must be discounted as a possible candidate. The most probable explanation is that some practical joker had slipped the letter into the archives while Eusebius was visiting Edessa, choosing a place where he would be sure to find it.

JOBSEEKING, GERT POSTEL STYLE

Postman Gert Postel (*b.* 1958) had no chance of studying medicine, as he did not have even so much as a secondary school certificate. But what he did have was a silver tongue, which he used on several occasions to be taken on as a doctor. His preferred discipline was psychiatry.

Under the name Dr Clemens Bartholdy he was employed by the health service in the north German town of Flensburg. He worked there for several months until he lost his identification papers, which were discovered to have two names but only one face.

When Postel saw a job vacancy for a psychiatrist at a clinic in the small town of Zschadrass (today part of the city of Colditz), he decided to kill two birds with one stone: earn a good salary and avenge the death of his mother, who Postel believed had committed suicide after not receiving adequate treatment for depression. He forged his qualifications and references and, as Dr Gert Postel, gave all the right answers during his job interview. Postel's career as a psychiatrist, which was to last a year and a half, started on 15 November 1995. In that time, in addition to his salary of 200,000 marks, he earned 44,000 marks writing psychiatric reports for the law courts.

Postel's success was partly due to his acting talent but also to the fact that, in any group of professionals, no one wants to appear stupid in front of their colleagues. At conferences, Postel could therefore throw around terms like 'a third-degree bipolar disorder' and 'cognitively induced distortions in the stereotypal formation of judgment' (Merkelbach, 2004) and no one dared admit that they had never heard of such disorders. In the clinic in Zschadrass, Postel made such a good impression that his superiors considered him for promotion. But fortunately it never came to that. One of the nurses at the institution had family in Flensburg. He was exposed and eventually sent to prison for four years.

J. R. BRINKLEY, THE TESTICULAR QUACK

John Romulus Brinkley (1885–1942) was born in rural North Carolina as the illegitimate offspring of a preacher and his sister-in-law. Brinkley's father was also an alternative healer and the boy followed in his footsteps, practising as a young quack at fairs and bazaars. In 1908 Brinkley settled in Chicago and took a course at the alternative Bennett Eclectic Medical College. The name sounds impressive, but the course certainly was not: the curriculum studied little more than herbs with healing powers. After being awarded his diploma in 1911, he paid to have it converted into a university degree from the Eclectic Medical University in Kansas City, which had a name for awarding degrees by the dozen. He then registered as a physician in Arkansas and Kansas.

Brinkley set up a practice in Milford, Kansas, and went about his business without doing much of note for five years. But that was to change in the autumn of 1917, when 46-year-old Bill Sittsworth attended his surgery. Sittsworth was suffering from impotence, a complaint for which Brinkley knew no treatment. During Sittsworth's visit, Brinkley was staring out of his window when he saw two goats romping around in a way that was clearly sexual. And it gave him an idea.

The pair of goat testicles that he implanted in Sittsworth seemed to work at first, and, as a sharp-eyed businessman, Brinkley encouraged his patient to spread the good news. When Sittsworth became a father less than a year later, it was worth its weight in gold in publicity. Brinkley had found his niche. Shortly afterwards, he opened the Brinkley Institute of Health, a luxury private clinic with sixteen rooms and only one operation on the menu: implanting goat testicles. The clinic was a great success, and in no time his emporium also offered associated treatments, such as Formula 1020, a potion to increase potency. Brinkley bought a number of powerful radio stations, giving him coverage across most of the country, and broadcast light entertainment programmes about pseudomedical claptrap interspersed with regular commercials for the Brinkley Institute of Health.

An important factor in this case was that, in the first four decades of the twentieth century, the medical profession in the United States was organizing itself and becoming more professional. Scientific standards were introduced for the registration of physicians. Universities like the Eclectic Medical University, where Brinkley had bought his degree, were banned. Serious medicine resolved to eradicate the practice of quackery. The leading figure in this fight was Morris Fishbein, editor of the *Journal of the American Medical Association*. And Fishbein's greatest enemy was John R. Brinkley. He explained that Brinkley's operations were a waste of time: as alien material, the testicles of *Capra hircus* would be immediately broken down by the human body's immune system. The fact that Sittsworth and other patients seemed to benefit from goat testicles for a short time was purely psychological. Furthermore, the operations were dangerous. Brinkley messed around with his patients' scrotums (and ovaries – for he was even implanting testicles in women!) without having had any surgical training. And the fact that Brinkley was frequently tipsy as he stood at the operating table did little to make the whole situation safer.

In 1930, after dozens of complaints from members of the American Medical Association and a series of mortalities in Brinkley's clinic, Fishbein took legal action. As a result, Brinkley's licence to practise as a doctor in Kansas was rescinded, as was his broadcasting permit.

Brinkley reasoned that if he held the highest political position in the state he could turn the tide and, in 1930 and 1932, stood for election as governor. After losing for the second time, he left for Texas where he set up a new radio station just over the Mexican border, in Villa Acuna. He could now ply his trade without interference from U.S. authorities. Although there are no exact figures on his income, it was certainly at least $1 million a year.

In 1938 Fishbein launched another extensive attack on Brinkley's fraudulent practices, causing the goats' testicles evangelist to instigate legal proceedings against him for slander. Brinkley lost, a sign that the efforts to clean up the medical profession in America were paying off and that public opinion on certain kinds of 'doctor' was changing. In 1941 Brinkley, his wife and half a dozen members of their staff were found guilty of mail fraud (throughout his career Brinkley distributed masses of brochures by post). But Brinkley would never be sentenced for his crimes: in May 1942 he slipped away forever while fast asleep.

JOHN ADAM, THE MODEL HOSTAGE

At the end of January 2005 the Al Mudjahedeen Brigade posted a statement on a website often used by Muslim fundamentalist groups. The organization claimed to have taken an American serviceman called 'John Adam' hostage and showed a photograph of a soldier with a gun pointed at his head and a banner behind him with the text: 'There is no god but Allah and Muhammad is his prophet.'

On Tuesday 1 February Liam Cusack, spokesman for the American toy manufacturer Dragon Models, was able to reassure the nation. The 'soldier' in the photograph was Special Ops Cody, a doll produced in 2003. The gun pointed at his head came in the box with the doll.

JOHN OLSEN, FORGETFUL FORGER

In 2002 Australian gallery owner Winifred Schubert instigated legal proceedings against Leonard Joel Auctioneers. She demanded that they pay her Aus$22,900 because two paintings by John Olsen (*b.* 1928) she had bought from them had not been marked as forgeries. The auction house had a simple defence: the paintings, *Escaping Mouse* and *Green Tree Frog and Pond*, had not been marked as forgeries because they were not forgeries. Schubert disputed this, saying that when Olsen had seen the paintings on her website, he had contacted her to warn her that they were not authentic. The auctioneers' lawyers suggested that in his long career Olsen might have sniffed too much turpentine. The artist had labelled his own works as forgeries before, only to change his mind after further consideration. When expressing his opinion on *Escaping Mouse* and *Green Tree Frog and Pond* Olsen also said that a third work, *Cat Drinking Milk*, was a forgery. He retracted that claim when a woman came forward and reminded him that he had painted it as a gift to her.

JOYCE HATTO, ARGUABLY THE WORLD'S GREATEST PIANIST

Joyce Hatto (1928–2006) started her career as a concert pianist in London in the early 1950s. She performed for some 25 years, but her sense of rhythm and her playing quality were not enough for her to break through to the top of her profession. She stopped playing in public in 1976, claiming that she had cancer (this was later refuted by her doctors). After that she lived the life of a virtual anchoress. Around 2000, however, Hatto seemed to have been reborn. Through the record company Concert Artist, owned by her live-in husband William Barrington-Coupe, she brought out some 100 CDs, all of which were received with nothing but praise by the critics. In 2005, one critic described her as 'the greatest living pianist that almost no one has ever heard of' (Edgers, 2007). When she died, an obituary in *The Guardian* said that she left behind 'a discography that in quantity, musical range and consistent quality has been equalled by few pianists in history' (Nicholas, 2006).

In early 2007 an American music lover was playing one of Hatto's CDs, Liszt's *Transcendental Studies*, using the Apple application iTunes. Now, iTunes does not identify music from the CD but from a database called CDDB. To his surprise, it was not Hatto's name that appeared on his screen but that of László Simon (1948–2009), a little-known German pianist. But iTunes also said that the CD had already been brought out in 1993 by BIS Records – not after 2000 by Concert Artist. The listener contacted a music magazine, which asked audio expert Andrew Rose to investigate. Rose concluded that ten of the twelve *Studies* by Liszt had been performed by Simon; the other two were from an album by Japanese pianist Minoru Nojima.

Hatto's oeuvre appeared not to be Hatto's at all. Her husband simply copied work from others and then played around with the speed and tone to disguise the plagiarism. When confronted with the accusation, Barrington-Coupe first tried to talk himself out of it, claiming that he had just tried adding pieces of recordings by others where his severely sick wife's groaning spoiled the recording. Faced with overwhelming evidence to the contrary, however, he had no choice but to confess. But he insisted that his wife never guessed that 'her' recordings were not actually hers at all – a claim that not a single music journalist took seriously.

K

KOUADIO KOUASSI AND HIS HOTEL BARS

The SoHo Grand Hotel in Manhattan is a 353-room island of luxury. All rooms are equipped with a gourmet minibar, Wifi and iPods with Bose Sound Docks; the bathrobes are designed by well-known names in the fashion industry. The magnificent Grand Bar, the hotel's website tells us, 'features a gold polished marble top oak bar, woven leather banquette seating, rich end-grain wood floors, and embossed leather bar stools with nail-head detailing'. It is the hotel where celebrities like to go for a private date, illicit or not.

Kouadio Kouassi, a poor immigrant from the Ivory Coast settled in Brooklyn, decided one day in 2006 that life would be better if he owned the SoHo Grand. And so a couple of days later he filed a deed with New York City authorities stating that the hotel was owned by Kouadio Kouassi, 46 years of age. When he came back a couple of days later to see whether ownership of the hotel had been transferred to him he was told that the deed had not been processed because it lacked the required signatures. Perhaps Kouassi did not get the message, as he returned several times to see if the city officials were making any progress with his case.

In the meantime, officials had contacted the owner of the hotel, the Hartz Group. They said they had never heard of Mr Kouassi and had no intention of giving him the hotel, which was valued at $76 million. 'We think that since we bought the land, built the hotel and have run it for 12 years that we actually own the hotel', said spokesman Ron Simoncini. When he eventually stopped laughing, he added: 'I guess we should take it as a compliment' (Buettner, 2006).

Kouassi was charged with fraud and filing a false document. He ended up spending a year in somewhat less salubrious accommodation, without an iPod and with all the bars on the windows.

L

THE LAND-GRAB *DONATION* OF EMPEROR CONSTANTINE

The *Donation of Constantine* (Donatio Constantini) is a forged document composed in the seventh century by an unknown Roman priest. Although only a few pages long, it had an enormous impact, from the ninth to the fifteenth centuries. The document was mentioned as early as 777 by Pope Adrian I, but became more widely known in the mid-ninth century when it was included in the Pseudo-Isidorian Decretals.

The *Donation* alleges that, in the early years of the fourth century, the Roman Emperor Constantine the Great (272–337) was plagued by leprosy. The disciples Peter and Paul appeared to the emperor in a dream and told him that he must be baptized by Sylvester, a priest who was a fugitive at that time, together with his followers. Constantine took their advice and, when the leprosy disappeared, he showered Sylvester with gifts. He also merged all the existing churches, which until then were autonomous institutions with their own Bibles, liturgies and so on, to form the Roman Catholic Church, under Sylvester's leadership. The priest became the first to bear the title Pontifex Maximus, 'Pope' for short. Constantine also transferred large parts of his empire to the Church, and gave it supremacy in all religious affairs worldwide.

As if this were not enough, in later centuries (and especially during the Investiture Controversy in the eleventh and twelfth centuries), the *Donation of Constantine* was interpreted increasingly broadly and the text was 'improved', notably by Anselm of Lucca (1036–1086). Eventually it came to signify that, according to Rome, all European monarchs were little more than lieges of the Pope. Furthermore, all islands in the world belonged to the Pope. This is an excellent example of the *Donation*'s influence. In 1155 Pope Adrian IV, the first and only Pope to have been born in Britain, invoked this broad interpretation of the document to claim ownership of Ireland. In his papal bull *Laudabiliter*, he granted power over the island to King Henry II of England, heralding the start of a relationship between the two countries which remains strained to this day.

The *Donation of Constantine* continued to be influential long after the Investiture Controversy, until Italian historian Lorenzo Valla exposed it as a forgery in the sixteenth century.

LAURA ALBERT AND HER MANY IDENTITIES

Laura Victoria Albert (*b.* 1965), aka Emily Frasier, Jeremy LeRoy, JT ('Jerome Terminator') LeRoy, Speedy and Terminator, is an American musician/telephone sex worker/author, active from 1996 to 2006. Together with her partner Geoffrey Knoop, Laura Albert was responsible for one of the most intriguing literary hoaxes that I have come across, which involved juggling fictional identities for eleven years. Even when the case seemed solved in 2007, it took a last, surprising turn in court.

At the beginning of the 1990s, Albert and Knoop performed with the bands Daddy Don't Go and Thistle. The songs, with titles like 'Vicious Panties', were pornographically tinted, with a tendency towards sadomasochism. It later became clear that it was not so much Albert's source of income – offering phone sex – that led to her interest in pornography as vice versa: her predilection for pornography caused her to earn her living in that way.

In her musical and pornographic activities, Albert – born and bred in Brooklyn – used a variety of accents, including British and African American and that of the Southern states of America. Albert was also trying to build up a career as a writer and wanted to get into contact with hip writers, but did not know how to go about it. She was aware that successful writers were not queuing up to help their less successful colleagues.

In 1994 Dennis Cooper, acclaimed author of gay literature, received a fax from a fourteen-year-old homosexual boy called Terminator. Cooper told a handful of writers about the teenager, and they were fascinated by his life story. Terminator was the son of a truck-stop prostitute working in the South. Before long his mother had started dressing him up as a little girl to hire him to truckers with a preference for young boys in drag. In 1993, when he was thirteen, with a whole life behind him, a bundle of sexual confusion and seriously messed up, Terminator was saved from his street life by a social worker called Emily Frasier, who referred him to psychologist Terrence Owens. It was Owens who had advised Terminator to commit his story to paper.

At the age of sixteen Terminator, who was now using a number of aliases including LeRoy and JT, made his literary debut. This was followed by publications in various magazines and anthologies. In 1997 he was offered a contract to write a novel. In the literary world rumours were going around about the young star, especially about his pathological shyness. According to some, this was because of his psychological insecurity, while others attributed it to a skin disease. LeRoy could only be contacted by phone, with calls sometimes lasting several hours, or by fax.

LeRoy's debut novel *Sarah*, published in 2000, was a critical and commercial success. The story of the young Jeremy who prostitutes himself out of love for his mother was translated into twenty languages. It was followed a year later by *The Heart is Deceitful above all Things*.

The cast of the film based on the book included Peter Fonda, Winona Ryder and Marilyn Manson.

LeRoy eventually accepted that he would have to show himself at some stage and decided to face the media attention he so feared. The scoop went to a German television channel. LeRoy appeared wearing a wig and sunglasses. The writer, so eloquent on the telephone, hardly uttered a word. It was the same story throughout the six-week European publicity tour: LeRoy appeared on stage (or preferably on the highest balcony he could find) in disguise and hardly said anything. His appearances continued in the same vein in the years that followed. Luckily he was supported by his friend Speedy, who was in reality Laura Albert. Albert and her partner Geoffrey Knoop had apparently taken LeRoy into their home. Speedy was such a good friend that she was able to answer even complex questions about LeRoy's work.

LeRoy's androgynous appearance led to many theories. One was that he was 'a boy pretending to be a girl pretending to be a boy' (Beachy, 2005). Another, medically acceptable explanation was that LeRoy's development had stopped in adolescence due to an AIDS infection contracted at a young age. LeRoy himself claimed that he had undergone the first, hormonal stage of a sex change. Amid all the commotion, the third book, *Harold's End*, appeared in January 2005.

What the author did not know was that Stephen Beachy, an author with whom LeRoy had regular contact (by telephone, of course), had started an investigation. The outcome, an article entitled 'Who is the Real JT LeRoy?', was published on 10 October 2005 in *New York* magazine. It came as a real bombshell.

Beachy was unable to find any trace of LeRoy at all until 1994, and after that, very little. He talked to dealers, prostitutes and clients who could have known LeRoy but found nothing. Of all the publications LeRoy had written for, not one seemed to have his social security number. The traces that Beachy did find all led back to one person: Laura Albert. Wherever LeRoy was, Albert was conspicuously close. LeRoy's share in the proceeds of his first book proved to have been paid to Jo Ann Albert, Laura's sister. The remainder of the payments had been made to Underdog Inc., whose president was Carolyn Albert, Laura's mother. Soon more disclosures followed. In January 2006 the *New York Times* reported that the person who performed publicly as JT LeRoy was Savannah Knoop, Geoffrey Knoop's 25-year-old half-sister. On 7 February 2006 Geoffrey Knoop admitted the hoax: JT LeRoy was Laura Albert.

In the aftermath of the affair, Albert was sued by Antidote International Films, which had contracted JT LeRoy on an option on the film rights of *Sarah*, for which they had paid $116,500. As LeRoy did not exist, Antidote considered the contract null and void and demanded the money be refunded. What started as a simple civil case developed into a psychological drama. As the court tried to establish where JT LeRoy came from, Albert's mother was the first to speak. She talked about her daughter's shyness, which was so acute that she did not dare to go to school. When her mother had a teacher come to the house, Laura only dared to have contact with him by telephone, with him in the living room and she in her bedroom. Details about Laura's psychological state emerged when she herself got to speak and told a story which showed marked similarities to JT LeRoy's biography. Albert described how she had been sexually abused in her childhood, how she had felt responsible for it, and how she had only felt free of the guilt when, still a child, she had asked a trucker to beat her during sexual contact. Shortly afterwards, she was admitted to a psychiatric hospital for the first time.

In her early twenties Albert moved to San Francisco, where she called psychiatric helplines from telephone cells. Too messed up to be herself, she took on the identity of a fictitious street kid, Jeremiah or Jeremy, an early incarnation of JT LeRoy. When the helpline psychologist wanted to meet her in person, Albert paid a street urchin to play Jeremiah/Jeremy and accompanied him as Speedy. The psychologist was none other than Terrence Owen, the man who encouraged JT LeRoy to write.

Albert made up JT LeRoy as more than just a way of making money, but the jury still found her guilty of fraud. She was ordered to pay back the $116,500 to Antidote and $350,000 for the legal fees. Publication of JT LeRoy's fourth book, *Labour*, was postponed indefinitely in April 2006, a postponement that continues to this day.[17]

LAUREL ROSE WILLSON, VICTIM OF EVERYTHING

In 1988, at the height of the hysteria about the satanic abuse of children (see DISMEMBERING *MICHELLE REMEMBERS*), Lauren Stratford published a book in the U.S. entitled *Satan's Underground*. For a book in this genre, the story it told was not unusual. At the age of six, her mother had allowed an odd-job man to rape her as payment in kind for services rendered. That was quickly followed by pornographic pictures and bestiality. When she was fifteen she fled and went to her father, who had long ago cut off all contact with his wife. Lauren's mother, however, succeeded in tracking her down. Slowly, Lauren realized that her mother was part of a network producing pornography which extended across several states. She found herself leading a double life, half schoolgirl, half porn star. When she met Victor, the leader of the network, he introduced her to satanism. When she refused to take part in the ritual murder of children, he shut her up in a metal drum with the corpses of four small children. She herself gave birth to three children, who were also ritually slaughtered. After trying to stay out of the clutches of Victor's henchmen for many years, Lauren found a sensitive therapist and everything turned out fine.

Although some of the details were true – her mother was hot-tempered and her father had taken to his heels – the horror stories of sexual abuse and satanic practices were complete fabrications. Several critics had already voiced their doubts. Recollections in which she refused to name important locations, names and dates aroused suspicion. Lauren's claim that she did so 'to protect the victims' (Passantino, 1990) just didn't wash.

The suspicions proved to be well founded when Lauren's sister Willow, who is not mentioned once in *Satan's Underground*, decided to tell the real story. First of all, her sister's real name wasn't Lauren Stratford, but Laurel Rose Willson (1941–2002). Second, the chronology in her book was all over the place. Her father did not leave when she was four, as she claims in the book, but when she was nine. That also undermined her claims of persistent sexual abuse. Furthermore, it was unlikely that any of that could have taken place without Willow knowing about it.

Other facts also seemed not to fit. You would expect a teenager who was being exploited in the porn industry to have problems of a social nature. But nothing could be farther from the truth. Laurel Rose Willson, who had taken singing, piano and clarinet lessons, achieved excellent results in music competitions and got top grades at school.

After dropping out of various study programmes and drifting from town to town, Laurel Rose – now about seventeen – started to tell stories of being sexually abused. First of all she accused Willow's husband, but the accusations proved unfounded and she was placed under the supervision of a psychiatrist. After being admitted to a new course of study, she again started talking about sexual abuse, this time by a member of the faculty staff. When this, too, proved to be untrue, she made her first attempt at suicide.

In the decades that followed a pattern emerged. Laurel Rose drifted through the wondrous world of American Christianity and made the most of its obsession with all the evil in the world, real or imaginary. There were always stories that focused attention on her. She inflicted wounds on herself and blamed her mother. For a while, she claimed to be blind. In chat groups and on radio programmes she talked about the abuse she had suffered.

When the mass hysteria about ritual child abuse broke in the 1980s, Laurel Rose jumped on the bandwagon. Until then she had never said a word about satanic practices. She now claimed that the many scars on her arms, the result of self-mutilation, had been inflicted on her during satanic rituals. She told stories about the two leaders of the movement, Elliot and Jonathan (prototypes who she later merged to form the character of Victor in *Satan's Underground*). It was as though she was trying out different stories in front of a live audience. Different groups of people heard different accounts but they all had the same response when the book was published in 1988 – it bore no resemblance at all to what they had heard. Some were certain that Laurel Rose had told them that her father had also been a satanist and had been involved in the abuse, while in *Satan's Underground* it was her father who she turned to for help when she was trying to escape the satanists.

The first holes soon appeared in the web of fabrication that *Satan's Underground* proved to be. Around two years after the book was published, in 1990, its status as non-fiction was completely in shreds. For Laurel Rose Willson, alias Lauren Stratford, this was a great disappointment. She had spent 30 years of her life arousing the sympathy of those around her with stories that had now been totally discredited. Nearly 50 years old and with no one to care for her, what could be expected of her? That she would see the light and work on how to interact with other people in a normal way? Not at all. When the sympathy dissipated, there was only one course of action open to her: to generate more sympathy.

And so Laurel Rose Willson was born again, as Laura Grabowski. The crucifix around her neck was replaced by a Star of David. 'Jesus lives!' became 'Shalom'. Laura Grabowski, survivor of Auschwitz-Birkenau, was ready for the warm bath of human pity.

In essence, she did not really have to change her stories very much. The many wounds that Laurel Rose had attributed to the satanists now became the work of Josef Mengele and his team of assistants. The newborn children allegedly taken for ritual sacrifice in her earlier incarnation were now used for genetic experiments.

This time she did not publish any books, but she did give lectures and piano recitals for Jewish charities. In 1997 she started to correspond with Binjamin Wilkomirski, clarinettist and author of fake Holocaust memoires. The two linked up and many a reception organized by Jewish organizations was graced with music by the duo Laura Grabowski and Binjamin Wilkomirski, both as Jewish as the late Yasser Arafat.

LAWSONOMY: A ZIG-ZAG THEORY OF LIFE, THE UNIVERSE AND EVERYTHING

In the midst of all the crackpots who become entangled in their own view of the world, Alfred William Lawson (1869–1954) is conspicuous in that he started off so normally. After a career as a professional baseball player, he emerged as a pioneer of aviation. In the first two decades of the twentieth century in America, aeroplanes were primarily used for military purposes and for delivering mail. The Lawson Airplane Company helped develop aircraft to transport passengers. In 1921, however, Lawson's chances of commercial success were dashed. He had built the largest aircraft ever made in the U.S. Designed to carry 26 passengers wishing to travel in the greatest luxury, it was fitted with berths and shower baths. But the mammoth liner crashed on its maiden flight, when the wing hit a tree.

Lawson's next career move was to become a pseudo-philosopher. He had already taken a first step in this direction in 1904, when he published a book called *Born Again*. Its subtitle, 'a novel', by no means covered the book's expansive content. It starts like any other novel might, with the adventures of seaman John Convert, but out of the ordinary elements soon make an appearance:

> Speaking once more I said, 'Madame, can you understand my language?' Then I received another strange but unmistakable impression which replied: 'I can understand your thoughts but not your babble.' 'Are you able,' she continued telepathically, 'to give an explanation of this extraordinary metamorphosis?' (Lawson, 1904)

Conversing telepathically with this woman, Arletta, Convert learns that she is the only survivor of her people. These people knew all the secrets of the Natural Law, and the rest of the book is filled with explanations of this law. It becomes less of a novel and more a pseudo-philosophical pamphlet addressing the moral shortcomings of humankind, including selfishness and eating meat:

> Good Christians are anxious to know when the time will arrive that the lion and lamb will lie down together in peace and harmony. Possibly the lamb would like to know if the time will ever come when its carcass will not be utilized to appease the voracious appetite of the Christian. (Lawson, 1904)

If *Born Again* can be seen as a novel by an idealist that has got out of hand, *Lawsonomy, Volume One* (1922) professes to be a scientific work and, as its author soon makes clear, not just a run-of-the-mill work at that:

> The birth of Lawson was the most momentous occurrence since the birth of mankind . . . In comparison to Lawson's Law of Penetrability and Zig-Zag-and-Swirl movement, Newton's law of gravitation is but a primer lesson, and the lessons of Copernicus and Galileo are but infinitesimal grains of knowledge. (Grant, 2006)

In 29 chapters, totalling a little less than 40,000 words, Lawson describes a world view that embraces cosmology, biology, physics, law, economics and much more. For the largest part, it contradicts accepted

Alfred W. Lawson.

scientific wisdom. That is of course because science has not understood anything properly but, fortunately, Lawson is on hand to explain everything. I suspect that, before starting to write his magnum opus, he may have taken more than a passing look at Spinoza's *Ethics*. In *Lawsonomy, Volume One* he tried to imitate the philosopher's mathematical writing style, unfortunately without success. His gobbledygook is almost impossible to decipher but I will do my best. To start with, a number of definitions from chapter One:

> Lawsonomy is the knowledge of Life and everything pertaining thereto. Lawsonomy is based on Life as it is and not upon a theory of what it ought to be. Theory, as espoused by so-called wise men or self-styled scholars has no place in Lawsonomy. Everything must be provable or reasonable or it is not Lawsonomy. Lawsonomy treats of things as they are and not as they are pretended to be. Facts, not fancies; Truth, not falsity; Knowledge not notions; is the foundation of Lawsonomy. (Lawson, 1935)

This is only the hors-d'oeuvre for the new physics that Lawson introduces. The most important law is that of Penetrability: all motion is based on the fact that objects of greater density penetrate objects of lower density. Lawson calls this Pressure. The same force seen from the perspective of the object with the lower density is known as Suction. Gravity does not exist. Objects do not float in the air because of the Suction exercised by the hollow centre of the Earth. Penetrability, Pressure and Suction explain all phenomena in human existence, including the human metabolism:

> The basic principle of a formation is to draw into itself external substances for growing purposes, and this is accomplished by a Suction movement which attracts these substances toward the center . . . Suction attracts toward a center, and Pressure throws off from a center.

The difference between the sexes can also be explained in Lawsonomic terms:

> The male sex of a formation is caused by a superabundance of internal Pressure. The female sex of a formation is caused by a superabundance of internal Suction. (Lawson, 1935)

Lawson's most curious discovery is Zig-zag and Swirl movement. This part of his 'theory' states that nothing can move in a straight line or a circle. Imagine that you are on board a ship following a northerly course. From the port railing, you cross directly to the starboard railing, for instance, from west to east. You may think you have walked in a straight line, but nothing could be farther from the truth. Seen from an absolute point, you have not only moved from west to east but also – because the ship itself is moving – from south to north. Depending on your speed relative to that of the ship, the 'straight' line is not straight at all, but crooked. Lawson has actually got this right, but it is so self-evident that no scientist has ever taken the trouble to encompass it in a law. The Law of Zig-Zag and Swirl is as useful as a law stating that water makes you wet.

Lawsonomy, Volume One was followed by two more volumes, *Mentality* and *The Almighty*. He also published several dozen other works. Since he considered himself the kind of teacher who comes along 'about every 2,000 years' (*Time*, 1952), in 1943 he bought the campus of the bankrupt Des Moines University and established the non-accredited Des Moines University of Lawsonomy. Registration was free but required endurance: the study programme lasted ten years. After 30 years you could be awarded the degree of 'Knowledgian'. Women were not admitted and the study consisted primarily of learning Lawson's writings off by heart. The federal government suspected the university of tax evasion.

One of Lawson's last public appearances was in March 1952, when he was questioned by the Senate Small Business Committee. Lawson had no time for the hearing. He snapped at 50-year-old senator Blair Moody: 'God, boy, if you want me to tell you all these things, you will wreck my mind . . . I'm thinking great philosophical thoughts for the benefit of mankind' (*Time*, 1952).

LEE ISRAEL AND HER BUSY OLD TYPEWRITERS

Lee Israel made a name for herself as the biographer of reporter and television presenter Dorothy Kilgallen and of actress and television presenter Tallulah Bankhead. But at the end of the 1980s things went downhill. Israel's biography of cosmetics queen Estée Lauder, published in 1985, was panned by reviewers and ignored by readers. 'I was not in the flower of mental health', Israel said later. Her apartment began to accumulate cat faeces and flies. A wild romance with a 'brilliant, beautiful bartender named Elaine' led to her drinking too much and financial worries (Mallon, 2008). When her 21-year-old cat Jersey died and his replacement, Doris, needed expensive veterinary treatment, Israel turned to crime.

As a biographer, Israel had access to the manuscript collections of many libraries. In the spring of 1990 she selected three rather ordinary letters by the actress Fanny Brice from a collection and smuggled them out of the library in her socks. She sold the letters to autograph dealers for $40 each. They taught her that the price increased as the content became more interesting, something Israel didn't need telling twice. She bought an array of vintage typewriters, invested in old writing paper and created history that never was. Her talent and experience as a biographer came in handy. The letters fitted neatly in the chronology of the lives of the 'authors' and the style was a perfect match. Israel even used real lines from her celebrity subjects. Movie star Louise Brooks (1906–1985), for instance, 'wrote' about her studio head Harry Cohn (1891–1951), 'My cat has spit up hairballs more attractive than him' (Mallon, 2008). She used an upended TV as a light box to trace the signatures. Autograph dealers flocked to buy the letters. Besides Brice and Brooks, Israel forged letters by playwrights Noël Coward and Lillian Hellman and writers Dorothy Parker and Edna Ferber. In around fifteen months Israel sold some 400 phony epistles.

Israel first got into trouble over a letter supposedly from Noël Coward (1899–1973). The letter came into the hands of a collector who had known Coward and who felt that the playwright seemed to be writing much more candidly about his homosexuality than he would expect. The danger blew over but Israel decided to change her tactics. She carefully studied original letters in collections and made replicas of them at home. On her next visit, she would swap the two. She then sold the original letters through a middleman – a 'wacky ex-con'. Israel felt no remorse. The letters, she said, 'were from the realm of the dead. Doris and I were alive' (Mallon, 2008).

In 1992 Israel found out that the FBI was keeping an eye on her. Each time she left her apartment, she took a bag containing a typewriter, which she dumped. Unfortunately the cops were at the door before she got rid of the whole collection. Thanks to a judge with a kind heart, Israel got off lightly with six months' house arrest and five years' probation.

In 2007 *The Letters Of Noël Coward*, edited by Barry Day, was published and received good reviews. By the time the paperback edition was issued, the collection was shorter by two letters – after a tip from Israel.

In August 2008 she published a short book about her days as a forger entitled *Can You Ever Forgive Me?* The title should not be taken too seriously: it is a sentence from one of Israel's forged letters by Dorothy Parker.

LIFE AT THE FINAL CHECK-OUT DESK

John Lennon Airport, Liverpool, 6 April 2010. On that day, three of the passengers queueing at the easyJet check-in desk for flight EZY 7223 to Berlin were Gitta Jarant, her stepdaughter Anke Anusic, 41, and Gitta's 91-year-old husband, Curt Willi Jarant. Curt, wearing sunglasses, was taking it easy in an airport wheelchair. He looked as though he was having a nap.

When they finally reached the check-in desk the old man snoozed on. The easyJet staff became concerned about his health, wondering if he was in a fit state to fly. They called medical staff, who concluded that Curt had nothing to fear from the flight: he had already taken his final journey. The police were informed. The mother and stepdaughter insisted that they had no idea that Curt had died. Finding it difficult to believe that they really thought he was just taking a nap, the police arrested the two women for failing to report a death.

An interesting detail was that all three travellers held German nationality. They were suspected of wanting to bury Curt in his homeland and were trying to save the big expense of shipping Curt in a coffin by buying him a much cheaper ticket for a seat on easyJet. Just to make the story even more bizarre, they had travelled from their home town of Oldham, Lancashire, to the airport in a taxi.

THE LOST STONE AGE TRIBE IN THE PHILIPPINES

In 1971 Manuel Elizalde, a businessman and Philippines' minister for cultural minorities, announced that a lost tribe had been discovered on the Philippine island of Mindanao. The tribe, known as the Tasaday, still lived in the Stone Age. Its members spoke a strange language, made fire with sticks, wore leaves for clothes, lived in caves and led a paradisiacal existence in which disputes were not settled by argument but by gentle persuasion. With the help of a much-talked-about report in *National Geographic*, the Tasaday became wildly popular and were favoured with visits from VIPs, including aviator Charles Lindbergh and actress Gina Lollobrigida (who wrote a coffee-table book about the tribe, together with her friend Imelda Marcos, the president's wife).

Within a short time Elizalde expressed concern that all these modern interferences would have a corruptive effect on the Tasaday. A foundation was created to protect the interests of the tribe, and at Elizalde's urgent request, President Ferdinand Marcos turned 180 sq. km of their land into a reserve, only accessible to outsiders with the minister's permission. As Elizalde allowed more celebrities to visit the reserve than anthropologists, scientists were as yet unable to say anything about the Tasaday.

In 1983 the political situation in the Philippines became very unstable and Elizalde fled the country, taking with him millions from the foundation set up for the benefit of the Tasaday. After President Marcos was deposed in 1986, Mindanao was again visited by foreign journalists, including Swiss anthropologist Oswald Iten, who was astounded to find Tasaday people sitting on the verandas of their houses, wearing jeans and smoking cigarettes. They also turned out to speak a dialect that other tribes did indeed understand. They told Iten that they had pretended to be Stone Age people at Elizalde's request. But this, too, was called into doubt later, when members of the tribe responded indignantly and insisted that they had only said what Iten had asked them to say.

Whether Iten and the tribe members were lying too is not clear, but Manuel Elizalde's guilt is in no doubt. Even if the Tasaday were an authentic discovery (which I highly doubt), the fact still remains that Elizalde lied about them for his personal gain.

LOTT'S FALSE RESEARCH AND HIS SHADY STUDENT

University of Maryland senior economics researcher John R. Lott Jr (*b*. 1958) was on the Right of American politics and published books with subtle titles like *More Guns, Less Crime*. In this book, Lott claimed that in 98 per cent of cases, just producing a gun is sufficient to change a criminal's mind. This was apparently based on 2,000 interviews he had conducted in the course of his research. When asked to make the interviews public, Lott said that the hard disk in his computer had crashed and that he had never made a back-up.

Lott was the object of merciless criticism on the internet. But in 2000, he seemed to have found an ardent supporter, in the guise of Mary Rosh, one of his ex-students, who nostalgically recalled his classes in an online posting: 'I have to say that he was the best professor I ever had' (Morin, 2003).

Blogger Julian Sanchez thought that Rosh's opinions were suspiciously similar to those of Lott and decided to investigate. He discovered that the unique IP (Internet Protocol) address of her computer was the same as Lott's. It also became clear that 'Rosh' had posted highly enthusiastic reviews of his book on the sites of various online bookstores. Unsurprisingly, Sanchez published his findings on the internet, asking, 'We're a little old to be playing dress up, aren't we Dr Lott?' (Morin, 2003).

LOURDES' APPARITIONS AND MIRACLE CURES

Lourdes, that pilgrimage town in the foothills of the Pyranees, is a 'double fake': Mary, the mother of Jesus, appears, after which 'miraculous healings' occur.

Marian apparitions – appearances by the Virgin Mary – are not especially uncommon. They may take the form of a hallucination (for instance, an appearance with no physical evidence of anything extraordinary) or an illusion, which is caused by the brain interpreting an external physical phenomenon incorrectly. A literature study for the 1928–1971 period turned up 210 Marian apparitions, almost five

The Blessed Virgin of Lourdes.

a year. These cases record only those which were reported by those who experienced them. How many people decide, after seeing an apparition, that they have been deceived by their own brains and how many decide to keep their imaginary encounter to themselves is of course unknown.[18] What makes Lourdes interesting is that, strictly speaking, it was not Mary who made an appearance. Between 11 February and 16 July 1858 Bernadette Soubirous (1844–1879) experienced an apparition on eighteen occasions in a grotto in Massabieille in Lourdes. Soubirous described the apparition as '*aquero*', meaning 'she' or 'her' in her Gascon-derived dialect, but her fellow villagers knew better and, after the third apparition, the local priest asked her whether it was the Virgin Mary. Soubirous denied this at first, claiming that the girl she had seen was the same age (fourteen) and size as she herself, which was not compatible with the official Vatican image of the Blessed Virgin in the nineteenth century. However, on 25 March, after talking to the priest a few times, Soubirous claimed that the girl had told her 'I am the Immaculate Conception' (Carroll, 1985). This was completely in line with the dogma defining the immaculate conception of the blessed virgin Mary announced fourteen years earlier by Pope Pius IX.[19] A little poetic licence in the reporting of what Soubirous had seen soon ironed out the creases in the story. Mary's age was increased slightly to 'sixteen to seventeen' and then to 'twenty' (Carroll, 1985). The statue of Mary that was placed in the grotto embodied the desired image: she was at least twenty years older and 40 cm taller than Soubirous' apparition, who she said looked nothing at all like the statue.[20]

Then we come to the second claim, that at Lourdes miraculous healings take place. It is useful to first define what a miracle is. Our world is defined by a number of fundamental physical laws. For example, everything that happens has a cause (if you see a chestnut tree, unless it has been planted there, it must have grown from a chestnut that fell to the ground there some years before). Furthermore, the same cause will always have the same effect (a chestnut tree grows from a chestnut and not from a dollar coin; only a chestnut tree can grow from a chestnut, not a dachshund or a delivery van). A miracle is an event that breaks at least one of these laws. A critical observer will conclude that a 'miraculous' healing already breaks the first law. With the best will in the world, it is impossible to establish a causal link between a visit to a damp and draughty French grotto or bathing in the dregs of hundreds of other pilgrims (the water in the baths is refreshed only once a day) and the sudden disappearance of pain in the joints. Even if this were possible, the phenomenon would fail to comply with the second law. A pilgrimage will very occasionally appear to heal a pilgrim, but more often than not, it won't. So the same alleged cause does not have the same effect. Perhaps the Virgin is not paying full attention? Unfortunately, I have disappointing news concerning even those very few cases in which Mary did seem to have been listening closely and a 'miracle' appears to have occurred. Miracles not only do not exist, they *cannot* exist.

One of the first to make this argument rationally was Benedict de Spinoza (1632–1677) in his *Tractatus Theologico-Politicus* (1670). A miracle requires temporary suspension of the laws of nature, as though gravity does not apply for a few minutes and I float around my study. Spinoza considered this absurd. He reasoned that the eternal, unchanging laws of nature were the work of the perfect insight and knowledge of God. This is not compatible with the idea that God suddenly changes his mind and decides that his perfect insight and knowledge does not apply in a certain situation (which after all implies that God's knowledge is *not* perfect). Stripped of the required seventeenth-century religious veneer, what Spinoza actually says here is that the world is nothing more than a consequence of the working of the laws of nature. The idea that below this outer skin there may be another world where these laws do not apply is absurd: breaking the laws of nature would mean that the world could no longer exist. What we call a 'miracle' is purely an event that occurs according to the laws of nature, but that we cannot yet understand plainly and distinctly.

All things considered, the 'miracles' of Lourdes are no great shakes. The 67 recognized 'miracles' that have occurred since 1857 include events qualified as 'supernatural healing'. That sounds promising but says nothing more than that doctors cannot establish a causal connection between the treatment (or other tangible influences) and the cure. That may seem surprising in this modern age, but it happens more often than you might think. Take, for example, multiple sclerosis – one of the illnesses that Mary has allegedly helped to cure in Lourdes. MS patients often spontaneously experience good and bad periods. In such cases, therefore, 'supernatural healing' is closer to Spinoza's 'event that occurs according to the laws of nature, but that we cannot yet understand plainly and distinctly' than to 'God's work delegated to Mary'. Around 5 million sufferers of all kinds currently visit Lourdes every year. That must have been much fewer in the nineteenth century, before the age of mass tourism but in a little over a century and a half, some 100 million believers have made the pilgrimage to the grotto. In the light of such numbers, 67 cases of medically inexplicable healing cases is slim pickings. If you study a 100 million people who have never visited a place of pilgrimage, you will probably find an equal number of medically inexplicable cures.

The best argument against the Virgin's medical practices is that her healings are exclusively 'supernatural' and never 'completely impossible'. These are remarkable claims since, as explained above, 'miracles' are not bound by the laws of physics. Yet no one suffering from Down's syndrome has ever left Lourdes cured because the extra copy of chromosome 21 has disappeared. A womb has never grown back after a hysterectomy, no one has risen from the dead. This was expressed succinctly by a man suffering from paraplegia in Cherry Duyns's documentary for Dutch television *Het genadeoord* (1977). Nodding at the grotto from his wheelchair, he said drily: 'As you can see, there are plenty of crutches hanging there, but not a single wheelchair' (Duyns, 1977).

M

MARTIN LUTHER, EARTHLING

A clergyman of the Holy Roman Empire, Martin Luther (1483–1547), believed that the earth was flat. After all, the Bible states that *all* the peoples of the world will witness the Second Coming of Christ. Luther reasoned that if the world was round, those living on the 'other side' would miss the show. Ergo: the earth is flat and is inhabited only on the upper side.

MARY TOFT, A REAL BUNNY GIRL

On 23 April 1726 Mary Toft, married since 1720 and the mother of three children, saw a rabbit in a field near her home town of Godalming, Surrey. She tried to catch it, but without success. For weeks, the only

Dr Martin Luther reading flat out in church.

thing she could think of was a delicious leg of rabbit. She even dreamed about it. This craving may have been due to her being a few weeks' pregnant at the time. Considering some women have a craving for ashtrays or cement when they are expecting, rabbit is quite a reasonable choice. What's more, rabbit was a luxury that Mary and her husband Joshua could rarely afford.

In July and August of the same year, Mary gave birth to two unidentifiable lumps of flesh within a period of three weeks. But she continued to display the symptoms of pregnancy. On 27 September, after being taken very ill and attended by her mother-in-law, who was a midwife, she gave birth to what appeared to be the lungs and guts of a pig. Joshua Toft informed John Howard, a surgeon who had practiced midwifery for 30 years and who lived in nearby Guildford. A few days later, Howard helped Mary deliver further parts of a pig. A month passed and Howard was once again called to Godalming, where Mary's pregnancy had taken a strange turn: she had started giving birth to rabbits at a rate of one a day.

John Howard wrote to a number of eminent colleagues about this strange case, and before long the newspapers were full of stories describing how the rabbits would jump around in the womb, sometimes for up to eighteen hours, before dying as they were born. Violent spasms in Mary's uterus would break their bones and the baby rabbits would come into the world in several pieces, often even without their skin.

After Mary had given birth to nine rabbits, Howard was so busy attending to her that he moved her to his home in Guildford, where he received visits from Nathanael St André, surgeon to the royal household, and Samuel Molyneux, private secretary to the Prince of Wales. St André was convinced by what he saw and heard and rapidly published a pamphlet, which became an immediate bestseller. King George I then sent a second surgeon from his household, Cyriacus Ahlers, to Guildford. When Ahlers reported back to the King on 21 November that he felt the whole case was an elaborate deception, a fierce debate erupted. Everyone had their own explanation for Mary's seeming ability to give birth to rabbits. Many saw it as confirming the traditional belief that pregnant women should stay away from animals, as it might have an effect on the foetus. Preachers of penitence claimed it to be the work of the Devil, while pamphleteers accused Mary of bestiality.

For one profession, the whole affair could not be over soon enough. Butchers had experienced a drastic fall in demand for rabbit, possibly due at least in part to a law in force in Elizabethan England that forbade the eating of anything that could be born of woman (Seligman, 1961).

George I made a wise decision. On 29 November Mary, who had by then given birth to seventeen rabbits and a collection of loose body parts, was transferred to Lacy's Bagnio (a kind of public bath) in London, and placed under the supervision of Sir Richard Manningham, a respected obstetrician. There she was observed and examined by

Mary Toft in 1726.

several doctors – not to mention many others whose interest was far from medical.

Although she continued to experience severe labour pains, no more rabbits appeared. A little later, she was exposed as a fraud. Thomas Howard, a porter at the Bagnio, made a statement on the evening of 4 December that Mary had persuaded him to secretly supply her with a rabbit. Mary still refused to admit the hoax, but soon changed her mind when Manningham informed her that he would be forced, in the name of science, to cut open her vagina and womb to solve the mystery. On 7 December 1726, she finally confessed that she had been lying.

She was imprisoned and threatened with prosecution, but was not ultimately charged and returned to Godalming, where she gave birth to a daughter, Elizabeth, at the end of January 1727.

Why would a 23-year-old woman insert dead rabbits into her vagina and so that she could 'give birth' to them shortly afterwards? A contemporary document described her as being 'of a very stupid and sullen temper' (Seligman, 1961). Her stupidity perhaps explains the nature of the deception, which lacked any systematic planning. If Mary had been capable of planning, she would have made sure that she had a few rabbits with her when she was taken to Lacy's Bagnio. It is also interesting that the first 'births' produced pieces of pig, rather than rabbit.

This is my hypothesis: Mary Toft, 23, married for six years and the mother of three children, living in poverty, did something one day that got her husband's attention (the first 'birth'). So she did it again (the second 'birth'). Mary even succeeded in attracting the attention of a professional midwife (her mother-in-law; the third 'birth'). If this really was what motivated her, she must have included her husband and mother-in-law in the plot after the third birth; she could not have continued the deception without the assistance of Joshua, at least. Perhaps he, too, shared her desire for attention. If not, perhaps his wife had persuaded him with the promise of the financial benefits it would bring them (and not without reason: while she was still producing rabbits on a daily basis, George I had mentioned the possibility of her receiving a royal grant). If this depressing hypotheses is correct, then Mary must have had a miserable life. The only time that history paid her any attention was when she became a suspected criminal.

The many pamphlets written about Mary Toft became collectors' items in the nineteenth century, and continue to be sought after today. Preferably compilations, and even more preferably bound in rabbit skin or fur.

MELVIN EARL DUMMAR'S ROADSIDE BUM

On 5 April 1976, eccentric recluse Howard Hughes (see GHOSTING AN AUTOBIOGRAPHY and PROJECT JENNIFER) died, leaving an estate worth an estimated $1–2 billion. In the weeks following his death, it gradually emerged that Hughes had not left a will. Although he had drawn up several during his lifetime, they had all been destroyed or lost or had not been signed.

On 27 April 1976, a senior official in the Church of Jesus Christ of Latter-day Saints, also known as the Mormon Church (see MORMON

SMITH), found an envelope on his desk. It contained a will signed by Howard Hughes, leaving a large amount of money to the Mormon Church. This is less odd than it might seem at first. In the twenty years before his death, Hughes had close contact with the Mormons, and the majority of the dozen or so members of his secret household also belonged to that church. The Mormons decided to hand the document over to the court dealing with Hughes's estate to determine its authenticity.

One of the people mentioned in the will was fuel-pump attendant – and Mormon – Melvin Earl Dummar. Dummar had an idea why Hughes might have remembered him. In January 1968, while driving through desert-like landscape in the state of Utah, he had seen a man lying at the side of the road. Dummar stopped, to find the man dressed in rags and bleeding from one ear. Dummar assumed the man was a bum or hobo but offered to take him to a hospital. The 'hobo' declined Dummar's offer, but asked if he would take him to Las Vegas, in neighbouring Nevada. Dummar agreed, and after a drive through the night he dropped the man off at the Sands Hotel, which was owned by Hughes. When the man asked Dummar for a quarter, he gave him one, after which his passenger revealed that he was Howard Hughes. The fuel-pump attendant assumed that this act of charity must have been the reason why, eight years later, Hughes left him $156 million.

This story fitted in perfectly with the myths forming around the reclusive Hughes, who spent fortunes on the most trivial matters. The court, however, stuck to the facts. And one fact in particular proved fatal for Dummar: his fingerprints were discovered on the will found in April 1976. In June 1978 the court declared the will a forgery.

Almost 30 years later, Dummar tried again. There was apparently new evidence to prove that Hughes had indeed left the hotel once at night. Furthermore, Dummar had found him in an area where Hughes owned a number of mines. But once again, in 2007, the judge tore the story to shreds.

Dummar was not the only one to try and benefit from Hughes's capital. After the billionaire's death, countless 'wives' and 'illegitimate children' staked a claim to his fortune. They even included two African Americans, whose story was very unlikely as Hughes was a virulent racist who would tolerate no non-whites around him.

Dummar's story was filmed in 1980 by Jonathan Demme, under the title *Melvin and Howard*.

MEMORANDUM 46

At the end of the turbulent 1970s a document entitled *Black Africa and the U.S. Black Movement* was circulated among African American activists. It soon became known as *Memorandum 46*. In the document, dated 17 March 1978, President Jimmy Carter's national security adviser, Zbigniew Brzezinski, outlined a government strategy to undermine the black leadership in the United States and contact between African Americans and African countries.

When *Memorandum 46* surfaced, the U.S. government realized how damaging it could be and did its utmost to convince African American activists that it was fake. The Carter administration declared with hand on heart that it was a forgery. In September 1980 the National Security Council pointed out that the memo contained nonexistent entities, such as an NSC Political Analysis Committee. In 1982 a director of the CIA said that *Memorandum 46* was one of a dozen suspected forgeries by the Soviet Union. There was also a genuine memorandum 46, a very boring theoretical analysis of U.S. policy on Central American issues. But it all fell on deaf ears. For more than three decades now *Memorandum 46* has been a cat that refuses to go back inside the bag and has continued to circulate, initially as a photocopy and now on the internet. Many African Americans are still convinced it is authentic and consider all attempts to prove it is a forgery as a cover-up.

A convincing argument for the falseness of the document was put forward by its supposed author, Zbigniew Brzezinski, who pointed out that 'the idiot-forger could not even spell my name correctly' (Lartigue Jr, 2007).

MENDEL'S PERFECT PEAS

In 1866 Gregor Johann Mendel (1822–1884), an Augustinian priest at St Thomas's Abbey, Brno, Moravia, published an article on experiments involving crossing peas. For decades, the article failed to make any impression, but from around 1900 his experiments in heredity began to be considered groundbreaking; today Mendel is known as the Father of Modern Genetics. But in 1936 statistician Ronald A. Fisher examined the results of Mendel's experiments and concluded that they were too good to be true. The question to what extent Mendel cheated will probably never be answered. Did he select only the best results? Did he make up data? Or was he perhaps fooled by the Abbey's gardeners, who knew which results he expected? This shows the importance of one of the unwritten rules of modern science: the 'rough data' on which a theory is based must remain available.

An anonymous entry in the journal of the American Society for Horticultural Science, *HortScience*, entitled 'Peas on Earth', sketched a possible scenario:

> In the beginning there was Mendel, thinking his lonely thoughts alone. He said: 'Let there be peas,' and there were peas and it was good. And he put the peas in the garden saying unto them: 'Increase and multiply, segregate and assort yourselves independently,' and they did and it was good. And now it came to pass that when Mendel gathered up his peas, he divided them into round and wrinkled, and called the round dominant and the wrinkled recessive, and it was good. But now Mendel saw that there were four hundred and fifty round peas and a hundred and two wrinkled ones; this was not good. For the law stateth that there should be only three round for every wrinkled. And Mendel said unto himself: '*Gott in Himmel*, an enemy has done this. He has sown bad peas in my garden under the cover of night.' And Mendel smote the table in righteous wrath, saying: 'Depart from me, you cursed and evil peas, into the outer darkness where thou shalt be devoured by the rats and the mice,' and lo, it was done and there remained three hundred round peas and one hundred wrinkled peas, and it was good. It was very, very good. And Mendel published. (Anon., 1972)

MESMER'S ANIMAL MAGNETISM

Theologist and doctor Franz Anton Mesmer (1734–1815) studied medicine in Vienna. He was a man of the Enlightenment, and strangely enough, it was this that made him go astray. Inspired by Sir Isaac Newton's ideas on gravity, Mesmer assumed that human health too was influenced by the planets. His dissertation, published in 1766, was entitled *De planetarum influxu in corpus humanum* (On the Influence of the Planets on the Human Body).

In the early 1770s Mesmer met Maximilian Hell, a Jesuit who told him about how he had used magnets to heal diseases. Mesmer combined his own theory with Hell's practical insights. In 1773 he treated a chronic hysteric, Fräulein Österlin, by giving her a fluid containing iron. When he then moved magnets over her body, she experienced flows of energy running through her. Österlin was cured. Soon after, Mesmer discovered that he did not even need magnets. Just moving a finger over the body was enough to influence what he called 'animal magnetism.' This was a subtle fluid which fills the cosmos and circulates between planets and people. When the magnetism can run freely through the body, a person is healthy, while obstructions cause illnesses.

To Mesmer there was nothing supernatural about his theory; he considered animal magnetism as real as gravity. One important difference however, as we now know, is that gravity exists while animal magnetism does not.

In 1777 Mesmer treated Maria Theresia Paradis, a seventeen-year-old pianist who had been blind since she was three. The result that Mesmer claimed to have achieved illustrates that he was becoming less and less enlightened and more and more of a quack. Maria Theresia was able to see again, but only when Mesmer – and no one else but Mesmer – was present. The laughing stock of Viennese physicians, he was forced to leave the city and settled in Paris, where magnetic treatments soon became fashionable. He managed to increase his income considerably by no longer treating his patients individually but in groups, a method that proved even more medically successful.

The secret of Mesmer's therapy had nothing to do with animal magnetism. His pseudo-therapy relied on suggestion and autosuggestion. A patient like Fräulein Österlin would be told beforehand what would happen during the treatment: 'The animal magnetism cannot run freely through your body and your hysteria is the result. By manipulating the flow of the animal magnetism we are going to remove this blockage. When the blockage has been removed, your hysteria will be healed.' Mesmer knew how to present this in a sufficiently persuasive way to influence how the patient experienced her own body. Although Mesmer would have hated the idea, as he thought he was dealing with a purely physical force, he is considered one of the founders of psychology. The reason the group treatment in Paris worked better than individual treatment was because of contagion.

Individual patients might have felt inhibited in surrendering themselves fully to Mesmer. But when they saw that someone else was responding to the treatment, they felt more free to respond themselves. And respond they did. Mesmer's patients screamed out loud, the perspiration flowed and they collapsed in convulsions.

Mesmer set up a business venture called Societies of Harmony to sell his treatment. Anyone who was interested could learn the tricks of the trade, if they took an oath of secrecy and paid him a large sum of money. Paris was divided. Half saw Mesmer as a visionary while the other half – including most of the local doctors – thought him a charlatan. The dispute became so heated that Louis XVI had to step in. He appointed two prominent scientists, Antoine Lavoisier and the American Benjamin Franklin, to draw up a report on mesmerism. They came up with a series of experiments, sixteen in total, to test Mesmer's ideas. Subjects who thought that they were being treated with animal magnetism were treated with complete nonsense while those who assumed that they belonged to the control group were actually treated with animal magnetism. The experiments proved that it was all a matter of suggestion: it was the thought of being treated with animal magnetism that 'healed' the patients. Cups of water and trees in a garden were magnetized but subjects could not distinguish them from non-magnetized cups and trees. In 1785 Lavoisier and Franklin concluded:

> Nothing proves the existence of Animal-magnetism fluid; that this fluid with no existence is therefore without utility; that the violent effects observed at the group treatment belong to touching, to the imagination set in action & to this involuntary imitation that brings us in spite of ourselves to repeat that which strikes our senses. (Shermer, 2002)

Mesmer moved to England and later returned to his native country, but his name lives on in the English term 'to mesmerize', meaning to spellbind. And his work left its traces, too: more than 225 years after Lavoisier and Franklin's report, trade in magnetic bracelets, insoles and cat beds is thriving.

A very valuable close-up of an electronic circuit board.

MICROPROCESSING MONEY

A kilogram of microprocessors is worth more than a kilogram of heroin. This, together with the fact that the trade in processors attracts less attention than trade in heroin, explains why forgers smell easy profits here.

First, they have to get hold of authentic processors. That is not difficult. Computer manufacturers who discover that they have bought too many processors in a given period will want to sell them as quickly as possible because they can rapidly depreciate in value, especially if a better or higher-speed model is introduced. Forgers buy them up through middlemen and use acid to remove the technical data. The chip is then provided with new data, for example a higher clock speed or a newer model number, to make it appear better or faster than it really is.

MISSING, PRESUMED TOTALLED: WILF KENDALL, AUTO PARTS DEALER

On 1 October 2001, shortly after the 9/11 attacks on the World Trade Center, Cyril Kendall reported that his thirteenth child, Wilfred Kendall, was missing. He produced a Guyanese birth certificate and described his son as about 5 ft 10 in. tall with dark-brown skin and a strong West Indian accent. According to Kendall, his son – who dealt in automobile parts for a living – had gone to a job interview in the North Tower of the World Trade Center on the morning of 11 September. As a result of his loss, Kendall received around $160,000 from the American Red Cross and the charity Safe Horizon.

Less than two years later, Kendall found himself on trial facing fraud charges together with his sons, Mark and Wilberforce. According to the prosecution the Kendalls had deceived everybody, as Wilfred Kendall only ever existed in their imagination.

The trial took five weeks. The fact that Wilberforce had already been in prison for five years for forgery at that time might have given the prosecution a slight head-start. No fewer than 33 witnesses were heard, including Wilberforce himself, who reminisced about his brother Wilfred.

But it was to no avail. On 7 August 2003 Cyril Kendall was found guilty of two counts of grand larceny, criminal possession of forged documents and offering false information. On 16 September Justice Ronald A. Zweibel sentenced him to 11 to 33 years in prison. The judge said he did not think that the defendant could be rehabilitated because Kendall was 'bereft of any moral values' (Saulny, September 2003).

MITTERRAND'S *AFFAIRE OBSERVATOIRE*

Some incidents in France in the final months of 1959 were destined to go down in history as the *Affaire Observatoire*. Even so, more than five decades later, the exact course of events is still veiled in mystery.

In the autumn of 1959 François Mitterrand (1916–1996), who had recently lost his seat in the French National Assembly, was a determined opponent of President Charles de Gaulle's Fifth Republic. Mitterrand's ambition to become leader of the Left was fraught with difficulties, because the left-wing camp was fragmented into endless variations of socialists and communists, all with their own leaders. In the preceding months, Mitterrand's political position had moved from moderate to extreme left, a shift expressed in his opinion that the French colony of Algeria should become independent – a view that was diametrically opposed to that of De Gaulle.

In the early hours of 16 October 1959, Mitterrand was driving to his home in the Rue Guynemer, at the northwest corner of Paris'

Jardin du Luxembourg, in his dark-blue Peugeot 403. Later, Mitterrand said that he had noticed he was being followed by a suspicious looking car. (Because of his opinions on the independence of Algeria, he had received death threats before.) To save his family from danger in what was possibly an attack on his life, instead of going directly home, Mitterrand drove on to the south end of the Jardin du Luxembourg. On the rue Auguste-Comte, near the old observatory, Mitterrand pulled over to the left and parked on the curb. He leaped out of the car and ran to the park, where he jumped over the railing and lay flat on the ground behind the cover of a hedge. As the suspicious car drove past, there was a burst of machine-gun fire. Later, seven bullet holes were found in the right-side door of Mitterrand's car, and a bullet had gone through the driver's seat. Mitterrand went to number 5, avenue de l'Observatoire, and asked the concierge for help. Alarmed neighbours had already phoned the police, who arrived soon afterwards.

In the days that followed, the Left united behind Mitterrand. A motley crew of anti-fascists, anti-Gaullists, anti-colonialists, socialists and communists, who would normally not give each other the time of day, expressed their horror at the attack. Mitterrand took every opportunity to suggest that his assailant should perhaps be sought not in Algerian colonial circles, but closer to home. The implication was that initiative for the shooting had come from the government and had been sanctioned by President De Gaulle. It was a clever political move that put Mitterrand on the map as an idol of the Left.

The victory, however, lasted less than a week. The events of the early hours of 16 October raised questions. The Algerian colonial movement and the French secret service had many professional soldiers in their ranks. Why would any gunman with proper military training open up on an obviously empty car? Five days later some astounding news appeared. On 21 October the right-wing newspaper *Rivarol* published an article based on interviews with Robert Pesquet, a somewhat shady figure who did odd jobs for the extreme Right. Pesquet revealed that it was Mitterrand himself who had commissioned the attack.

In the week that followed, it emerged that the politician had had several meetings with Pesquet and there were letters showing that the attack had been discussed in detail. Mitterrand tried to make the best of it. On 30 October he published a kind of confession, admitting that the attack had been staged. He said that Pesquet had convinced him that he, Pesquet, had been contracted to kill Mitterrand but did not want to do it. By faking the attack the politician could stay alive without Pesquet arousing suspicion in far-right circles. Many were not convinced by Mitterrand's confession and his ambition to lead the Left remained unfulfilled, for the time being.

MORMON SMITH FINDS PLATES – GOES WEST – GETS ALL SHOT UP

It is too simple to blame his parents for everything, but the heady world of magic, myth and religion within which Joseph Smith (1805– 1844) was raised certainly contributed to his later career. His father was a farmer by profession, but a treasure digger by calling. His reasons were more than purely financial, even though the Smiths could certainly have used the money. Digging for treasure had a curious eschatological component, as if finding it could bring redemption. It

Joseph Smith.

was not an exclusively Christian outlook; it also contained elements of common witchcraft. Smith senior had dreams about being saved at the eleventh hour, which were written down by his – if possible even more religious – wife. Not a bad home environment for someone aspiring to a pseudo-religious career.

At the age of fourteen, when the family was living in New York state, Smith junior had his first visitation from two religious entities, who introduced themselves as the Father and the Son. They told him that no single religious community had a monopoly on the truth: Smith would therefore have to establish his own community. His fellow villagers took little notice of him: it was just twaddle produced by a troubled adolescent with a vivid imagination. In September 1823 Smith had a visitation from Moroni, an angel that would give him his great breakthrough. From this point Smith's account of the facts becomes unclear. According to one version it was Moroni who led him to a big treasure; according to another, Smith found the treasure while digging with his father. In any case, what Smith found, according to his own version, was a number of golden plates with an illegible text. Between around 1827 and 1830 the plates were supposedly also seen by a handful of other people. Unfortunately, the statements date from a considerably later period and there are none from people not belonging to Smith's entourage.

During this period, Smith deciphered and translated the text into English. He had received assistance in reading the text, which he claimed had been drawn up in 'Reformed Egyptian', by Urim and Thummim, two seer stones set in silver bows fastened to a breast plate (the details remain vague).

What Smith finally wrote down, the Book of Mormon, is a kind of quirky nineteenth-century historical novel, although Smith failed to conduct the research this genre requires. *The Wanderings of Jesus Christ* would probably have been a more gripping title, though it would not have made the actual text – pseudo-biblical piffle open to every, and consequently to no, interpretation whatsoever – more exciting.

For a forger it is not difficult to imitate another era; the trick is keeping your own era out of the forgery. Here Smith failed miserably. When reading 'it shall be a land of liberty' (II Nephi 1:7, anon. [Smith, Joseph], 1976) you can almost hear the Star-Spangled Banner trumpeting out.

The most important premise of the Book of Mormon is that the continent of America is populated by the lost tribes of Israel. However, because they live in sin and their souls are dark, their skin has also become dark. The result: the Native Americans. If the gospel of Christ can be preached to these ungodly souls, all will be well: 'And then shall they rejoice; for they shall know that it is a blessing unto them from the hand of God; and their scales of darkness shall begin to fall from their eyes; and many generations shall not pass away among them, save they shall be a white and a delightsome people' (II Nephi 30:6, anon. [Smith, Joseph], 1976). A race clearly only has any value if it's white.[21]

Nineteenth-century ideology was well suited to the period for which it was intended: the nineteenth century. In 1830 Smith founded the Church of Christ. His followers, known as Mormons, shared his objective of establishing Zion, a kind of paradise on earth. Smith had several revelations revealing the site for Zion, but they never proved workable in practice. Wherever the Mormon flock settled, the locals turned out sooner or later with their pitchforks and buckshot to drive them out of the county.

A religious movement always benefits from martyrs, and in 1838 Smith had his first shot at martyrdom when he was put behind bars for five months. The authorities had had more than enough of the quarrelling between the Church of Christ, by then called the Church of Jesus Christ of Latter-day Saints, and the local population. Like a Moses in the making, Smith led his followers on a trek across the United States. The church had not been united for some time, and this division led to problems. In April 1844, after the church had settled in the small town of Nauvoo, Illinois, opponents of Smith published a newspaper, the *Nauvoo Expositor*, to expose his failings as a leader. Smith, by then mayor of the town, banned the paper. This proved to be a step too far. Charged with inciting a riot to destroy the *Expositor*'s press, Smith was sent to prison in nearby Carthage. There, on 27 June 1844, the mob took the law into their own hands. They stormed the jail and shot to death Smith and his brother Hyrum.

The Church of Jesus Christ of Latter-day Saints survived and eventually found a home in the state of Utah, where few others wished to settle. It still exists, although the percentage of suicides among homosexual Mormon teenagers is higher than that of any other group in the United States. When Mormons die, they become God over their own planet, no less, and they marry an infinite number of partners of the opposite sex. This heterosexual perspective explains why the Mormon Church has such a hatred of homosexuals. In November 2008 California voted on Proposition 8, which aimed to overturn legalized same-sex marriage. Mormons, who account for only 2 per cent of the Californian population, had provided 71 per cent of the funding for the campaign for Proposition 8 (why do sects always have such difficulties with sex?).

Crazy as the teachings of Mormonism are, their practices are even crazier. The church baptizes people who are long dead. To do this, it collects huge quantities of genealogical material. If you ever find an ancestor in an archive that has been copied by Mormons, there is a good chance that they have since been baptized as a Mormon. When it emerged that the church had also applied this 'posthumous proxy baptism' to victims of the Holocaust (after all, the Nazis kept excellent records), there was great indignation among relatives of the victims. The Jewish religion does not accept the New Testament, so a post-mortem annexation based on a nineteenth-century copy – especially one written in such bad taste – is equally hard to swallow. The Mormons announced that from then on they would baptize Holocaust victims only if they were direct ancestors of current members of the church.

In the 1990s one of the church's central dogmas also turned out to be wrong. DNA tests showed that Native Americans did not come from the Middle East, but from Asia. Mormon theorists fabricated a counter-argument that the lost tribes of Israel had stayed in Asia for some time before leaving for America. Something Moroni must have forgotten to mention.

MOTHER'S BOY

Thomas Prusik-Parkin supplemented his disability benefit with money and property belonging to his mother Irene. In 1996 he forged her signature on a document transferring ownership of a building in Brooklyn from mother to son. Prusik-Parkin then sold the building but soon lost the proceeds by speculating in real estate together with his accomplice Mhilton Rimolo.

When Irene died in 2003, Prusik-Parkin had a problem. His mother's monthly pension of $700 was a welcome addition to his disability benefit. So he made sure that, on paper, at least, his mother was still in the land of the living. By giving the funeral director a false social security number and date of birth, he was able to prevent his mother's death from being registered.

In the years that followed, Thomas drew his mother's pension to a total value of $52,000. Now that she was completely under his control, he started devising ways to benefit even more. He decided that she should file for bankruptcy, which brought in a further $65,000 in rent subsidies.

Sometimes Prusik-Parkin could not avoid his mother having to appear in person. So he donned a wig and make up and, to ensure that she did not have to talk too much, he took Rimolo along, who, posing as her nephew, helped the poor old lady find her way through the bureaucratic jungle.

In 2008 the mother, despite being as dead as a doornail, initiated a lawsuit against a creditor wanting to sell her house to collect his debt. During the process, the parties accused each other of false allegations, which attracted the attention of the authorities. They started to suspect that Irene was dead, but had no evidence until they finally acquired a photograph of her grave.

Early in May 2008 investigators called to say that they would visit the house on the 11th of the month to discuss details of the case. To their surprise they found Prusik-Parkin in full fancy dress as Irene, with an oxygen mask on her face and with her loyal nephew at her side. Rimolo explained that his aunt was very ill and could not speak. When the investigators made it clear that the game was up and literally and figuratively unmasked the fraudster, he claimed that he had done nothing wrong, saying, 'I held my mother when she was dying and breathed in her last breath, so I am my mother' (BBC News, 2009).

N

NEW SIGNINGS – A SPORTS ROUNDUP

Probably no other market today has as many fakes as the trade in sports memorabilia. Ice hockey pucks, baseball bats, football shirts and so on, preferably autographed, are worth enormous amounts of money. In the United States alone, where there is more trade in these items than anywhere else in the world, it is an industry worth an estimated $2–4 billion a year. During one investigation,

Operation Bullpen, the FBI confiscated forged memorabilia worth some $200 billion.

The number of forgeries has increased sharply since 1994. That year there was a Major League Baseball strike in America. It cost the sport many fans, as a result of which the demand for memorabilia decreased strongly and many dealers went bankrupt. A large number of them resorted to forgery as this reduced their purchase prices and because much-sought-after items could be fabricated and there is always a market for them, even when demand is falling. Subsequently, autographed pictures of Joe DiMaggio and his wife Marilyn Monroe (which are by definition fakes as DiMaggio refused to sign anything showing a picture of his wife), and baseballs autographed by John F. Kennedy and, curiously enough, Mother Teresa, appeared.

As a result a business evolved which, according to the FBI, consisted almost entirely of forged material (En-Lai, 2002). In Britain some 60 per cent of all sports memorabilia offered is estimated to be fake, in Canada this is 70 per cent and in the United States 90 per cent, a percentage which is even higher with items involving big names like basketball player Michael Jordan or golfer Tiger Woods.

One factor that encourages the forgery of sports memorabilia today is that it is relatively simple. In the case of baseballs the modern lettering is removed with sandpaper, they are varnished to give them an old-looking colour and then surrounded with dry dog food for a couple of weeks to make them smell mouldy. The balls are then 'autographed' by DiMaggio (who, of course, died back in 1999!) or some other baseball hero. Because of the coarse, round surface of the ball and the fact that autographs tend to be signed quickly one after the other, there is no need for the writer to be an accomplished forger. Together with a home-made statement of authenticity (supposedly drawn up by a dealer who has gone bankrupt and can no longer be consulted), the item is put up for auction online. Prices of up to $500 a ball are common.

A small group in the industry, mainly the producers of authentic memorabilia and the agents of the sports heroes who autograph the items, are doing their utmost to combat the fraud. For instance, some pieces are fitted with a chip with a unique code referring to a register of traded items. Nowadays, autographs are signed with a PenCam, a camera that records the actual signing. The buyer gets a DVD with the recording, along with a code showing where and when it took place.

The U.S. authorities tried to introduce legislation that would require dealers found guilty of selling fake memorabilia to pay triple damages to the buyer. The proposal did not make it into law partly because of fierce opposition from dealers.

The sports heroes themselves are not completely innocent either. Many are known to promote items they know to be forged, not only with their own autographs, but also with those of others.

NOT-SO-CLEVER HANS: KARL KRALL'S UNDER-PERFORMING HORSES

In 1905 Karl Krall (1863–1929), a jeweller from Elberfeld near Wuppertal in Germany, bought a horse called 'Clever Hans' (Kluge Hans) from amateur ethologist Wilhelm von Osten, a retired schoolteacher who had been performing with animals since 1891 to show that they possessed superior intelligence. Von Osten claimed that he had taught Clever Hans arithmetic. Apparently the animal could undertake addition and extract cube roots. In the years that followed, Krall added a number of other clever horses to his menagerie, including Muhamed, Zarif, Amasis, Aroun, Bento and a pony called Hänschen (Little Hans). The horses answered by tapping their hoofs (left for single numbers, right for tens). They almost always got their sums right.

Initially Krall, like Van Osten, sincerely believed in the mathematical prowess of his horses, but that was because both were bad

Karl Krall in 1909, teaching Zarif to do complex sums.

researchers. When a competent scientist, Oskar Pfungst, studied the case, the myth collapsed. First of all, Pfungst discovered that the horses could perform calculations very well when Krall was present, but if he was not around the number of correct answers was no higher than to be expected on the basis of coincidence. Pfungst found that Krall was making ideomotor movements – small movements he was not aware of. When a horse had to answer, Krall would lower his head slightly and look at the appropriate hoof, which the horse immediately started to tap. After the correct number of taps Krall unconsciously raised his head again. From his movements, the horses deduced what was expected of them.

Pfungst's discovery demonstrates the importance of double-blind tests, in which the researcher also does not know the correct answer to prevent him or her from involuntarily influencing the outcome. In honour of Pfungst and his study of the horses, the phenomenon of influencing experiments involuntarily has since been referred to as the Clever Hans Effect.

Although Krall now knew how it worked, he refused to accept Pfungst's conclusions. He voiced a number of objections, including the fact that Bento was blind. But this horse too, was only capable of performing calculations when Krall was present. Although visual hints were out of the question, Bento obviously had another way of understanding when he had to tap his hoofs.

Krall remained convinced of the intelligence of his horses, and until his death published extensively on the theme.

NOTHING'S SO NICE AS BASMATI RICE

Connoisseurs consider basmati rice, which grows in the foothills of the Himalayas in northern India and Pakistan, one of the finest and most delicious kinds of rice in the world. As basmati is difficult to grow, little is produced and the price is high. This makes it the perfect prey for fakers. Because of its characteristic aroma, it is impossible to fake basmati rice completely, but it can be mixed with other, cheaper varieties.

In 2003, 363 brands of basmati rice were tested in Great Britain, and only 54 per cent proved to consist of pure basmati. The remaining 46 per cent of producers mixed it with cheaper varieties. In the case of 31 brands, more than 60 per cent of the 'basmati' was made up of

Basmati rice – but is it real?

other kinds of rice. The estimated cost to the consumer in 2002 was €6.6 million.

O

OMAR KHAN, THE STRAIGHT-A STUDENT WHO WORKED NIGHTS

Omar Shahid Khan lived in a well-to-do gated housing development in Orange County, California, and was a student at Tesoro High School. The school often appeared in *Newsweek* magazine's annual list of best high schools. Good grades secured students a place at a prestigious university. But Omar Khan's grades were not at all good. He regularly got an F, the lowest grade in American schools.

In 2008 Khan applied to both the University of California and the University of Southern California for a place. Understandably, his applications were rejected. A few weeks later, Kahn requested copies of his transcripts, listing the subjects he had taken and his grades, from Tesoro High School, so he could appeal against his rejected application. While printing the records, a school administrator noticed that Khan's abysmal grades had miraculously metamorphosed into top scores: every F had turned into an A.

The police initiated an investigation and reconstructed what had happened. They discovered that between January and May 2008 Khan had entered the school on several nights using a skeleton key. After breaking into the computer network, Khan had changed his grades and those of twelve other students. He had also installed software that allowed him to access the network from his home. In the weeks that followed, Khan downloaded many tests, some of which he forwarded to dozens of other students.

What had seemed like a great prank in the 1986 movie *Ferris Bueller's Day Off* was not appreciated by the Public Prosecutors in 2008. Khan was charged with 69 offences, including altering and stealing public records, computer fraud, burglary, identity theft, receiving stolen property and conspiracy. The prosecutors demanded a stiff 38-year sentence. But that was going too far, even for the judge, who allowed Khan to plead guilty to five charges in March 2011. In the end he was sentenced to a month in prison, 500 hours of community service and a fine of $14,900.

OMID AMIDI-MAZAHERI, THE DEMON DENTIST

Mogjan Azari is a Swedish-Iranian former dentist who practised in south London. One ill-fated day around 2002, she met Iranian refugee Omid Amidi-Mazaheri and Cupid's arrows found their mark. Amidi-Mazaheri decided that he would also like to be a dentist, and wondered if Azari could teach him a thing or two. After instructing her boyfriend in the basics of dentistry, Azari allowed him to practise on her own patients. They writhed in the chair from the horrific pains Amidi-Mazaheri inflicted on them, while the fillings he gave them crumbled within days. Once, while administering an injection, Amidi-Mazaheri dropped one of his instruments down the patient's throat. (He and his fellow sufferers would have been pleased to know that around £30,000 of the money Azari claimed from the National Health Service was for work that was never actually undertaken!) Financially, things were going very well for Amidi-Mazaheri. He dashed from one nightclub to another in a top-of-the-range Mercedes. Not adverse to earning even more money, the couple decided to open a private dental clinic in April 2003, where Amidi-Mazaheri was to treat the patients. Because treatment had to be declared in the name of a registered dentist, they took on an older colleague, Johannes Kidane. Rather conveniently, Kidane died from a stroke in January 2004; but he continued to be registered at the clinic and Amidi-Mazaheri simply took on his identity.

During his career as a dental demolition expert, Amidi-Mazaheri tortured some 600 patients in his chair. Such damage and such suffering!

The duo's downfall came after a fourteen-month investigation by Scotland Yard's Economic Crime Unit and the NHS Dental Fraud Team. Amidi-Mazaheri was estimated to have made £120,000 from his illegal practice.

In March 2005 he received a two-year prison sentence. Furthermore, the judge expressed serious doubt about his suitability to remain in Britain, which meant that he would be deported after serving his time. Azari was sentenced to twelve months in jail and, in early 2006, the General Dental Council barred her from practising dentistry. The NHS deemed it necessary to ask all the clinic's patients to come forward, not only for dental check-ups but also – as hygiene was not one of Amidi-Mazaheri's strong points – for blood tests to screen for hepatitis B and C and for HIV.

007 IMPERSONATOR MICHAEL NEWITT

In 2005, after an earlier bankruptcy, Michael Newitt's latest business was also on the verge of collapse. He was having difficulty paying his bills, including the mooring fee for his £200,000 motor yacht. When the harbour master of a marina in Suffolk moved the yacht, Newitt (*b. c.* 1967) came up with a story that boosted his low self-esteem. He told the harbour master that he was a secret agent and that the yacht was part of his undercover operation. He even persuaded the man to sign a pledge of secrecy under the Official Secrets Act.

In the period that followed, Newitt purchased the attributes required to live the life of a spy: weapons (realistic-looking replica pistols that he left on his bedside cabinet, so that even his wife believed his lies), a revolving light and siren for his car (which he used to arrest a drunk driver on the M6 motorway who he turned over to the local police), four police radios with earpieces (none of which worked) and identification documents. Newitt awarded himself the title of Companion of the Order of St Michael and St George (CMG), the same distinction presented to James Bond in *From Russia with Love*.

Throughout his career as a con artist, Newton regularly fooled the police, but one officer refused to be taken in. In April 2008 Newitt reported to the police station in Hinckley and claimed to have information about drugs transactions. Lee Smith, who had a military background, became suspicious when his guest presented himself as a Commander, the same rank as James Bond. Smith investigated Newitt more closely, discovered his false identity and arrested him shortly afterwards. When he was seized, Newitt was in possession of a truncheon and three air rifles. In October 2008 he was sentenced to two years in prison.

OPERATION ANDREAS: THE BIG MONEY GAMBLE

In 1939 SS officer Alfred Naujocks (1911–1966) revived a traditional practice of the German government: producing counterfeit foreign currency. He proposed printing English banknotes on a large scale with the aim of destabilizing the British economy. His boss Richard Heydrich (1904–1942) decided they should go a step further and counterfeit not only sterling, but also U.S. dollars. The plan, Operation Andreas, was set in motion in 1941.

To make sure the counterfeit notes were of high quality, they even found out how the Bank of England devised its serial numbers. The first sterling notes were tested at the end of 1942. A secret agent went to a bank in Switzerland, told them he had bought a large quantity of sterling on the black market, and asked if they could test them as he had doubts about their authenticity. The notes were declared authentic.

As a result of internal politics, Naujocks was dismissed from his post. The new leader of the project was Bernhard Krüger, who renamed it Operation Bernhard. From 1942, a search was instigated in concentration camps to find inmates with experience in the graphics industry. One of those who came forward was Adolf Burger (*b.* 1917), who had been imprisoned for producing illegal documents for the Communist Party in Slovakia. Burger's wife had been gassed in the autumn of 1942, and he was himself facing the abyss.

Burger was transferred to the concentration camp at Sachsenhausen, where he found himself in a surreal situation. The counterfeit notes were produced in two blocks in the camp, 18 and 19, which were completely cut off from the outside world. The prisoners slept on beds with proper bed linen, were fed reasonably well, were permitted to wear normal clothes, did not have their heads shaved, and were issued with soap and towels. To complete their isolation, the group even had their own Jewish barber and a Jewish doctor. The idea behind this strategy was that, if the operation were ever wound up, the whole team could be sent to the gas chambers, leaving no witnesses. The ss guards were changed so regularly that they could never have an inkling of what was going on, while in the whole hierarchy of the secret service, right up to Hitler himself, only a handful of people knew about the operation.

The underlying rationale of allowing the group to live in relative luxury was of course driven purely by considerations of efficiency. Many inmates of concentration camps became completely apathetic, lost all contact with reality, and were no longer able to respond to anything at all. The luxury, including access to books and newspapers, was intended to prevent this kind of depression, which would after all be bad for productivity.

What started in September 1942 with a small team of 26 had grown by the autumn of 1944 into a full-fledged, innovative printing shop, employing 144 inmates. Besides printing money, the 'company' also took on other assignments. When ss chief Heinrich Himmler found himself depicted on counterfeit German postage stamps made by the British, he retaliated by ordering Operation Bernhard to produce fake British stamps bearing the Star of David, images of the British monarch and Joseph Stalin. This counterattack was known as Operation Watergolf, after the watermark on the paper used to print the stamps.

In September 1944 Himmler issued the order to speed up the printing of dollar bills, something that had eluded the group until then. With this in mind, a new member was added to the team, Salomon Smolianoff, the only professional counterfeiter in the group. Full of professional pride, he launched himself into producing the bills with great enthusiasm. A little too enthusiastically for some people's liking. Adolf Burger and a Dutch colleague, Abraham Jacobson, decided to sabotage his efforts. The dollar bills had to be produced using the collotype process, which entailed printing an image of the bill on a plate of glass with a layer of gelatine and then exposing it to light. No matter how hard Smolianoff tried, the process went wrong no less than 200 times. Perhaps there was something wrong with the gelatine? Or perhaps he should have exposed it for a shorter time? In this way, Burger and Jacobson succeeded in preventing the production of the bills. Bernhard Krüger was aware that someone was sabotaging the operation and, within a short time, Himmler issued an order that a counterfeit dollar bill had to be produced successfully within a month, or the whole team would be executed. At his 250th attempt, Smolianoff produced a perfect bill. On 12 February 1945, with the outcome of the war now relatively certain, Himmler ordered the team to produce $1 million a day.

A month later, with the Allies on the doorstep, a chaotic withdrawal started. The tension in the group built up as everyone was aware that, paradoxical as it sounds, the end of the war would mean certain death for all of them. The retreat came to an end at the camp in Ebensee. The German guards, convinced that the war was at an end, lost interest and, on 5 May 1945, the group was liberated.

After the war, some 40 per cent of the British banknotes in circulation, with a total value of £135 million, proved to have been produced by Operation Bernhard. The Bank of England first recalled all notes worth £10 and more, and then all £5 notes. They were all eventually replaced by notes with new designs. Not one of the counterfeit dollars ever went into circulation.

In the years following the war, there were many stories about large quantities of money and weapons that the Nazis had stored in the Alps in preparation for the time that they would regroup and fight to establish the Fourth Reich. In 1959 the German weekly magazine *Stern* started to investigate the allegations. In July of that year divers found chests containing millions of pounds and a large number of documents on the watery bottom of the Toplitzsee. It was largely the documents – with lists of agents, middlemen and others – that fascinated the German public. But before any conclusions could be drawn, *Stern's* directors ordered the investigation to be abandoned. Clearly, pressure had been applied behind the scenes; there were too many careers at stake in the new Germany.

More than 40 years later, America's CBS TV set up and filmed a new diving operation. Among those present when the first pounds were retrieved from the water was Adolf Burger. Burger could not conceal a feeling of pride as the notes proved to be still in perfect condition after lying 65 m underwater for 55 years.

In 2008 *Die Fälscher* (released in English as *The Counterfeiters*), based on Burger's memoirs, won an Academy Award for Best Foreign Language Film.

Percival Lowell, American astronomer, *c.* 1904.

P

PERCIVAL LOWELL'S LIFE ON MARS

Percival Lawrence Lowell (1855–1916) was on the one hand a patient and painstaking scientist, and on the other a dreamy and inspired artist. After graduating as a mathematician, he went to work in the family business. He quickly made his fortune in the United States through a series of successful investments and started to travel the world. An interesting but apocryphal account describes how Lowell was en route from Japan to the U.S. in 1893 when he heard that the eyesight of astronomer Giovanni Schiaparelli was failing rapidly.[22] Lowell decided there and then that he would become Schiaparelli's successor. The following year he built an observatory near Flagstaff, Arizona, and another year later published his first book, *Mars*, about the lines he had observed on the red planet. Even this first work was a combination of science and creative thinking. Those who did not believe in the lines pointed out that, to be observable from earth, the canals would have to be at least 50 km wide. Lowell solved this problem by claiming that the lines were not only the canals themselves but also the vegetation that grew alongside them amid the otherwise barren landscape of the planet, just like the banks of the river Nile in Egypt. Lowell discovered no fewer than 183 canals.

The book drove a wedge between Lowell and other astronomers. While he was popular with the wider public because he wrote interesting and readable books and newspaper and magazine articles, his colleagues produced texts that could only be deciphered by other astronomers. They took Lowell less seriously with each publication. Some no longer considered him a colleague: sitting in an observatory and staring at the sky doesn't make someone an astronomer any more than holding a scalpel makes them a surgeon. William Wallace Campbell described Lowell as 'a trial to sane astronomers' (Crossley, 2000). These sane astronomers were being criticized by the public for their inability to make the same observations as Lowell. Astronomer Edward S. Holden, perhaps Lowell's fiercest critic, tried to give the public a lesson in proper scientific procedure:

> I remember I was asked, in 1890, to telegraph my opinions as to the land and water on Mars, etc. I replied that our observations at the Lick observatory up to that time enabled us to construct an accurate map of the dark and of the bright regions of the planet; but that neither I nor any one could say which regions were land and which were water. This telegram was received with a certain air of disappointment, natural enough, I suppose, to those who have been fed on (alleged) certainties, and who could not conceive that such fundamental matters were still unsettled . . . 'I do not know,' is a scientific answer, though it is, undoubtedly, a disappointing one when it replies to a question in which the whole world takes a vivid interest. But scientific men are in honor bound to make this answer on so far as it is true, and to be scrupulously exact in their dealings with the public which supports observatories and which has a right to know where certainty ends and speculation begins. (Crossley, 2000)

Holden's lesson fell on deaf ears, however, as far as Lowell was concerned. His subsequent books, *Mars and its Canals* (1906) and *Mars as the Abode of Life* (1908), were scientifically very unsound and critics ripped them to pieces. They claimed that Lowell the poet was too explicitly present in the work of Lowell the (pseudo)scientist. Lowell also had the dangerous habit of reasoning too often by analogy. That can make a story more readable and more convincing to readers who are not aware that the analogy has no value at all as hard evidence. Take this passage from *Mars as the Abode of Life*:

> Viewed under suitable conditions, few sights can compare their instant beauty and growing grandeur with Mars as presented by the telescope. Framed in the blue of space, there floats before the observer's gaze a seeming miniature of his own Earth, yet changed by translation to the sky. Within its charmed circle of light he marks apparent continents and seas, now ramifying into one another, now stretching in unique expanse over wide tracts of disk, and capped at their poles by dazzling ovals of white. It recalls to him his first lessons in geography, where the Earth was shown him set ethereally amid the stars, only with an added sense of reality in the apotheosis. It is the thing itself, stamped with that all-pervading, indefinable hallmark of authenticity in which the cleverest reproduction somehow fails. (Lowell, 1908)

It is easy to explain why such texts enjoyed such popularity with a broader public. It was as close as they would ever come to a space telescope (it was still difficult to photograph planets at the start of the twentieth century. Even the best images were vague, because of the long exposure times). Lowell took advantage of this situation, catching their interest with romantic prose and then serving them up complete twaddle:

> Young Martians must be born mathematicians and then never outgrow the faculty . . . The system [of canals] betrays a wonderful unity of purpose for it girdles the planet from pole to pole. Race prejudice, national jealousy, individual endeavour are there all subordinated to the common good. (Crossley, 2000)

Although people who could not immediately be dismissed as charlatans continued to defend the existence of canals on Mars after Lowell's death, since the 1930s the subject has received little attention. In the 1970s photographic images of Mars showed that one or two of the lines that Lowell identified as canals were caused by natural relief on the surface of the planet. The remaining more than 180 existed only in Lowell's overactive imagination.

There is, however, one achievement that mitigates history's hard judgement of Lowell. On the basis of calculations (by others), he concluded that there must a ninth planet somewhere in our solar system. In 1906 he started to search for this 'Planet X', as he called it. When he died in 1916 he left $1 million to the Lowell Observatory to continue the search.

On 18 February 1930 astronomer Clyde Tombaugh announced that, on the basis of photographs taken the previous month, he had discovered the planet. The planet was christened Pluto and given the astronomical symbol ♇, in honour of *P*ercival *L*owell.[23]

THE PERILS OF COOKING UP STORIES

During his military career, Philip Anthony Sessarego (1952–2008) twice took the entrance test for the elite Special Air Service (SAS). Each time he was turned down. So Sessarego was left with no choice but to make up a heroic past. He was especially fond of talking about his experiences in Afghanistan, where he claimed he had trained the mujahideen to fight the Soviet army:

> The butt of my deadly Kalashnikov pressed into my shoulder as I let go a long, vicious burst of fire. A Russian special forces soldier and two Afghan regular troops clambering over the wall only noticed me as they were poised in mid-air. By then it was too late. My weapon bucked and climbed as it spewed out bullets. They had no chance . . . All three were dying as they flopped awkwardly into the dust. (Gillan, 2009)

In the early 1990s, probably to avoid repercussions meted out by indignant SAS members, Sessarego spread the rumour that he had been killed by a car bomb in Bosnia. Later, he surfaced again as 'Tom

Carew'. Under this name, he published his memoirs, *Jihad!*, which sold some 50,000 copies. Years later, after the 9/11 attacks on the World Trade Center, this made him a much sought-after commentator. But the media attention was to be his downfall. On 14 November 2001, the BBC current affairs programme *Newsnight* exposed him as a fraud.

His wife and children, whom Sessarego had abandoned years before, did not have a good word for him. His daughter Claire made no effort to disguise her feelings:

> He is a twat . . . He's just a fantasist who's trying to make money on the back of other people's reputations. There are a lot of former SAS men who have scores to settle with him . . . I wouldn't care if somebody killed him because he's brought it all on himself. (Gillan, 2009)

In 2008 Sessarego was living in Belgium under the assumed name Philip Stephenson. In January 2009, the landlord of the garage Sessarego rented came to collect six months' worth of unpaid rent. Inside the garage he found Sessarego's decomposed body, together with a mattress, a small cooker and some leftover food. Sessarego had presumably died there of carbon monoxide poisoning the previous summer. It was ostensibly an accident but conspiracy theorists pointed out that SAS men leave no traces at the scene of a crime.

PERU'S FAT GANGSTERS

In November 2009 General Félix Murga announced at a press conference that a criminal gang of dealers in human fat had been rounded up in the Peruvian province of Huánuco. Murga claimed that the gang, consisting of four members, had killed between 40 and 60 people and had used candles to extract human fat from the corpses. Their customers were plastic surgery clinics in Europe and in the United States. At the press conference Murga showed two bottles filled with human fat and played a video of one suspect confessing. The spectacle received worldwide media attention.

Soon it became clear that Murga's story was full of holes. Human organs are worth tens of thousands of dollars on the black market, but there is no trade in human fat. And why would plastic surgery clinics want to buy fat? Apart from the question of what they would do with it, the clinics themselves throw away litres of the stuff every week.

Further investigation revealed a much more horrific story. Murga had made the whole thing up to cover up the fact that in that year, his police force had executed 47 suspects rather than handing them over to be tried.

PETER CHAPPELL, THE HARMONIC HOMEOPATH

Like many homeopaths Peter Chappell can turn his hand to curing anything, whether it is multiple sclerosis, Parkinson's disease, Alzheimer's, anorexia, asthma, chronic fatigue syndrome, hepatitis, a spastic colon, fibromyalgia, infertility, Lyme disease, Ménière's disease, prostate problems, traumas resulting from rape, torture and genocide, or malaria. You name it, Chappell can treat it.

In December 2007 Chappell presented his newest 'discovery': he claimed to be able to compose and supply musical remedies for illnesses. Even 'AIDS in Africa', he said, 'could be significantly ameliorated by a simple tune played on the radio' (Goldacre, 2007). Perhaps to prove that he was not only after the money, visitors to his website could download a free tune to combat bird flu. When there was an outbreak of swine flu in the spring of 2009, the tune was replaced by the Swine Flu Healing Download MP3.

PHILOSOPHY AND ETHICS REVISITED

In 1953 Elisabeth Ströker (1928–2000) obtained her doctorate with the thesis *Zahl und Raum* (Number and Space). It was the start of a beautiful career and in 1965 she became a professor of philosophy.

In 1990 Ströker published a collection of texts on the ethics of science. Maybe this was courting disaster as, shortly afterwards – 37 years after the publication of her thesis – she was accused of plagiarism. She had allegedly copied for her thesis large sections from works by Bertrand Russell and Ernst Cassirer without crediting the sources. While her employer, the University of Cologne, conducted an investigation, Ströker had the cool-headedness to give a course on the ethics of science. Eventually the accusations were ruled valid and the university sacked her. Unabashed, in the year of her death Ströker published *Im Namen des Wissenschaftsethos* (In the Name of the Ethics of Science) defending her actions.

THE PILTDOWN TURKEY

When the first *Archaeopteryx* fossil was found in Bavaria in 1861, Thomas Henry Huxley (1825–1895), an avid supporter of Charles Darwin, formulated the theory that dinosaurs had not simply become extinct but had evolved into birds. For almost a century and a half the theory was the subject of heated discussion. Those who condemned the theory challenged its proponents to come up with a transitional fossil, a creature that exhibited clear traits of both species.[24]

In 1999 a fossil seemed to have been found that was up to the challenge. It originated from the Chinese province of Liaoning, the site of many thousands of dinosaur fossils. The fossil – roughly speaking, a bird with a long, bony tail – was smuggled from China into the United States and sold to Stephan Czerkas, owner of a palaeontological museum, for $80,000.

In November 1999 the discovery was presented in *National Geographic* under the name *Archaeoraptor liaoningensis*. This magazine, known for its rigorous fact-checking procedures, invested a lot of money examining the fossil. Communication between the scientists conducting the examination and the editors of the magazine was obviously not very good, for when *National Geographic* published the article, it was already known behind the scenes that there was something not right about the fossil. The left and right feet were mirror images of each other, suggesting that a single piece of stone had been split into two, producing an imprint and a counter-imprint. Later research published in *Nature* magazine showed that *Archaeoraptor liaoningensis* was a composite of between two and five different fossils. Furthermore, they were not just different fossils of the same species but fossils of different species. *Archaeoraptor liaoningensis* was a cross between a dinosaur-like bird and a bird-like dinosaur.

Normally, this would mean an inglorious end for the fossil, which – in reference to Piltdown Man – had been dubbed Piltdown Turkey. But in 2001 and 2002 the separate parts of the fossil turned out to be of palaeontological interest in themselves. By trying to create a highly marketable fossil, the composer had used parts which – when seen separately and in the right context – were much more valuable than the fake. The bird parts turned out to belong to a fish-eating bird, *Yanornis martini*. The tail was identified as belonging to a previously undiscovered species of dromaeosaurus, *Microraptor zhaoianus*. The *Yanornis* had teeth, like a dinosaur, while the *Microraptor*, the smallest dinosaur ever found, had feathers and lived in trees. Separately, therefore, the parts strongly supported Huxley's thesis and were of great scientific value. They are now back in China and have an estimated value of several million pounds sterling.

PINKHAM'S PANACEA

There was nothing that could be called conservative about the Quaker upbringing of Lydia Estes (1819–1883). Spiritualism, votes for women, the Greenback Labor Party, the abolition of slavery and the death penalty – as long as it was radical, she was in there like a shot. She was well educated and became a teacher. In 1843 she married widower Isaac Pinkham, who earned a living in real estate. But Isaac had little talent for the business and money was scarce in the Pinkham household.

In the economic crisis of 1873 Pinkham's real estate company went belly up. The couple tried a number of ways to earn money, and one proved to be a goldmine. Lydia Pinkham believed in alternative healing and had a particular aversion to conventional gynaecologists. She concocted a herbal remedy, which she called Vegetable Compound. Like all medicines offered by quacks it was a panacea, a cure-all. It was especially intended for 'women's problems', which embraced everything from menstruation pain and nausea during pregnancy to urinal infections and prolapse of the womb.

The whole Pinkham family was mobilized to sell the remedy. The sons distributed advertising leaflets and peddled it door-to-door. Lydia herself was responsible for the most important element that made Vegetable Compound such a great success: the marketing. Her grandmotherly face adorned the labels on the bottles and the newspaper advertisements. It was these adverts that made Vegetable Compound a household name. They contained easy-to-remember rhymes like 'Elsie W. had no children / There was nothing in her blouse / So she took some Vegetable Compound / Now they milk her with the cows' (Renckens, 2002).

At the end of the nineteenth century, the anti-alcohol movement

Advertisement for Lydia E. Pinkham's Vegetable Compound, 1882.

MRS. LYDIA E. PINKHAM, OF LYNN, MASS.,

LYDIA E. PINKHAM'S

VEGETABLE COMPOUND.

Is a Positive Cure

for all those Painful Complaints and Weaknesses so common to our best female population.

It will cure entirely the worst form of Female Complaints, all ovarian troubles, Inflammation and Ulceration, Falling and Displacements, and the consequent Spinal Weakness, and is particularly adapted to the Change of Life.

It will dissolve and expel tumors from the uterus in an early stage of development. The tendency to cancerous humors there is checked very speedily by its use.

It removes faintness, flatulency, destroys all craving for stimulants, and relieves weakness of the stomach. It cures Bloating, Headaches, Nervous Prostration, General Debility, Sleeplessness, Depression and Indigestion.

That feeling of bearing down, causing pain, weight and backache, is always permanently cured by its use.

It will at all times and under all circumstances act in harmony with the laws that govern the female system.

For the cure of Kidney Complaints of either sex this Compound is unsurpassed.

LYDIA E. PINKHAM'S VEGETABLE COMPOUND is prepared at 233 and 235 Western Avenue, Lynn, Mass. Price $1. Six bottles for $5. Sent by mail in the form of pills, also in the form of lozenges, on receipt of price, $1 per box for either. Mrs. Pinkham freely answers all letters of inquiry. Send for pamphlet. Address as above. *Mention this Paper.*

No family should be without LYDIA E. PINKHAM'S LIVER PILLS. They cure constipation, biliousness, and torpidity of the liver. 25 cents per box.

Sold by all Druggists.

was very popular in America. The Pinkhams, too, were believers in temperance but Lydia claimed that the herbs in her Vegetable Compound could only be properly preserved in a solution comprising 19 per cent alcohol. Consequently, many female teetotallers were happy to take a regular slug of Vegetable Compound – purely for medicinal reasons, of course.

The Pinkhams no longer had to worry about money. By 1881 their monthly turnover had risen to $30,000 and Lydia was the first woman in the United States to become a self-made millionaire.

After she died in 1883 the company carried on using her famous face as its trademark, while advertisements still encouraged women to send her their questions and comments. Vegetable Compound continued to thrive for many years, until the business found itself in trouble in the 1920s and '30s. There were long-running conflicts in the family, and national guidelines were making it more difficult to make medicinal claims in advertisements. The factories and the brand name remained in the hands of the Pinkham family until 1968. Nothing more was heard of the brand until 1987, when the new owner re-introduced Lydia Pinkham's Herbal Compound, which now had completely different ingredients to the original remedy. Herbal Compound is still on the market today, and Lydia's portrait still appears on the label.

POLES APART: HOW TO REACH AN INCREASINGLY ICY RELATIONSHIP

The name Robert E. Peary (1856–1920) is inseparable from that of Frederick Albert Cook (1865–1940). The two American friends shared expeditions for many decades, but became embroiled in the controversy about the North Pole that erupted in September 1909.

By the early twentieth century the world had pretty much been fully explored. There were only two regions left where the intrepid could make their name: the North Pole and the South Pole. Peary and Cook were serious adventurers with experience in both the Arctic and the Antarctic, although neither had reached either Pole when Cook left for the North Pole in 1907. Peary's expedition followed the year after. In September 1909 they returned to the civilized world, only five days apart – Peary to Greenland and Cook to Denmark. Peary sent a telegram home to say that he had reached the North Pole on 6 April

1909. What he did not know at that point was that Cook had announced a few days before that he had made it to the same Pole on 21 April 1908. His team had not returned until 1909 as bad weather conditions had forced them to spend the winter on the ice. When they heard each other's news, Cook congratulated Peary on his achievement.

Peary realized that the fame he had pursued for 23 years would now evade him. At first, he was too dumbfounded to respond, but it was not long before he contested Cook's claim. This led to a controversy over the North Pole that continues to this day.

The former friends started taking steps to get their rival claims approved. Cook handed over a number of notebooks to Copenhagen University containing navigation notes and observations, while Peary started a telegram campaign, contacting as many geographical societies around the world as he could think of. He had a strategic advantage in the form of two influential American sponsors: the National Geographic Society and the *New York Times*. Since these two institutions had a stake in the success of Peary's expedition,

Photogravure of Robert Peary in furs by Benjamin B. Hampton, 1909.

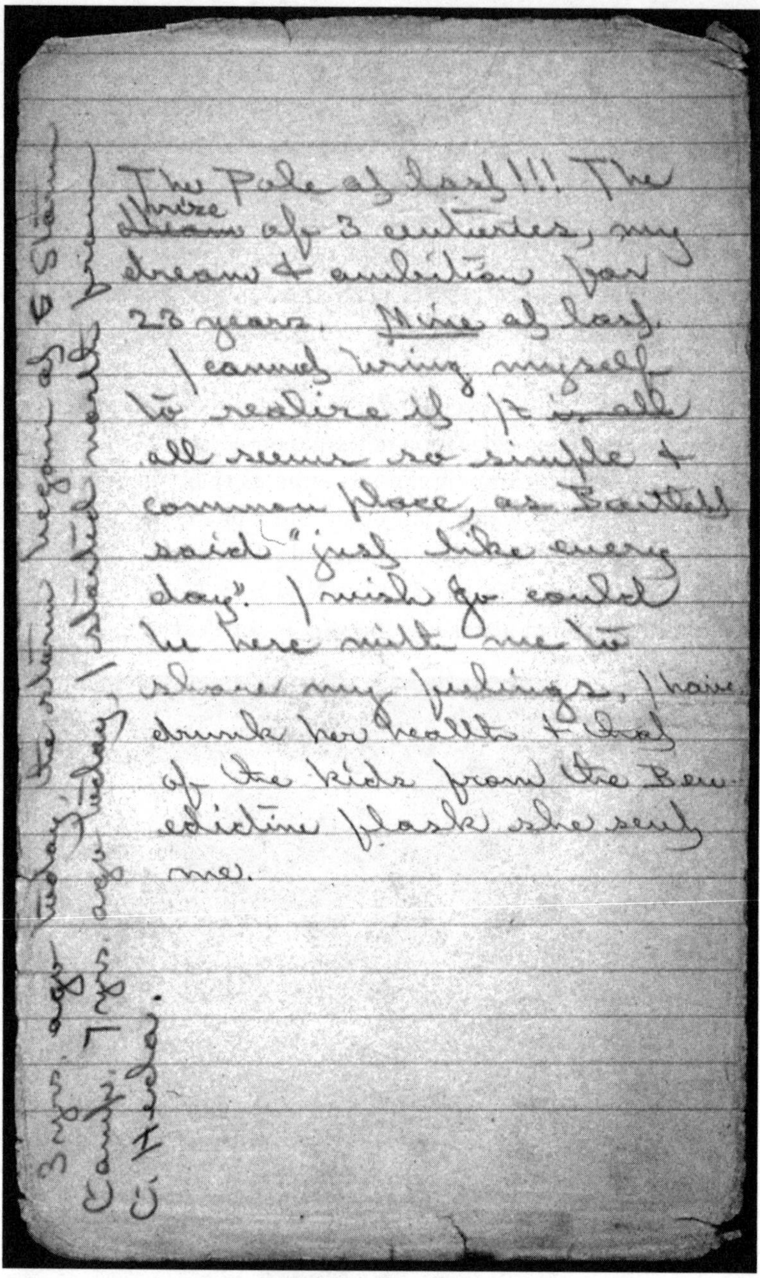

The Pole at last!!! The ~~dream~~ prize of 3 centuries, my dream & ambition for 23 years. Mine at last. I cannot bring myself to realize it. It all seems so simple & common place, as Bartlett said "just like every day". I wish Jo could be here with me to share my feelings. I have drunk her health & that of the kids from the Benedictine flask she sent me.

3 yrs. ago today the storm began at 6 S Storm Camp. 7 yrs. ago today I started north from C. Hecla.

A page from the diary of Robert E. Peary, beginning 'The Pole at last!!!'

both financially and in terms of their reputations, they were perhaps less critical than they should have been. Newspaper articles repeatedly contained biased remarks. In an article on 12 September 1909, the *New York Times* reported Peary as saying that the public should not take Cook's story 'too seriously'. In October, the paper quoted Captain William Armstrong, who had climbed Mt McKinley with Cook, as saying, 'Cook is a good fellow, a great self-advertiser, but, in my opinion, the worst prevaricator in the world (the *New York Times*, October 1909). Headlines like 'Peary found no trace of Cook at Pole' are also misleading, to say the least (the *New York Times*, 8 September 1909).

That same month, a three-man commission examined a few loose papers from Peary's notes and some of the material from the expedition and upheld his claim. Two years later, a committee dismissed the commission's inquiry as nonsense (Gibbons, 1990).

Meanwhile, the libellous conflict raged on unabated. The October article was extremely damaging for Cook. In 1903 and 1906 he had undertaken expeditions to Mt McKinley, the highest mountain in North America, and claimed to have reached the summit in 1906. The newspaper reported that Edward Barrill, who had accompanied Cook on the expedition, had confessed that they had not reached the summit. The pair had not even got half way. The article was factually correct – Cook had indeed lied – and it appeared to be a triumph of good investigative journalism by the newspaper. What it failed to mention, however, was that Barrill had made his statement after being paid a sum of money by Peary's camp. That may not make the article incorrect, but it does illustrate the lack of scruples in the dispute.

In 1910 neither camp was very effective in producing evidence of their adventures on the ice. Cook came no further than the notebooks submitted earlier. It was clear that there were parts missing and that they provided a very sketchy report of the route. Peary's expedition had been sponsored by the government and in the spring of 1910 he was invited to appear before a committee of inquiry. He refused to attend, claiming it was in breach of his contract with his publisher. His notes, too, left much to be desired. After he had returned, his chronometer was discovered to run ten minutes fast, making all his navigation data unreliable – to the degree that Peary's position could have been 29 km from the actual Pole. Besides, the data itself said very little. As Peary admitted to the inquiry in January 1911, notes can be made without actually being at the stated position. Peary's journal also raised questions. There were a number of unexplained blank pages and on 6 April a loose sheet of paper had been inserted stating: 'The Pole, at last!!!' (Wilford, August 1988). The journal has nothing at all to say about what Peary did in the 30 hours he spent there. What also casts doubt on his account are the enormous distances he claimed to have covered. British polar explorer Wally Herbert had this to say about that in 1988:

> This works out (adding a modest 25 per cent for detours) at 71 statute miles a day – nothing less than phenomenal! No explorer, before or since, has claimed such distances across the polar pack over the same number of consecutive days, neither with dog teams nor even snowmobiles. (Wilford, August 1988)

The American government was in two minds. Peary was promoted from Commander to Rear Admiral, but when he retired in 1911, the official word of thanks from Congress mentioned only his 'Arctic discoveries'. The passage that originally followed – 'and discovery of the North Pole' – was scrapped (Gibbons, 1989).

During the twentieth century, the widely held opinion was that Peary had been at the North Pole and Cook was lying. Cook still has some supporters today, but the majority of those in the know no longer take his claim seriously. His notes are too summary and simply contain too many errors. But, from the 1970s on, Peary himself also came under fire. Wally Herbert concluded that Peary got no closer to the Pole than 30 to 60 miles, while Dennis Rawlins believed it was as far away as '121 miles'. In 1989 the Navigation Foundation concluded that he had been only 5 miles from the Pole, close enough to allow him to retain the honour of being the first to reach it. Finally, in 1997, Robert M. Bryce calculated that Peary had been around 100 miles off the Pole and accused him of intentionally falsifying his journals.

Whatever happened at and around the North Pole in April 1909, it is clear that Peary's evidence offers minimal support for his claim. Others learned a lesson from this drama. During Norwegian Roald Amundsen's expedition to the South Pole in 1910–12 (he was the first to reach it, on 14 December 1911), he made sure that the evidence was overwhelming, including getting different people to take navigational readings, independent of each other.

PROFESSOR BEHE ON INTELLIGENT DESIGN

Professor Michael J. Behe (*b.* 1952) is one of the leading figures of the intelligent design movement, a predominantly American pseudo science. The popularity of this pseudo-theory in the U.S. is thanks to the First Amendment of the United States Constitution, which guarantees the freedom of religion. The separation of church and state means that schools are not permitted to make statements of a religious nature. This is a thorn in the side of the country's many fundamentalist Christians, who watch with horror as the theory of evolution is taught in schools.[25] Although it is not a religious doctrine, it is clearly incompatible with their belief that all the species on earth were created by God some 6,000 years ago, and have not changed since.

Christian fundamentalist groups have been trying to smuggle the story of Creation into the school curriculum since the 1970s. One ruse was to invent a new 'creation science', which they argued should be taught alongside the theory of evolution. But creation science is not scientific. Science means drawing up hypotheses, testing them and then, depending on the results, rejecting or accepting them, at least until they are proved inadequate. As religion is concerned with supernatural phenomena, which cannot by definition be tested; it cannot be scientific. In 1987, the Supreme Court ruled that creation science is religion in disguise, and that teaching it violated the First Amendment.

Christian fundamentalists responded by designing a new form of camouflage. They stopped using not only the name of God but also the word 'creation'. They came up with a new 'theory': the world is so perfectly constructed that it must be the result of intelligent design.[26] Three guesses who they have in mind as the designer.

The Center for Science and Culture at the Discovery Institute in Seattle plays a leading role in propagating this nonsense. This misleadingly named 'scientific' institute is an Astroturf body (see ASTROTURF – PLANTED OPINIONS) funded by fundamentalist Christians. Michael Behe is a senior fellow of the Institute and, as a prestigious professor of biochemistry, one of the heroes of the intelligent design movement, which is delighted to finally have a genuine professor among its members.

In 1996 Behe published *Darwin's Black Box*, in which he introduced a concept that appears to give intelligent design a touch of scientific respectability: irreducible complexity. Using three examples, Behe claimed that some systems are only useful as they are and not if they are in development. The tail that a bacteria uses to move does not work if part of it is missing; blood does not clot if one of the components is missing; and the immune system does not work if one of the components is missing. Behe concluded from these examples that their design entails forethought about the desired final result, which implies that there must have been some form of intelligence to do the thinking, which in turn requires the existence of an intelligent designer. Very little of this argument makes any sense, either formally or substantively.

First, two formal objections. There is nothing new under the sun: Behe's argument is simply the latest incarnation of the teleological 'design argument' ('if something is complex, it must have been designed by a process of intelligent thought'; 'watermelons are divided into neat sections, so God must have designed them for us'). This argument was shown to be flawed long ago, and Behe cannot be so stupid that he does not know that. That explains why he published his ideas in book form and not in a scientific journal. A peer-reviewed journal would make mincemeat of them. Second, irreducible complexity cannot be an argument for intelligent design. Even if the theory of evolution proved unable to generate complex systems, it would be an argument against evolution but not necessarily in favour of intelligent design.[27]

Substantively, too, little of Behe's argument holds water. Take blood clotting, for example; Behe claims that the series of chemical processes in the body that allow the blood to clot cannot work if one of the steps is missing. There are, however, fish where not only one, but three, of the steps are missing, and yet the process works perfectly.

At the start of the twenty-first century, Christian fundamentalist William Buckingham led a coup in the Board of Education of the district of Dover in Pennsylvania. Buckingham succeeded in ensuring that a statement had to be read out in biology lessons to the effect that the theory of evolution was just one theory among many. Anyone interested in the alternatives was advised to read the book *Of Pandas and People*, published by a Christian fundamentalist Astroturf body, the Foundation for Thought and Ethics. A number of parents caught a whiff of religion in the move and took the Board to court.

The case of *Kitzmiller et al.* v. *Dover Area School District et al.* was tried from 26 September to 4 November 2005 before Judge John E. Jones III. No one could accuse Jones of holding progressive ideas: a conservative Republican, he was appointed by born-again Christian George W. Bush in 2002.

While preparing for the trial, the plaintiff's lawyers made an astounding discovery. In *Of Pandas and People*, wherever there were references to intelligent design, previous editions had used the term 'creation science' which, as we have seen, had been banned in schoolbooks by the Supreme Court. The publisher had literally replaced the banned term with its new alias by cutting and pasting.

The trial turned into a tortuous ordeal for Behe and co. Accustomed only to preaching to the converted, the creationists were at a loss to answer every critical question. After six weeks of humiliation, Jones's 139-page report was the final blow. The judge had nothing good to say about the creationists' testimonies. Besides their tendency to lie under oath, they also presented a distorted view of the facts. Their claim that there was disagreement among scientists about the theory of evolution is simply not true. There are of course discussions about the theory, but very few do not adhere to it. By contrast, Jones concluded that intelligent design is 'a religious view, not a scientific theory'. This was the final nail in the coffin for the creationists (Jones, 2005).

Behe's career never really recovered after the trial. His employer, the Department of Biological Sciences at Lehigh University at Bethlehem, Pennsylvania, was so embarrassed by the antics of their staff member that they placed a statement – 'Department Position on Evolution and "Intelligent Design"' – in a prominent position on their website, which is still there today:

> The department faculty, then, are unequivocal in their support of evolutionary theory, which has its roots in the seminal work of Charles Darwin and has been supported by findings accumulated over 140 years. The sole dissenter from this position, Prof. Michael Behe, is a well-known proponent of 'intelligent design'. While we respect Prof. Behe's right to express his views, they are his alone and are in no way endorsed by the department. It is our collective position that intelligent design has no basis in science,

has not been tested experimentally, and should not be regarded as scientific.

Behe just made things worse for himself. His second book, *The Edge of Evolution*, published in 2007, was panned en masse by the critics. In a review in the *New York Times* Richard Dawkins wrote: 'I had expected to be as irritated by Michael Behe's second book as by his first. I had not expected to feel sorry for him' (Dawkins, 2007).

PROJECT JENNIFER'S MURKY DEPTHS

In March 1968, the Soviet submarine *K-129* sank in international waters about 1,200 km off Hawaii. Unlike their counterparts from the Eastern Bloc, who spent weeks searching in the wrong place, the U.S. Navy knew the exact location of the wreck. For the CIA this was an excellent opportunity to learn about the latest Soviet technology. They were interested in not only the torpedoes and nuclear missiles on board the vessel, but also the encryption apparatus that made it so difficult to listen in on the sub's communications with Moscow.

To keep the Soviets in the dark about the salvage operation, known as Project Jennifer, it needed a cover. So the CIA contacted the organization run by eccentric billionaire and recluse Howard Hughes (1905–1976). Not only did many of Hughes's companies have close ties with the U.S. Defense Department, but Hughes also had a reputation as a crazy inventor. The fact that he was almost paranoid about secrecy was also a plus for the CIA.

On 1 November 1972 Hughes's Summa Corporation started building the 189-m-long *Hughes Glomar Explorer*, a research vessel that was to search the ocean floor for manganese nodules (rock concretions that can contain minerals like nickel, copper and cobalt). The media swallowed the story and dutifully published articles about Hughes's visionary new enterprise. The *Hughes Glomar Explorer* had a bottom that could be opened and a grapple that could be lowered to a depth of 4,900 m. The ship, intended to be used only once, cost more than $350 million to build. With the exception of the 40 'scientists' on board, the crew had no idea of the true objective of the expedition.

In July 1974 the ship arrived at the site of the wreck. The *K-129* proved to have broken in two, so the crew tried to raise the fore section, which was some 40 m long. But when it was halfway to the surface, this section also broke in two and the most important part sank back to the ocean floor in pieces. Or so the story went.

Meanwhile, back on the mainland, the CIA's cover had quickly unravelled. On 5 June, a month before the *Hughes Glomar Explorer* had even reached the site of the wreck, there had been a burglary at a depot belonging to Summa Corporation. The burglar had also taken personal documents describing Hughes's involvement in Project Jennifer. As they were no use to him, he had given them to a journalist. They proved to contain sufficient information to set the press on the right track. Confronted with difficult questions, the CIA appealed to the media's sense of responsibility and asked them to keep quiet about the project until it was over. In exchange for press cooperation, CIA director William Colby gave the journalists regular briefings on the progress of the project. It would be March 1975 before the *New York Times* revealed the true nature of the expedition.

In December 1976 it became clear that Project Jennifer had salvaged the entire submarine, from bow to stern, and had retrieved the bodies of crew members, who were buried at sea with full military honours. The 1974 briefing by the CIA had been a white lie, intended to give the Soviet Navy a false feeling of confidence that its secrets were safe.

PROTOCOLS OF THE ELDERS OF ZION

The *Protocols* are anti-Semitic literary forgeries, probably written in 1898 by Mathieu Golovinski, a Russian living in France who, according to some sources, worked for Okhrana, the Russian secret service. They were first published in 1905 by Russian 'mystic' Sergei Nilus.

The *Protocols* are allegedly the minutes of a meeting, held at the end of the nineteenth century, of the leaders of a Jewish plot to disrupt the world order and seize power. As in all conspiracy theories of this nature capitalism, communism, liberalism, the Freemasons, Darwinism and the media are all instruments devised by international Jewry to corrupt healthy societies. In terms of style the *Protocols* are better than most, because much of the text was plagiarized from *Dialogue aux enfers entre Machiavel et Montesquieu* (1864) by French satirist Maurice Joly. In Joly's version Machiavelli is the villain of the piece; in the *Protocols* his place is taken by the Jews.

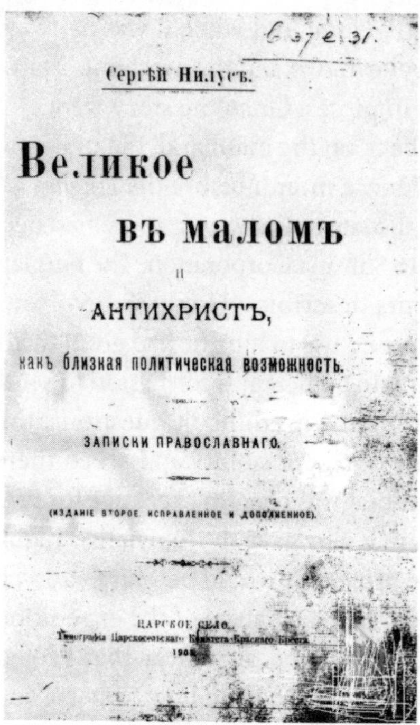

Сергѣй Нилусъ.

Великое

въ маломъ

и

АНТИХРИСТЪ,

какъ близкая политическая возможность.

ЗАПИСКИ ПРАВОСЛАВНАГО.

(ИЗДАНІЕ ВТОРОЕ ИСПРАВЛЕННОЕ И ДОПОЛНЕННОЕ).

ЦАРСКОЕ СЕЛО.

Типографія Царскосельскаго Комитета Краснаго Креста.

190[illegible]

The *Protocols of the Elders of Zion* (cover of the first book edition), *The Great within the Miniscule* and *Antichrist.*

The first English edition of the *Protocols* was published in 1920. Less than a year later, *The Times* produced convincing evidence that the document was a forgery. Apologists ignored the evidence, and still do to this day, arguing that the media is in Jewish hands and is therefore by definition not to be trusted.

Adolf Hitler quoted from the *Protocols* in *Mein Kampf*. In the U.S. Henry Ford published the *Protocols* and offered a free copy to anyone who bought one of his cars. In the 1960s and '70s King Faisal of Saudi Arabia gave them to visiting heads of state as a gift. The information service of the Palestinian National Authority placed the text on its website (it has since been removed after complaints from other countries), and parts of the *Protocols* can be found in the charter of the Islamic organization Hamas.

The 9/11 attacks revived interest in the *Protocols*. Rumours quickly spread that not a single Jewish American died in the attacks, because they were warned in advance. This could all be traced back to the *Protocols*, which became so popular that they were on sale in Walmart supermarkets.

THE PUB CURE FOR CANCER

Sometimes a few sentences are enough. In December 2007 Huub van Griensven, chairman of the Regional Medical Disciplinary Board in the Dutch city of Eindhoven, questioned quack Patrick van Eeghem, a self-proclaimed 'internist' and 'gastroenterologist':

> VAN GRIENSVEN: Just to go back to the jenever. The contents of a litre bottle are transferred into small bottles, which are then sold at 35 euros a piece. That's a profit of €1,000 a litre.
>
> VAN EEGHEM: A special kind of energy is added to it.
>
> VAN GRIENSVEN: And you prescribe that to your patients?
>
> VAN EEGHEM: Yes. When I cannot help people any further with regular medicine. There are no side effects. And it makes people feel better. (Vermeulen, 2007)

Witness the achievements of 2,500 years of medicine, Van Eeghem-style: people feel better after a couple of slugs of jenever. Your local publican knows that too, and he charges nothing for the advice and much less for the jenever.

Patrick van Eeghem and his coworker Carine Bolijn, a self-styled 'orthomolecular therapist', belong to that most reprehensible scum of the forger's profession: those who take advantage of other people's suffering and fear. They run the Integraal Medisch Centrum Maria Magdalena in Roosendaal, where they promise to cure cancer patients for whom regular treatment has been unsuccessful.

The methods used by this pair of quacks would not have been out of place at a medieval fair. Patients are diagnosed using a Lecher antenna (a modern version of a divining rod) and treated according to the principles of energetic medicine. This means that the patient lies down on a couch for half an hour to an hour.

Is that all? Not according to Van Eeghem and Bolijn. While the patients are on the couch, divine guides spring into action and start doing the real work. Removing cancer, repairing an organ or making a whole new one: the guides can turn their hands to anything. What is so nauseating is that Van Eeghem sells this nonsense as medicine.

So it was that in 2007 the Dutch Health Care Inspectorate investigated the duo. It reported them to the police and brought the case before the Regional Medical Disciplinary Board in Eindhoven. The Board suspended Van Eeghem for 'deception of the worst kind' in January 2008 (Van Bemmel, 2008). A disciplinary board in Belgium took the same decision. Even the united 'orthomolecular therapists' – a professional group from which you would not expect too much common sense – expelled Bolijn from its ranks.

PYRAMID SMYTH INCHES HIS WAY OUT OF THE ROYAL SOCIETY

In 1864 there was a proposal to introduce the metric system in Great Britain to replace the imperial one then in use. Most scientists were in favour, as it would simplify communication with their European colleagues. However, a number of their more nationalistic colleagues, including the astronomer John Herschel, denounced the proposal, if only because the metric system was an invention of the accursed French. Herschel received the support of his Scottish colleague Charles Piazzi Smyth (1819–1900).

What Smyth created was pure pseudoscience, a combination of nationalism, religion, mathematics and insanity. He had heard that one of the cornerstones of the Great Pyramid at Giza had been exposed and was 63 cm long. Smyth started doing calculations: 63 divided by 25 is 2.52, which is very close to an inch (2.54 cm). He felt that this could not be a coincidence and concluded that 2.54, the 'pyramid inch', was the true universal measure of all things.[28] No matter what he calculated – the distance between the poles and the centre of the earth, or the dimensions of Noah's Ark – the outcome was always a neat round number in pyramid inches. He then traced the pyramid inch back to the sacred cubit, seeing this as yet more proof that God intended the British to rule the world.

Smyth's *Our Inheritance in the Great Pyramid* (1864, latest reprint in 1979), which is liberally spattered with biblical texts, is worth a read. It is a delightful example of how everything can be linked to everything else.[29] His pursuit of pseudoscience caused Smyth's reputation much harm, resulting in friction with his scientific colleagues. In the end Smyth did something unheard of for a British scientist: he resigned his fellowship of the prestigious Royal Society of London for the Improvement of Natural Knowledge, founded in 1660.

Q

QUESTIONABLE QUIZZING IN THE 1950S

On the NBC quiz show *Twenty One*, which was sponsored by a pharmaceutical company, two contestants were given the same questions and, if they gave the correct answers, they were awarded a number of points of their own choosing between zero and eleven. The idea was to end up with 21 points, or at least closer to 21 points than your opponent.

On its first showing, the show was not at all popular with the viewers and the sponsor threatened to withdraw. Producer Dan Enright (1917–1992) wondered what he could do to make the programme more interesting. The answer was simple: introduce a little drama. From then on, the show always pitted an attractive, sympathetic contestant against one who was unattractive and unsympathetic. To keep the viewers – and therefore the sponsor – happy the sympathetic contestant had to win most of the time. The programme was a set-up. Enright played his own game very cleverly. Each contestant had the impression that he was the only one to have made a deal with the producer. They were all promised that, even if they had to intentionally lose at a

Quiz show *Twenty One* host Jack Berry turns towards contestant Charles Van Doren as a fellow contestant, Vivienne Nearing, looks on, 1957.

certain point in the quiz, they would still be able to go home with quite a large sum of money.

In November 1956 Herb Stempel, a nerdy man with glasses, topped the quiz for several weeks. He was not popular with the viewers and Enright realized this was a good opportunity to introduce a little drama. Stempel's new opponent was Charles Van Doren. Van Doren was an 'all-American boy'. He came from a family of well-known writers and taught literature at Columbia University. He made his debut on 28 November 1956. The excitement increased as both contestants closed the show with 21 points. On 5 December they faced each other again. The show attracted a record 50 million viewers. A 'stupid mistake' brought Stempel's winning run to an end. When asked which movie had won the Oscar for best film in 1955, he answered – as he had been instructed – *On the Waterfront*, even though he knew better.

Van Doren stayed on the quiz until 11 March 1957. Every week, out of sight of the cameras, he was given detailed instructions about what to do during the broadcast. He was not only given the right answers, he was also told exactly when and how he should pause, cough, sigh and lean on the desk. Van Doren became a national celebrity, appeared on the cover of *Time* and was seen in the company of famous actresses. This was all stage-managed to generate publicity. In real life, he was happily married.

In the show broadcast on 11 March 1957, Van Doren successfully gave the names of the kings of Norway, Denmark, Sweden, Jordan and Iraq but, as agreed, could not remember what the king of Belgium was called. It was the end of his run on the quiz, but his cooperation had earned him $128,000 in prize money.

NBC was so pleased with Van Doren that they offered him a well-paid job in the corporation. That marked the start of a short and unhappy career in the world of TV. A few years later he took an 80 per cent salary cut to become an editor at the *Encyclopaedia Britannica*, where he was much happier.

Producer Dan Enright's methods came to light when Herb Stempel decided to spill the beans on his time as a contestant on *Twenty One*. It led to an investigation by the Public Prosecutor, resulting in hearings in front of a committee of the U.S. Congress. The hearings made it clear that nearly all of the 24 quiz shows running in America at that time were rigged. There is simply too much money at stake in the world of commercial television to leave such things to chance.

The *Twenty One* affair was made into a film in 1994, directed by Robert Redford and entitled *Quiz Show*.

R

REJECTION, A TALE

Dermatologist William Talley Summerlin claimed that he had used a new procedure to perform four skin transplants in Minnesota. After the tissue had been removed from the donor it was kept in a chemical solution for a couple of weeks to 'acclimatize'. This meant that, after the transplant, there were fewer symptoms of rejection. On the basis of this pioneering discovery, Summerlin started working as a professor at the Memorial Sloan-Kettering Cancer Center in New York in the autumn of 1973. His work could possibly reveal why the human immune system sometimes does not work properly – one of the causes of cancer. In New York Summerlin continued three lines of research he had set up in Minnesota: skin was transplanted between genetically unrelated mice of different colours, organs were transplanted between genetically unrelated mice, and human corneas were implanted in the eyes of rabbits. The results seemed overwhelmingly positive. 'Old Man', for example, a speckled mouse which had had a skin transplant from an albino mouse in November 1971, was still alive and kicking with a fully accepted skin allograft. Summerlin also showed photographs of rabbits where the eye that had been implanted with a non-cultured cornea had gone cloudy, while the eye with the cultured cornea was clear.

During the first three months in his new job, Summerlin lost a lot of goodwill. Colleagues were critical of his sloppy methods of work and organization. Scientists from all over the world who had been unable to replicate his results and had asked for help were simply ignored.

Two researchers working under Summerlin, John Ninnemann and John Raaf, happened to talk independently to the surgeon who performed the cornea transplants for Summerlin. Both were astounded to hear that the cultured and non-cultured corneas were implanted in two separate groups of rabbits. No wonder that in Summerlin's photographs one eye looked perfectly fine: nothing had been done to it!

When they asked Summerlin for an explanation, he just brushed them off, only to calmly show the same photographs at a congress a couple of weeks later.

In March 1974 Ninnemann wanted to publish a paper describing his failure to reproduce Summerlin's transplant successes. As project leader, Summerlin would be named as the co-author. If Summerlin were a real scientist, he would have no objection to this: information that negates a thesis is more important than information confirming it. But Summerlin objected to the publication. On 26 March 1974, while this was going on, he had an appointment with his boss, Robert A. Good. To illustrate his success, Summerlin took along some albino mice that he had grafted with skin from black mice. In the elevator to Good's office, Summerlin inked the edges and the hairs of the grafted skin black. This turned out to be unnecessary, as Good was not interested in the mice but in the methodological sloppiness of Summerlin's most recent article. Later that same morning, however, laboratory assistant James Martin discovered that the beautiful black patches of skin on the mice looked significantly less beautiful after rubbing them with a ball of cotton soaked in a little alcohol. Summerlin was immediately suspended and a peer review committee set out to work. When the committee published its report on 17 May 1974, the conclusion was clear. Summerlin's work was useless and his 'successes' were statistically insignificant. This meant that millions of dollars had been wasted on futile research all over the world.

And what of 'Old Man'? Well, he (or she, to be precise) turned out to be an F1 hybrid, a mouse genetically related to the albino, which explained the acceptance of the skin. And Summerlin had also grossly exaggerated the success of his four skin transplants in Minnesota. The committee of peers was remarkably mild in its conclusion: 'some actions of Dr Summerlin over a considerable period of time were not those of a responsible scientist' (Hixon, 1976). Summerlin was sent on medical leave for a year and then given the ultimate rejection: he was fired.

Summerlin now works as a dermatologist in Rogers, Arkansas. As he did not work as a doctor at the Sloan-Kettering Center, his professional profile correctly states that he has never received any disciplinary measures.

The 'Sloan-Kettering Affair' unleashed a heated debate on whether, in the battle for funding, scientists focussed more on sensation than on serious research. As a colleague of Summerlin put it at the time: 'I have some advice for young researchers in biology. Stay out of cancer research because it's full of money and just about out of science' (Hixon, 1976).

RELICS

Primary relics are the alleged remains of saints, most often teeth or pieces of bone. Apostles and martyrs are particularly popular. Secondary relics are objects that Jesus or the saints have touched, while tertiary relics are objects that have been in contact with relics. All are attributed with miraculous powers, including the cure of various illnesses.

Relics have been popular since medieval times. In the late Middle Ages, some rulers added to their status by assembling collections numbering many thousands of objects. The churches, too, sought to add to their prestige by possessing relics. Their motives were largely economic – relics attracted pilgrims and pilgrims put money in the churches' coffers.

Relics are ideal objects for forgers. Demand is much greater than supply and it is almost impossible to verify authenticity. In the Middle Ages, medicine was primitive, still based on bloodletting, and it would be several hundred years before modern science emerged, enabling 'ancient' objects to be quite accurately dated. There was a lively trade in relics, which also made it difficult to establish their origins.[30]

Potential material for relics was in plentiful supply. There were as yet no registers of births and deaths, so people could easily disappear without trace. Furthermore, since many churches did not start to lay out proper graveyards in their grounds until the eighteenth century, and then not on a grand scale, churches and their charnel houses had any amount of human bones stacked up or under the floor.

As objects capable of performing miracles, all relics are by definition fake, as miracles contravene the laws of physics and are therefore impossible (see LOURDES). But are all relics, as remains of a certain long-dead individual, necessarily fake? In theory it is possible that a relic genuinely comes from a specific person, but we should not be under any illusions. Around AD 400, even before the appetite for relics had gathered momentum, St Augustine expressed his disgust at 'hypocrites in the garb of monks for hawking about of the limbs of martyrs, if indeed [they are] of martyrs' (Brewer, 1901). Today we should also assume that relics with miraculous powers do not exist and that relics as the physical remains of saints are fake unless it can be proven otherwise.

An examination of the history of relics is a celebration of the human imagination. Here are some of the most ingenious of all:

> The first relic came into the world only moments after Jesus himself: several churches claim to possess straw from Christ's crib.
>
> His first visitors, the Three Wise Men from the East, followed shortly afterwards. Their skulls can be found in Cologne. Finger bones are a popular relic, especially those of the Apostles Paul and Andrew, and – believe it or not – the Holy Ghost. Two heads of John the Baptist have survived, as have two of St Agnes.
>
> The chains that held St Paul when he was freed by angels have been preserved. It is not clear why his jailors, who were not too keen on the early Christians, let the chains go.
>
> The Apostles left us several teeth. One belonging to St Peter was found near his grave 600 years after his death, after the Apostle had appeared to the finder in a 'vision'. A tooth supposedly belonging to St Paul, but most likely coming originally from some 'monster of the deep', was so impressive that the owner remarked 'Don't you think that St Paul had a fine set of grinders?' (Brewer, 1901).
>
> Mary's breast milk has produced its share of relics. She used to feed her beloved son in the Crypta Lactea in Bethlehem. If a drop fell to the floor the stone would turn white. Women who have trouble breastfeeding can find solace by touching stones from the grotto, which have made their way around the world. There is a similar cave in Souillac, France (Mary obviously got around a lot). Anyone wishing to see the real thing would have to visit Charles v of France (1337–1380), who owned an ampoule of milk from Mary's breast.

The Milk Grotto, Bethlehem, a shrine where the Holy Family took shelter during Herod's slaughter of the Innocents.

St Briocus (aka Brieuc) left two ribs, an arm and a vertebra. When the bones were reunited in the cathedral at Angers they 'jumped for joy at the honour conferred upon them' (Brewer, 1901).

The bones of St Paul, bishop of León, were burned to a powder during the Reformation. In the nineteenth century his right arm and one of his fingers reappeared – miraculous indeed.

Over the centuries three churches have claimed to possess the body of Mary Magdalene. A fourth had to make do with a foot.

The bones of St Ursula and her 11,000 virgin martyrs are to be found in a convent in Cologne. As one author commented, the healing powers of the bones were clearly not affected by the fact that they had originally belonged to men (Brewer, 1901). The bones were alleged to have come from a graveyard that that was cleared to provide sufficient bones.

Jesus must have had a painful childhood, as no less than six churches claim to possess his foreskin. Other churches have one or more of his nappies. His pap spoon and a number of milk teeth have also survived.

The cathedral in Metz has one of the stones used to kill St Stephen. The bishop also has a flame from the burning bush.

While St Michael was fighting with Satan, someone managed to gather a phial of his sweat.

A particularly exceptional relic is a container holding some of the rays of the Star of Bethlehem.

A pair of slippers that Enoch wore before the flood have also survived.

A tear that Jesus shed at the grave of Lazarus was given to Mary Magdalene by an angel and is preserved in a phial.

A leg and the tail of the donkey that Jesus rode into Jerusalem in triumph have been preserved.

On 3 May 326 Helena, the mother of Constantine the Great, found the cross on which Christ was crucified. The Catholic Church still celebrates the discovery every year on this date, the Feast of the Cross. Splinters from the 'true cross' can also be found in many places.

Some 103 churches and one museum have thorns from the crown of thorns.

The sign that was nailed to the cross ('Jesus of Nazareth, King of the Jews') has reproduced itself. There are now at least three.

Nails used to fix Jesus to the cross can be found in Rome, Paris, Trier and many other places. At least 34 are known.

RENÉ-PROSPER BLONDLOT'S RADIATION WAVES

The French physicist René-Prosper Blondlot (1849–1930) was no scientific lightweight. His achievements included being the first person to prove that electricity moves through a wire at a velocity approaching that of the speed of light. Nevertheless, his name will always be associated with his one great mistake, 'N-waves', and he will forever be the textbook example of a scientist who suffered from cognitive prejudice.

The blunder started with a success. In 1903 Blondlot showed that x-rays really are waves and not a succession of particles. He proved this experimentally using a detector in which an electric spark was created if it came into contact with waves. During a subsequent experiment, in which Blondlot did not need the detector, he directed x-rays through a prism. Suddenly, he saw something remarkable out of the corner of his eye: the spark in the detector had lit up. How was that possible? After much thinking and testing, Blondlot reached a spectacular conclusion: there must be as yet undiscovered waves in the laboratory that were responsible for igniting the spark. He also concluded that these waves had remarkable properties. They could, for example, pass through wood, but not through water, and were generated by all kinds of everyday objects, such as pebbles.

Blondlot announced his findings to the world on 23 March 1903. He called the waves after the town in which his university was located: Nancy waves, N-waves for short. The whole country was delighted with the discovery. Alpha waves, beta waves, gamma waves, x-rays . . . after all these physical phenomena discovered in other countries, it was now France's turn!

Other universities quickly replicated the experiments, but a number of laboratories reported that their results had not been positive. Blondlot responded by saying that it was a matter of looking properly. First, the eyes had to be well accustomed to the dark before the experiment started and second, it was important to not look directly at the spot where the spark – or fluorescent screen – was expected to light up, but out of the corner of the eye. As with cats in the dark, the phenomena were more visible when seen out of the corner of the eye. Scientists in many a laboratory, especially outside France, started to wonder what was wrong with their eyesight. No matter how carefully they prepared and conducted the experiments, the effects of the N-waves remained invisible to the majority of them.

Although the N-waves were a hit and dozens of articles about them were published in scientific journals, scientists slowly but surely started to have their doubts about whether Blondlot had interpreted what he had seen correctly. American physicist Robert Wood (1868–1955) was sent to Nancy to see the experiments with his own eyes. On 21 September 1904 he visited Blondlot's laboratory. The experiment started with a simple test: according to Blondlot, fluorescent paint would light up more brightly in the darkened room if it were exposed to N-radiation. Wood was quick to admit that he had seen a difference but added that it could have been a trick of the light. He suggested modifying the experiment by placing a lead screen between the fluorescent paint and the source of the N-waves at random moments. In the dark laboratory, Blondlot would be unable to see when he placed the screen. Blondlot's observations caused Wood to fear the worst. Sometimes the French scientist would say that the paint glowed less brightly when Wood had not placed the screen in the way; at other times, he would see the paint glow more brightly when the screen was in the way. He also reported differences when Wood had left the screen in the same position.

A subsequent experiment involved a clock illuminated by a very dim light. Blondlot stood far enough away from the clock to say he could not see it. When he held an iron file against his head, however, he claimed that he could even see the hands on the clock face. Wood, however, also managed to sabotage this experiment successfully (though it was not really sabotage; on the contrary, Wood turned a faulty experiment into an excellent one). He found a pretext to suggest that he should hold the file against Blondlot's head. But, unknown to Blondlot, he exchanged the file for a ruler made of wood, which allegedly did not conduct N-waves. The result was astounding. No matter whether it was iron or wood, as long as there was an object floating in front of his eyes, Blondlot was able to see the hands of the clock. When the object was removed, he could not see the clock any more.

Wood's final, decisive discovery was to become a classic in the history of science. There was a spectroscope in the laboratory. Normally a spectroscope contains a glass prism to break up white light so that its individual components can be studied. Blondlot's spectroscope, however, contained a prism made of aluminium to divide up the N-waves so that the frequencies could be read on a scale. After Blondlot had made a number of readings in Wood's presence, the American asked his host to do them again, just to be certain. Without Blondlot's knowledge, Wood deftly removed the prism. Despite the fact that a spectroscope cannot function without a prism, Blondlot registered the same readings as during the first session. Distressed that such an eminent scientist should lose face in such a fashion, Wood secretly replaced the prism after the experiment.

Anyone reading the report on Wood's visit, published eight days later in *Nature*, can only conclude that he was a man of integrity. Wood knew that it was his scientific duty to reveal what he had discovered, but considered it equally important to minimize the damage to Blondlot's reputation. He did not mention the French scientist's name in the article and avoided any suggestion of intentional deception. In fact, the text is so subtle that anyone reading it today with no knowledge of the background to the case would probably ask themselves what it was about. Back in 1904, the readers of *Nature* knew the significance of the article, showing how much fuss there was about Blondlot's N-waves at the time.

Scientists who had never been able to observe the effects of N-waves breathed sighs of relief and went back to their daily business. Those who were not sure what they had seen, packed up the apparatus for the experiment and quietly stashed it away somewhere. But Blondlot continued to believe resolutely that N-radiation was a genuine phenomenon and, in 1905, he published an expansive book on the subject.

Was Blondlot a bungler who continued to hang on to his theory long after it had been proven wrong as that may have been the only way to preserve his good name? Or was he really convinced that his observations were correct, because he was unable to admit to himself that he had clearly not seen what he thought he saw?

Blondlot continued to work inconspicuously as a physicist at the university in Nancy for another six years and, after he retired in 1910, disappeared into obscurity. Where the Nobel Prize had seemed within reach in 1903 and 1904, all that was left was loneliness and eternal notoriety in the history of science as an example of how it should not be practised.

RENIER CHALON AND THE FORTSAS RARE BOOKS AUCTION

On 1 September 1839, Jean-Népomucène-Auguste Pichauld, Comte de Fortsas, died. The Count owned a collection of books that were literally unique, in that only one copy of each was known to exist. In the summer of 1840, more than 100 European bibliophiles received a catalogue entitled *Catalogue d'une très-riche mais peu nombreuse collection de livres provenant de la bibliothèque de feu Mr. le Comte J.-N.-A. de Fortsas* (Catalogue of a very rich but very select collection of books from the library of the late Count . . .), which listed 52 volumes. Most of them would have been of interest to bibliophiles even if they were not unique.

Take, for instance, a *Corpus juris civilis* (Body of Civil Law) from 1663, the only copy printed on vellum. A handwritten note by the publisher D. Elzevir stated that the book was made for the States of Holland. The Count concluded that it was 'perhaps the finest book in existence' (Klinefelter, 1941). Or how about a *Disputatio philosophica* (Philosophical Discourse), once owned by Gottfried Leibniz (1646–1716) bearing his signature and annotations in his hand? Or the *Evangile du citoyen Jésus, purgé des idées aristocrates et royalistes, et ramené aux vraix principes de la raison, par un bon sans-culotte* (The gospel according to citizen Jesus, purged of aristocratic and royalist ideas, and reduced to the true principles of reason, by a good sans-culotte) from year III of the Republic? The book did not survive the turmoil of the French Revolution, with the exception of this one copy, of course.

In book-loving Europe, there was great excitement as the day of the auction, 10 August 1840, approached. The printer of the catalogue had already received many high bids by post. On the day itself, collectors flooded to the Belgian town of Binche, where the auction was to be held at the offices of Maître Moulon, rue de l'Eglise no. 9. But the excitement soon turned to confusion. Not only had no one ever heard of Maître Moulon, but his address also turned out not to exist. The chaos only increased when pamphlets were distributed announcing that the auction had been cancelled and that the municipality of Binche had acquired the whole collection for its public library. When the bibliophiles tried to at least *see* the books, they discovered that Binche had no library. Confused and dejected, they gave up and went home.

The Fortsas Hoax, as it came to be known, was the work of Renier Chalon (1802–1889), a retired army major who had invented both Count Fortsas and his collection. Chalon had made up each of the 52 titles listed in the catalogue with one or two specific European bibliophiles in mind. Chalon knew exactly who would fall for what.

An interesting by-product of the Fortsas Hoax is that it made its own contribution to bibliophily. Today, the catalogue – of which there are 120 copies on white paper, ten on coloured paper and two on vellum – is a collectors' item, as is the auction's cancellation pamphlet, of which there are some 75 copies.

RICHARD MEINERTZHAGEN: SHAM ORNITHOLOGIST AND MAYBE MURDERER

Everything about Richard Nery Meinertzhagen (1878–1967) looked impressive, larger than life. As a British soldier he fought in Africa, India and the Middle East, where many enemies felt the sharp end of his bayonet. Meinertzhagen was known to be very violent and completely without scruples. On 19 October 1905, for instance, while shaking hands with a Hindu leader during peace negotiations, he took out a gun with his left hand and shot him dead.

After becoming interested in the natural world through his second wife, the ornithologist Anne Constance Jackson (1889–1928), Meinertzhagen collected 587,610 different species of lice, mites and flies. His next project resulted in more than 25,000 mounted birds, caught in the wild during trips to exotic places. In 1954 he donated this collection to the Natural History Museum in London. For many decades rumours circulated that there was 'something not quite above board' about the collection, but doubts about Meinertzhagen's integrity were not expressed in black and white until 1993. In the ornithological journal *Ibis*, Alan Knox wrote that he had studied dozens of birds from the Meinertzhagen collection and had concluded that they were the work of different taxidermists – and therefore not by Meinertzhagen alone. On the basis of her research, American ornithologist Pamela Rasmussen concluded that many birds showed signs of having been remounted. Slowly but surely the awareness grew that Meinertzhagen's birds had not been captured in the wild, but in museums. He had remounted them to conceal the working method of the original taxidermist. This was understandable, as many of them worked at the

Natural History Museum. The birds that Meinertzhagen donated to the museum in 1954 had previously been stolen from its collection (and probably also from other collections: one Swedish museum discovered that it was missing 50 specimens after a visit from Meinertzhagen). One disastrous consequence of the fraud for science was that Meinertzhagen changed at least some details of each specimen, for example its generic name and/or the place and date of capture. As a result, the 25,000 birds had hardly any scientific value left.

A very dark aspect in the whole affair was the death of Anne Constance Jackson. In 1928 she died at the age of 39 from a gunshot wound to the head sustained during target practice with her husband. Although ruled an accident at the time, it was later suggested that Meinertzhagen had murdered her because she was about to reveal his fraud of the mounted birds.

ROMANOVS

On 17 July 1918 former Tsar Nicholas II ('Nikolai Romanov'), his wife Tsarina Alexandra Feodorovna, their daughters Olga (*b.* 1895), Tatiana (*b.* 1897), Maria (*b.* 1899) and Anastasia (*b.* 1901) and their son Alexei (*b.* 1904) were shot and bayoneted to death by Bolsheviks in the basement of a house in Yekaterinburg located in Russia's Ural Mountains, together with the family's doctor and three servants. The revolutionaries made a hash of disposing of the bodies, first attempting to put the bodies in a mineshaft and making it collapse on top of them, and then deciding to cremate them and bury the ashes.

A royal family believed to have been killed but whose fate was not conclusive: it was only a matter of time before the first 'survivors' made themselves known. In the first seven or eight decades after the executions, dozens of Romanovs staked their claims. Anastasia and Alexei were particularly popular, though a number of Olgas, Tatianas and Marias also rose from the grave (male pretenders had only one choice, compared to four for their female counterparts). The pretenders simply ignored undeniable historical obstacles. All of the Alexeis, for example, had miraculously been cured of the incurable haemophilia from which the young heir apparent had suffered.

Some of the pretenders succeeded in attracting public attention for quite some time. The most well-known was Franziska Schanzkowska (1896–1984), a Polish factory worker with a history of mental illness.

In 1920 she was fished out of the water in Berlin after what was officially described as a failed suicide attempt (it is, of course, possible that Schanzkowska never intended to kill herself but that this was the first step in her deception). At first she refused to disclose her identity but in 1922 she claimed to be Grand Duchess Anastasia of Russia, who had miraculously escaped the slaughter of her family in Yekaterinburg. From then on she called herself Anastasia or Anna. She did not gather many supporters, but enough to keep her and her story alive for some time. In 1968 she emigrated to America, where she lived as Anna Anderson. She died in 1984.

In 1991 the remains of the tsar, his wife and three of their four daughters were found buried in ground a few miles north of Yekaterinburg. DNA material provided by a number of related royal houses confirmed their identities. At that time, the only available remains of Anna Anderson, who had been cremated, was a lock of her hair and medical samples of her tissue. DNA tests showed that she was not related to the Romanovs and was therefore not the as yet untraced daughter.

When the remains of Alexei and the fourth daughter were found near Yekaterinburg in 2007, it seemed to close the door permanently to any other pretenders. But, with so many fantasists around, you never know.

ROSEMARY BROWN, THE COMPOSERS' COMPOSER

In 1964 Rosemary Isabel Brown (1916–2001) took up transcribing new, original works for a number of well-known composers. They would tell her which notes to transcribe or get her to sit down and play the piece herself, after which the compliant Rosemary would write the music out in the form of notation. Strangely, in addition to sharing Rosemary, these busy musicians had an additional circumstance in common: they were all as dead as doornails. When not out at work in south London as a school dinner lady, Rosemary Brown was at home at the piano and receiving visits from Chopin, Schubert, Debussy, Bach, Rachmaninov and numerous other geniuses, although the most regular was Franz Liszt.

In the spiritual 1960s and '70s, some music experts were receptive to Rosemary Brown's claims and saw similarities with the works the composers had produced in their lifetimes. Others were less convinced. André Previn, conductor of the London Symphony Orchestra, commented that, if the compositions were genuine, they would be better off left on the shelf.

Brown's contacts with the composers were not limited to music. She watched television with Chopin, who was 'appalled' by it, and went shopping with Liszt, who was apparently intrigued by the price of bananas.

Was Brown an unabashed forger or simply self-deluded? Although she liked to present herself as someone who couldn't play a note, she was known to have had courses of piano lessons several times earlier in her life. Second, after the death of her mother and her husband in 1961, Brown started to move in spiritualist circles. If you hang around with such people long enough, you will start to hear 'voices from the other side' if you want to be taken seriously in the group. Third, Brown claimed that Liszt had already visited her when she was only seven years old; he had told her that when she grew up he would 'give her music', but she did not make this claim until after 1964, so its authenticity as a childhood mental experience cannot be corroborated, nor is the statement itself verifiable (Martin, 2001).

One reasonable interpretation of the facts is that in 1964 Rosemary Brown, who was widowed at the age of 45 and had very little to look forward to, decided to create a more significant life for herself.

ROYAL PRETENDER, KARL WILHELM NAUNDORFF

The Naundorff Affair originated in 1793. That year, during the French Revolution, Louis XVI and Marie Antoinette were executed by guillotine. The eight-year-old crown prince, Louis-Charles, was interned in the tower of the Temple prison, where he died of natural causes on 8 June 1795.

As royalty once again became popular in Europe in the nineteenth century, at least 43 people claimed to be the long-lost crown prince, including a number of female and black pretenders. The stories they told displayed a lot of similarities: while Louis-Charles was imprisoned in the Temple, Royalists had switched him for another child. It was this child who died, while the crown prince was still alive and kicking.

The most successful of this motley crew of royal pretenders was Karl Wilhelm Naundorff, whose suspected true identity is Carl Benjamin Werg (*c.* 1777–1845). While being tried for counterfeiting money in Brandenburg in 1825, he presented a very original argument to bolster up his defence. It would be outrageous to convict him, he claimed, as he was in reality Louis-Charles de Bourbon, the rightful King Louis XVII of France.

A number of facts appeared to refute Naundorff's story. He did not know how to spell the name 'de Bourbon', initially writing it phonetically as 'de Borbong', and he could not speak a word of French. Defenders of the self-appointed King of France blamed this all on what we would today call post-traumatic stress.

In a perfect display of wishful thinking, Royalist Europe took Naundorff to its heart. How better to forget the Republican Terror than to believe in a crown prince who had risen from the dead? Karl Wilhelm was fêted at many a palace. He presented himself as an inventor, especially of explosives, and spread the word that he had developed a 'secret weapon'. The Dutch king William II liked the sound of Naundorff's idea, and in the early 1840s appointed him director of the Pyrotechnic Laboratory in Delft. The Kingdom of the Netherlands paid Naundorff 100,000 guilders to produce the weapon. Although he never succeeded in perfecting an effective device, he did blow up the laboratory a couple of times.

Karl Wilhelm died in Delft, where his grave is today one of the few remains of what used to be a cemetery. His descendants continue to fight for recognition of his blue-blooded credentials. The real De Bourbon family continued to take legal steps to prevent the Naundorffs from using their name, in their view illegitimately, until 1954. The De Bourbon-Naundorffs, however, refused to budge, and when, in March 1998 DNA testing showed conclusively that they were not related to Louis XVI, they claimed – not surprisingly – that the test had been conducted incorrectly or sabotaged. The 'royal family' still comes together regularly in a Paris restaurant.

S

THE SAD TALE OF KATE HUME'S DECEIT

In September 1914, seventeen-year-old Kate Hume had a shocking message for her father and stepmother. She told them she had been visited in her home town of Dumfries, Scotland, by a nurse called Mullard, who had given her two letters. One was from Mullard herself, describing how she had worked on the battlefields of Belgium with

Kate's 22-year-old sister Grace. The other was a farewell letter from Grace herself:

> '6 Sept.
>
> Dear Kate,
> This is to say good-bye. Have not long to live. Hospital has been set on fire. Germans cruel. A man here had his head cut off. My right breast has been taken away.
> Give my love to ——
> Good-bye,
>
> Grace, x'

When the letter was published in the *Dumfries & Galloway Standard* it caused great consternation among the local people. A number of men from the area were fighting in Flanders and the letter showed that no mercy could be expected for those taken prisoner by the Germans. The concern quickly made way for amazement when a telegram and a letter arrived from Grace Hume, who was alive and well and working as a nurse in Huddersfield, England. The police investigated the case and soon began to suspect Kate Hume.

Charged with 'alarming and annoying the lieges' (other people), Hume appeared in court in Edinburgh on 28 and 29 December 1914 (*The Times*, 29 December 1914). A sad picture emerged from her statement and those of her father, stepmother and landlady.

The Humes were a musical family. Kate's great-grandfather had set the words of Robert Burns's poems to music, her father was a music teacher and Kate was also considered to have great talent. But in the past few years, things had not gone so well for the youngest daughter of the family. The girl, described as ' bright' and 'intelligent', had achieved little. A double tragedy had cast a shadow over her life: the deaths, in quick suggestion, of her mother and especially of her favourite brother, John. Twenty-one-year-old John Hume had been the leader of the ship's orchestra that played the hymn 'Nearer, My God, to Thee' as the *Titanic* sank on the night of 14 April 1912. When Kate did not get on with her new stepmother, she moved into lodgings in August 1912, where she felt sad and lonely. When her sister Grace left for England and nothing was heard from her for a long time, Kate's imagination went wild. Fuelled by the many newspaper reports describing the atrocities of war in great detail, Kate became convinced that her sister had become a nurse in the warzone and was dead. She wrote the letters as she thought Grace would have written them if she had had the opportunity. Her counsel called the letters 'a literary creation' and said that in writing them the suspect was a slave to her own emotions. Two doctors gave their opinions on Kate's mental health. They did not believe she was suffering from mental illness, but spoke of 'adolescent hysteria' (*The Times*, 30 December 1914).

After hearing the arguments, the jury only needed a quarter of an hour to reach a verdict of guilty, but with a recommendation to leniency. Given the fact that Kate had already been detained in custody for thirteen weeks, her age and her good character, the judge ordered her immediate release. The verdict was received with applause in the courtroom.

THE SCIENTIFIC SHAMBLES OF COLD NUCLEAR FUSION

> 'As parents scare their children with stories of ghosts and ogres, so professors scare their students with stories of Pons and Fleischmann'. (*The Economist*, 2002)

They were a remarkable pair, the electrochemists Martin Fleischmann (1927–2012) and Stanley Pons (*b.* 1943). Fleischmann, who worked in England at the University of Southampton, was a man full of ideas. 'Ninety per cent of the ideas are crazy', said one of his colleagues, 'and the rest excellent' (Broad, 1989). Fleischmann was not one for details. When he had an idea, it would first be tested to see if it was feasible and, if so, it would be passed on to an assistant to develop it further. Pons, after graduating from the University of Utah, first reluctantly made a career in the family textiles business but then, in his thirties, he decided to finish his PhD. In the United States this would have meant more or less starting from scratch, so Pons moved to England, where he met Fleischmann. The two became friends, both inside and outside the laboratory.

A decade later Pons had climbed to become head of a department at the University of Utah. Fleischmann was approaching retirement. During one of the hikes the friends took together from time to time, the talk turned to cold nuclear fusion. The fusion of atoms, in which energy is released, normally takes place under high pressure at extremely high temperatures. As the atoms do not 'want' to fuse, it takes energy to force them. Fusion requires more energy than it produces, leading Fleischmann and Pons to start wondering if there might be another way to achieve it. They decided to carry out some experiments with cold fusion. Because of the controversial nature of the subject – apart from a few marginal figures, nobody took cold fusion seriously – they decided to use their own money to cover the costs. They eventually invested around $100,000.

The crucial experiment itself was reasonably simple. Two electrodes, one of palladium and the other of platinum, were immersed in heavy water (D_2O – water in which hydrogen (H) is replaced by deuterium (D), hydrogen with an extra neutron). The electrodes (one positive, one negative) were hooked up to a battery. The resulting current separated the water into oxygen and deuterium atoms, and the deuterium was absorbed into the palladium electrode. After some time the electrode started to give off heat. When the palladium and deuterium atoms fused, cold nuclear fusion occurred, generating an energy output many times greater than the input. The practical end result was a simple and cheap solution to all the world's energy needs.

On the basis of temperature rises (one electrode went up in smoke; the melting point was at 15,540 degrees Celsius) the two concluded that cold fusion had taken place. Elsewhere in Utah, Steven Jones of the Mormon Brigham Young University reached the same conclusion, albeit on different grounds. Jones's team did not measure temperature rises but looked for – and found – by-products of fusion (such as helium). From February 1989 the two teams compared notes. Their experiments appeared to prove conclusively that cold fusion existed. Fleischmann and Pons wanted to continue experimenting for another eighteen months, but Jones had a lecture date on 4 May which he could not get out of, and he was already sure what news he wanted to reveal. They decided to share the honours and, on 24 March 1989, submitted articles on both research projects to *Nature*.

Much later, when the affair was over, the University of Utah stated that it had not wanted to risk another institute (that is, Brigham Young University) patenting the cold fusion procedure. Another explanation might be that every scientist knows that only being first counts. If you come second, you will be forgotten. Either way, on 23

March 1989, Fleischmann and Pons announced at a press conference that they had created a fusion reaction at room temperature and under normal pressure. 'Fusion in a flask!' shouted the headlines. Steven Jones had come second.

The scientific world was perplexed. First of all, since when did scientists announce research findings at a press conference instead of having them tested in a peer reviewed scientific journal? Second, since when was cold nuclear fusion possible – wasn't it contrary to the laws of nature? The third response was to dash to the laboratory to reproduce the results.

Fleischmann and Pons shut themselves in their laboratory for weeks – and with good reason. At the press conference they had told a little white lie, claiming that they too had detected fusion by-products, thereby stealing Jones's alleged results. They didn't even have the required measuring equipment.

In the weeks that followed, things developed rapidly and in different directions. When Jones published his article some saw it as confirming cold fusion. Others calculated that the by-products detected by Jones were around 1 million times too small in quantity to account for the temperatures recorded by Fleischmann and Pons. But the latter's findings were also confirmed by various laboratories. Just how hastily and sloppily research was being conducted in the spring of 1989 became clear on 10 April, when researchers at Georgia Tech announced that they had detected by-products of fusion – only to retract the claim three days later. Now that the impossible seemed possible, it was only a matter of waiting for news even more shocking than the impossible. It was not a long wait. In Italy the commercial Frascati Research Centre announced that they, too, had detected fusion effects, despite their experimental apparatus not even being hooked up to a power source!

When Pons appeared in public again, he didn't make things any clearer. Asked why he had not done a control experiment with 'normal' water, H_2O, he muttered that this would not necessarily be a good baseline. When he was pushed to clarify his answer, Pons replied in a roundabout way that cold fusion had also been detected when using regular water!

After a couple of crazy months, there was a general feeling that the sceptics were gaining the upper hand over the believers. The majority of laboratories were unable to replicate the results claimed by Fleischmann and Pons. There were indications that the phenomena they had observed were chemical rather than nuclear. The scientific community returned to the order of the day.

Fleischmann and Pons belong in this encyclopaedia not because they intentionally took everybody for a ride – there is no reason to assume that. They did, however, switch off their critical faculties, which made them prone to talking nonsense. If you don't question whether something you claim to be true really is, you are responsible when it turns out to be untrue.

The first mistake the duo made relates to the funding of their research. There is nothing wrong with scientists using their own money to pay for their activities. On the contrary, more of them should do it. It would reduce the percentage of half-baked research and increase the number of genuinely impassioned scientists. What Fleischmann and Pons should have realized, however, is that self-financed research increases the risk of cognitive prejudice. Sensory data only become observations in our brains, and the rest of our personality plays a part in that process. In plain words: you are more likely to see an alien if you believe in them than if you don't (how many militant atheists have visions of the Virgin Mary?). Fleischmann and Pons did not invest their money in research they did not believe in. Again, there is nothing wrong with that, but it does mean you have to be on the alert. If you are not careful, you might easily interpret an ambiguous result as affirmative.

The second mistake Fleischmann and Pons made was that they had allowed themselves to be put on the spot by Steven Jones and by their own University of Utah. In their meeting with Jones at the end of February/early March 1989, they made it clear that they wanted to continue with their experiments for another eighteen months. However, afraid that Jones would announce successful cold fusion in May, Fleischmann and Pons decided on the joint publication in March. The University of Utah's appeal to prevent someone else from patenting the discovery also weighed heavily. The all-too-human urge to want to achieve something proved stronger than the professional requirement to conduct careful research.

The third mistake Fleischmann and Pons made was their inability to admit that they had been wrong once their experiment had been consigned to the scrapheap. If – after publication – they had questioned their own theory in time, the scientific world could have concluded that 'this was not "it"' and could have returned to the question 'so what then is "it"?' But Fleischmann and Pons stuck with their theory of cold fusion. It cost them their scientific careers, although they both continued to work in a commercial laboratory for a number of years.

And what about cold nuclear fusion? It has enjoyed something of a revival in recent years but it has a new name, low-energy nuclear reactions (LENR), and the names Fleischmann and Pons are taboo.

SEEING DOUBLE IN THE AUCTION HOUSES

In 1965 Ely Sakhai, who was born in Iran, emigrated with his family to the United States, where he initially worked for his brothers in their antiques/junk shop. But he longed for a better clientele and more status. When he noticed that there was hardly any difference between a genuine Tiffany lamp and a cheap copy, Sakhai attached the Tiffany label to the copy and sold it for the price of the original. He had found his modus operandi.

In the 1980s he bought many 'lesser' works, mainly by artists such as Chagall, Modigliani, Renoir, Klee and Gauguin, at auction houses. They were paintings in the $50,000 to $200,000 range. There was a big market in Japan for works by these painters, a market Sakhai knew well through relations of his Japanese wife. Sakhai had the paintings copied by Chinese artists who had emigrated to the United States, for whom copying Old Masters had been an important part of their education. Sakhai sold the copies in Japan as originals, using the genuine certificates of authenticity (which he could always replace). After a couple of years, he would then sell the original on the American market. It was a well-thought-out method that solved a couple of problems: the copy could be made directly from the original, which is always better than copying an image of the original, and the copies could be furnished with a genuine certificate of authenticity. As the works were not top pieces, they attracted less attention at auction. And even if a buyer were to find out that he had bought a copy, his Japanese upbringing would probably stop him from admitting his error. Sakhai committed the same fraud with around 25 works, in some cases having several copies made. With the profits he improved his social standing in New York by opening a chic gallery and financing the Ely Sakhai Torah Center.

His business foundered when the inevitable happened: in May 2000 Gauguin's *Vase de Fleurs* came up for auction at both Christie's and Sotheby's. The Christie's painting had been put up for sale by its Japanese owner, while the other had been sent to Sotheby's by Sakhai himself. When it was discovered that the work at Christie's was a forgery and that its owner had bought it from Sakhai, the net tightened. Sakhai was arrested in March 2004 and was later sentenced to 41 months in prison. He also had to pay a total of $12.5 million in compensation to his buyers and forfeit eleven paintings.

SEX IN SPACE: THE EMISSION LOG

This hoax started seriously. In 1983, *Sexuology Today* ran an article on whether it is possible for people to make love in a state of weightlessness and if so, how. The article contained useful tips for the amorous astronaut:

> There will be a few problems with zero-gee lovemaking, but most are comparatively minor and probably may be overcome by superior technique. First, the redistribution of body fluids causes extra blood to pool around the heart, creating the false sensation that the body contains too much liquid. This depresses the sense of thirst, which can lead to dehydration unless people force themselves to drink. Also, sweat flows more freely in the dried space station air, so lovers may become further dehydrated if they keep at it for too long without a break. (Freitas, 1983)

After the arrival of the internet – the greatest collection of nonsense ever brought together – it was a matter of waiting for further documentary evidence to come to light. That happened in 1989. 'Document 12-571-3570', allegedly written by NASA, contained a short report on a sexual experiment performed during Space Shuttle flight STS-75. Using elastic belts and inflatable tunnels, two human guinea pigs tried to have sexual intercourse in ten different positions. The results offered little solace for prospective lovers during long space missions.

The document is clearly a forgery. Space Shuttle mission STS-75 did not take place until seven years later, in 1996. The crew of the mission was all male, while the document described heterosexual sex.

Nevertheless, 'Document 12-571-3570' enjoyed considerable popularity in the 1990s, perhaps partly because NASA clearly wished to stay clear of the whole topic. 'NASA is so puritanical that the subject is difficult for them to broach', said Royce Dalby, editor of space magazine *Ad Astra* (Broad, 1992).

In 1992, French scientific writer Pierre Kohler wrote a book called *The Final Mission*, in which the whole farcical business was once again presented as authentic. It is unclear whether Kohler – who writes copiously on astronomy, space and UFOs – knew that the document is a forgery or if he had also been taken for a ride. This time, NASA itself issued a response. 'We categorically deny there is any such document', said a spokesman, adding that it and the event comprise nothing more than an 'urban legend' (Oberg, 2000).

SEX TIP NO. 1: BE YOURSELF

In September 2008, Sabbar Kashur met a Jewish woman in the centre of Jerusalem, where he lived. The couple had sex, with no pretensions of affection. According to a newspaper report, 'Kashur left the building without waiting for the woman to get dressed' (Zarchin, 2010).

Later the woman found out that Kashur, who had pretended to be a bachelor, was in reality in a relationship. An unpleasant discovery maybe, but one you ought to be prepared to accept with these kinds of casual arrangements. What the woman did find unacceptable, however, was the fact that Kashur posed as Jew, while he is in fact an Arab.

The woman filed a complaint of 'rape by deception', claiming that if she had known Kashur was an Arab, she would never have had sex with him. In July 2010, a court of three judges sentenced Kashur to eighteen months in prison. Summing up, they said:

> When the very basis of trust between human beings drops, especially when the matters at hand are so intimate, sensitive and fateful, the court is required to stand firmly at the side of the victims . . . otherwise, they will be used, manipulated and misled, while [the offender pays] only a tolerable and symbolic price. (Zarchin, 2010)

This sounds noble but it is not thought through. For a start, it is doubtful whether people who have casual sex experience it as 'intimate' or 'sensitive'. More important, the concept of 'rape by deception' could have far-reaching consequences. It may be only a matter of time before we see the first case of rape in which one person had sex with another because he or she was told by the other, for the first or the thousandth time, that they were in love.

SHINICHI FUJIMURA BURIES THE PAST

Shinichi Fujimura (*b.* 1950), a self-taught archaeologist, appeared to be a natural. In 1981 he discovered the earliest remains of civilization ever found in Japan, dated at 40,000 years old. In the next two decades, his finds pushed the dates back even more, sometimes by tens of thousands of years at one leap, to between 600,000 and 120,000 years ago. Fujimura was given the nickname 'God's hands' and made his way up to be vice-chairman of the Tohoku Palaeolithic Institute.

At the end of 2000 Fujimura proved not to be so divine after all. A Japanese newspaper printed pictures of him burying archaeological artefacts in the early morning, so that they would be 'found' later in the day. At first, Fujimura insisted that this was a one-off transgression but he later admitted that he had buried artefacts at 42 archaeological sites. Japanese scientists were then forced to set about revising textbooks on the Palaeolithic era, which for Japan were based mainly on Fujimura's finds.

Fujimura was expelled from the Tohoku Palaeolithic Institute and the Japanese Archaeological Association. The disgraced scientist checked himself into a psychiatric hospital.

SHOOTING A SELFIE, GUATEMALA STYLE

Until April 2009 Rodrigo Rosenberg led the kind of life that was unremarkable for a Guatemala lawyer in his late forties. He had a good education, including studying at Harvard and Oxford. As a partner in a law firm he was comfortably well-off. He had an acrimonious divorce behind him and no longer saw his children, who lived with his ex-wife in Mexico. He was having an affair with a married woman, Marjorie Musa. In short, nothing out of the ordinary.

In April 2009 Marjorie's father, the 74-year-old coffee baron Khalil Musa, died in a shower of bullets fired by an assassin from the back of a motorbike. Marjorie was hit and died along with her father.

This, too, was nothing out of the ordinary. It is not unusual in Latin America for business or personal disputes to be solved in this way. Guatemala is a haven for mass murderers and 98 per cent of murders there are never solved.[31] This time, however, according to Rosenberg, there was no question of a business dispute or personal conflict. He claimed that Khalil Musa was about to expose a network of corruption in the government of President Álvaro Colom. In the weeks following the murder, Rosenberg immersed himself in the case. He told close friends about the clandestine world in which he found himself. Officials he spoke to seemed willing to act as whistleblowers, but it was easier for them to pull the right strings to frustrate Rosenberg's attempts to get at the truth.

On 10 May 2009 what Rosenberg himself had predicted in his more sombre moments came to pass. In the expensive part of Guatemala City where he lived – Distrito 14, full of diplomats and the heirs to great fortunes – Rosenberg was gunned down on 2da Avenida from a souped-up Mazda. He died immediately.

At the funeral the following day Rosenberg's close friend Luis Mendizábal handed out an extraordinary video, a 17-minute statement that Rosenberg had shot a few days previously:

> If you are listening to this, it's because I was murdered by President Álvaro Colom, with the help of [the president's private secretary] Gustavo Alejos and [businessman] Gregorio Valdez . . . The last thing I wanted was to deliver this message . . . because this won't make my children any better. But I hope Guatemala will be better. I hope my death helps get the country started down a new path. Guatemalans, the time has come. (Franklin, 2010)

When the video was uploaded to the server of a Guatemalan newspaper and to YouTube, servers in Guatemala started crashing. The country had never experienced as much traffic on the digital highway. Conservative opponents of the left-wing president took advantage of the opportunity. In a country where corruption is endemic and many criminals enjoy immunity, tens of thousands of protestors took to the streets, most of them from the upper classes.

The Colom government responded by claiming that the whole affair had been stage-managed by the country's right-wing politicians in Guatemala, who opposed Colom's plans to raise business taxes and provide equal treatment for the country's largely powerless Maya majority. In the weeks that followed, Guatemala's ruling elite tried to weaken Colom's political position. Many a politician stood in the wings to step in and replace the president at the first sign that he had been involved in Rosenberg's murder. For several weeks it was touch and go for the government, but eventually it came through the affair unscathed.

The investigation into Rosenberg's death was conducted by the International Commission against Impunity in Guatemala. This UN commission was set up in an attempt to reduce corruption in the investigation and sentencing of criminals in Guatemala. While the investigation was under way, the people of Guatemala were resigned to the possibility of the two possible outcomes: either Rosenberg was murdered because he knew too much about corruption in the public sector or he was killed by right-wing conspirators hoping to create that very impression.

The commission took its time and did its work thoroughly. When it published its findings in January 2010, they came as a complete surprise to those on both sides of the political fence. The investigators concluded that Rosenberg had committed suicide with the intention of making it look like a murder. Although he was a lawyer, Rosenberg apparently knew little of how to commit a crime, as he made a number of fundamental errors. The wealthy residents of Distrito 14 are keen to keep hold of their riches and there are more security cameras there than anywhere else in the country. The cameras not only showed that Rosenberg had indeed been fired at from a Mazda, but also that he had cycled up the 2da Avenida, stopped and sat waiting at the roadside until his killers arrived and shot him three times in the head. His second mistake was getting his bodyguard/ chauffeur to buy two prepaid mobile telephones after the death of Marjorie Musa. The commission discovered why he needed the phones. He used one to communicate with his killers and the other to record death threats on the answering machine of his own landline. His third mistake was to ask his bodyguard to repair his bicycle, which had been standing unused on the balcony of his apartment for some time. He needed the bicycle to meet his killers without the bodyguard being present.

Rosenberg recruited the killers through two cousins of his ex-wife, telling them he was being harassed by a man who was extorting him. He asked the cousins if they knew of a hitman and they passed the request on to what was obviously the right person: the head of security of a pharmaceutical company. The man proved well worth his salary: the hitmen he arranged were paid U.S. $40,000 for doing the job and communicated on several occasions with their client who was, unknown to them, also their victim.

The reason that Rosenberg wanted to die was that he led a miserable life and, after the death of his lover, saw no reason to carry on living. Can anyone blame him for wanting to give his death some grain of significance? Is a suicide that brings about what Rosenberg at least considered a noble political reversal worth more or less than a suicide that has no meaning at all? The question is hypothetical, since Rosenberg's plan completely misfired. After the revelations of the UN commission, it was president Colom who emerged the victor, proving that he was not the kind of leader who could be forced into rash action by populist sentiment.

SINGING ALONG WITH MILLI VANILLI

Music is often manipulated. Classical albums are typically patchworks of the best of many recordings of a piece. In pop music, the lightweight department, it is not unusual for songs to be performed by different people to 'the face of the band'. Well-known examples include The Monkees, the Village People, the Bay City Rollers and the Spice Girls. Nor are live performances always what they seem. Using instrumental and vocal backing tapes is common practice and many artists (ranging from Dolly Parton to Britney Spears) no longer take the risk of singing when performing. But cheating, and not even very surreptitiously, is different to receiving the highest American music award without ever singing a note.

Popular musical duo Milli Vanilli was created by German record producer Frank Farian (*b.* 1941), who was also responsible for Boney M, another band whose songs were sung by people other than those appearing on the cover. In the spring of 1988 Farian was working on the song 'Girl You Know It's True'. He had no complaints about the vocal qualities of singers Brad Howell, Johnny Davis and Charles Shaw, but did not feel they were appealing enough visually. A solution presented itself shortly afterwards when Farian came into contact with Fab Morvan and Rob Pilatus. The two singers aspired to a musical career. Farian felt that they lacked the talent, but they did have the looks and showed some talent for dancing. One advantage for the producer was that except for the recording engineer, the performers and the odd studio musician, no one knew who did what in Farian's music. Even the record company, Arista, had no clue. With Morvan and Pilatus as the frontmen of the band, 'Girl You Know It's True' became a big hit, and was soon followed by a successful debut album, on which Howell, Davis and Shaw again provided the vocals. The album was released in various versions, with the titles *Girl You Know It's True* and *All or Nothing*. Milli Vanilli's next three singles also reached the top of the European and American charts.

In January 1989 Morgan and Pilatus won three American Music Awards, followed a month later by the highest accolade, a Grammy for Best New Artist. Around this time, however, rumours were already spreading that something was not quite right. A couple of months later, in July 1989, a technical failure during a concert caused the vocal backing tape of 'Girl You Know It's True' to jam, repeating the first line over and over, funnily enough without the word 'true'). At the end of the year, Pilatus and Morvan fled from the stage during a performance when their tape refused to start. Once they were back in their dressing room, the song finally boomed out, vocals and all.

It was not only the ever increasing rumours that shattered the illusion but, above all, the ambitions of Pilatus and Morvan. They demanded that Farian allow them to sing on the follow-up album. Farian – with good reason – thought this was a bad idea and, on 14 November 1990, made it known that Pilatus and Morvan were not the real vocalists on Milli Vanilli's recordings. The deception, which had lasted two and a half years, had resulted in sales of 11 million albums and 30 million singles.

The disclosure left the jury members of the Grammy Awards feeling betrayed. The credits on the *All or Nothing* version of the group's debut album read 'Vocals: Fab and Rob' (this was removed from the later *Girl You Know It's True* version). On 19 November 1990 Milli Vanilli were ordered to return the Grammy.

A number of American consumers subsequently instituted legal proceedings against Pilatus, Morvan, Farian and record company Arista. In 1991 this resulted in modest refunds being offered to anyone who had bought a single ($1), an album ($2), a CD ($3) or a concert ticket ($2.50).

Farian's career did not suffer as a result of the fraud. Arista was satisfied with the profit it had made and had every confidence in the producer's future projects. Pilatus and Morvan decided to continue under the name Rob and Fab. Their self-financed debut single, 'We Don't Give Up a Fight', was a flop, selling only 2,000 copies. They muddled on in the music business for another eight years but Pilatus in particular, as a heavy cocaine user, was a walking time bomb. After a suicide attempt in 1990, conviction for a sexual assault on a 25-year-old woman, a series of fights and breaking into a car, his life came to an end in a Frankfurt hotel room, where he died from an overdose on 2 April 1998. In 2007 there were plans to make a film of the duo's career, but nothing has yet come of them.

SIR ISAAC NEWTON'S FRAUDULENT REPORT

British physicist Sir Isaac Newton (1643–1727) is known to have been guilty of at least two deceptions.[32] First there is a scientific lie in his masterpiece, *Philosophiae Naturalis Principia Mathematica* (1687). One of Newton's basic principles is that his system must unite theory and practice. To achieve this, he regularly juggled with figures to achieve the desired results, which, we now know, were incorrect. Newton's theory is, for example, correct about the speed of sound:

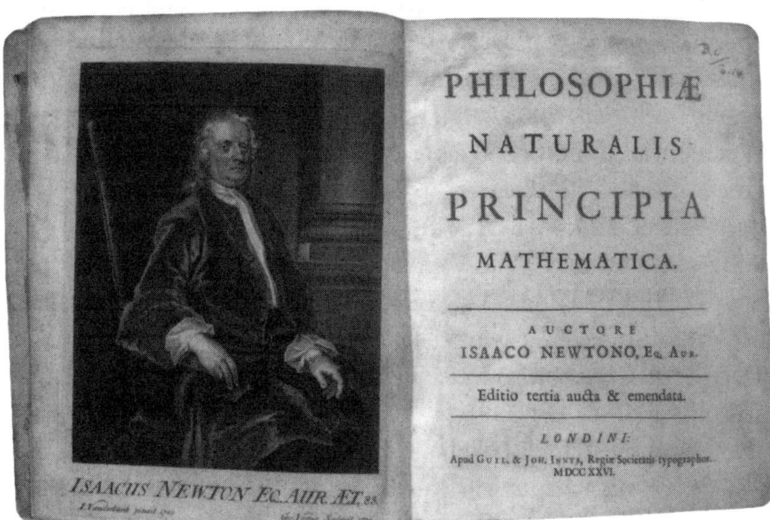

Frontispiece and title-page of the 1726 edition of Sir Isaac Newton's book on the mathematical principles of natural philosophy, first published in 1687.

applied properly, it will produce the right result. But the calculation uses variables that were still unknown in Newton's time. Newton's own sums led him to conclude that the speed of sound is 1,142 feet per second: this was the prevailing opinion in his time, but is not correct.

Newton's second known deception is connected to his dispute with Gottfried Leibniz (1646–1716) about who invented calculus. Both scientists claimed this honour and their argument smouldered for many years until, in 1711, it erupted into a full-blown public row. The Royal Society set up a commission to investigate the affair, which submitted its report in 1712. Since Newton was President of the Royal Society, the introduction to the report took great pains to insist on the independence and impartiality of the commission's members. It later emerged that the report, which chose in favour of Newton, had been written by the physicist himself, including the hypocritical foreword.

SOUTH AFRICAN SALAD COMBATS THE AIDS CRISIS

Few of the many cases of wilful denial in this book are as poignant as that of South African president Thabo Mbeki (served 1999–2008) and his health minister Manto Tshabalala-Msimang, who insisted that there is no link between HIV and AIDS. Mbeki compared AIDS scientists to Nazi concentration camp doctors and accused black South Africans who believe that there is a link between HIV and AIDS of being 'self-repressed victims of a slave mentality' (Goldacre, 2007). When international organizations tried to impress on her the importance of scientific research, Tshabalala-Msimang's response was one which could only come from someone who does not want to understand science: 'Whose science?' (Goldacre, 2006). Given their high-ranking positions in the South African government, the reprehensible attitude of the two politicians resulted in widespread deaths. Treating an HIV-positive patient with an anti-retroviral medicine like azidothymidine (AZT) costs $1,200 a month. Perhaps seeing this as Western oppression, Mbeki had a medicine developed 'in Africa, for Africa' (Goldacre, 2007). The drug, Virodene, cost $6 a month and was based on an industrial solvent called dimethylformamide, which is toxic, potentially lethal and completely ineffective in treating HIV or AIDS.

South African president Thabo Mbeki during a press conference after a meeting with the German chancellor in Berlin.

At an HIV/AIDS conference in Toronto in 2006, delegates called South Africa's stand the 'salad stall'. On the table, the government displayed an impressive array of weapons to combat HIV and AIDS: garlic, beetroot and African wild potato. Objective (that is, not financed by the government) research showed that use of the wild African potato in particular might be positively dangerous. One experiment had to be stopped because participating patients developed severe bone marrow suppression after a couple of weeks. A comparable study on cats infected with AIDS showed that death occurred within a relatively short period.

Given that contamination with HIV – as became clear in western Europe – no longer has to be lethal in the short term, Mbeki and Tshabalala-Msimang were guilty of the perhaps unnecessary deaths of some 2 to 3 million South Africans during their terms in government. This certainly makes them the deadliest fakers in this Encyclopaedia.

After her patron Mbeki was shown the door by the African National Congress in 2008, Tshabalala-Msimang was immediately fired as minister. Two weeks before she died in December 2009 she was able to witness the new South African government relegating her disastrous policy to the scrapheap. A year later the effects of the new policy were already visible: a quarter of the country's coffin builders and undertakers had gone bankrupt. As one of them put it: 'We are burying old grannies again' (Vermaas, 2010).

STIRRING UP THE SCIENCE WARS

In 1996 the postmodernist magazine *Social Text* received an article for publication entitled 'Transgressing the Boundaries: Towards a Transformative Hermeneutics of Quantum Gravity'. It was published in the next issue.

Shortly afterwards the editors felt rather foolish when the author, New York University physicist Alan Sokal, announced that the article was complete nonsense. It was a hoax intended to test intellectual rigour. He had adopted the dense style of writing of postmodernist French philosophy so revered by *Social Text*. The article was gobbledy-gook followed by a long list of references. The hoax led to strained relations between representatives of the humanities and a number of scientists.

T

TIP-TOP GUNS

On 24 August 2010 a Henan Airlines passenger plane crashed in the Chinese province of Heilongjiang, killing 42 and injuring a further 54 of those on board. Around a week later it emerged that the plane's pilot, who 'had shown earlier in his career that he had not entirely commanded the skill of landing' (Garschagen, 2010), was not qualified to hold the rank of captain, as he did not have the required experience to be promoted from co-pilot.

Another week passed and it became clear that the Civil Aviation Administration of China had long been aware of this problem. As early as 2008 the organization had established that 192 Chinese pilots had falsified their training qualifications and flight experience to be eligible for certain jobs.

The cause of the problem – besides the human penchant for corruption – was the explosive growth of civil aviation in China. With a shortage of trained civil pilots, airlines took on a lot of ex-fighter pilots. They had not been trained for flying passenger jets as thoroughly as those who had passed the modern, American-style civil training, but this produced too few pilots to meet the growing demand. And the airlines were not too selective about taking on and promoting pilots, as long as their planes could keep flying.

THE TOXIC SAUSAGES OF FRÉDÉRIC PAGÈS

Bernard-Henri Lévy (*b.* 1948) was a philosopher with the ego of a pop star. BHL, as he is known in France, was always suntanned, had recently visited the coiffeur, and wore his shirts open to the waist. The loudest of the *nouvelles philosophes*, the young intellectuals who fiercely criticized Marxist philosophy in the 1970s, BHL turned every book presentation into a media event. He was the kind of man who you sometimes wanted to see fall flat on his face.

And this is exactly what happened in February 2010. Lévy was presenting his newest book, *De la guerre en philosophie* (On War in Philosophy), in which he criticized Immanuel Kant (1724–1804), calling him 'raving mad'. He based one of his arguments on the work of French philosopher Jean-Baptiste Botul (1896–1947), who, according to Lévy, had shown 'in his series of lectures to the neo-Kantians of Paraguay that their hero was an abstract fake, a pure spirit of pure appearance' (Crace, 2010). BHL had based his critique on one of the two works published by Botul, *La Vie sexuelle d'Emmanuel Kant* (The Sex Life of Immanuel Kant); Botul's other book was entitled *Nietzsche ou le démon de midi* (Nietzsche, or the Midday Demon). In *La Vie sexuelle* Botul claimed that Kant's thought can be traced entirely back to his sexual frustration, and BHL agreed.

It would have been advisable if Lévy had acquainted himself a little better with Botul. He might have become suspicious on discovering that his school of thought is known as *Botulisme*. Or perhaps he would have doubted the reliability of his source if he had been aware of the exceptionally wide range of subjects Botul addressed, including phenomenology, cheese, sausages, women's breasts and luggage transportation in the 1930s. He could also have attended a meeting of the philosopher's fan club. At these meetings, held almost monthly, the *botuliennes* discuss such matters as the metaphysics of flab.

Simply typing the name 'Botul' into Wikipedia.com would have shown Lévy the error of his ways. Botul is fictitious, a character invented by Frédéric Pagès, a drop-out student of philosophy and journalist who worked for the satirical weekly *Le Canard Enchaîné*. 'My source of information is books, not Wikipedia', Lévy responded sourly (Carvajal, 2010). Furthermore, Lévy added that Botul may have been fictitious, but that does not make his comments on Kant any less valid. Botul's analysis, he said, was completely in line with his own (*NRC Handelsblad*, 2010).

BHL later tried to repair his damaged reputation in an opinion piece. He had clearly realized that praise was a better approach:

> It was a truly brilliant and very believable hoax from the mind of a *Canard Enchaîné* journalist who remains a good philosopher all the same. So I was caught, as were the critics who reviewed the book when it came out. The only thing left to say, with no hard feelings, is kudos to the artist. (Carvajal, 2010)

In 2010 the *botuliennes* awarded Lévy's book their annual literary honour, *Le Prix Botul*.

U

'UNDER THY SHADOW BY THE PIERS I WAITED . . .': SELLING BROOKLYN BRIDGE

By the end of the nineteenth century New York had two iconic symbols, Frédéric Auguste Bartholdi's Statue of Liberty, erected and dedicated in 1886, and the majestic Brooklyn Bridge suspended over the East River, designed by the German-born J. A. Roebling and opened in 1883. Brooklyn Bridge was a great challenge to con artists as well as to the many poets and painters it inspired, because the greatest challenge of all was to *sell* it.[33]

The second feature of the bridge that made it an attractive sales option to swindlers was the close proximity of Ellis Island in New York Harbor, where a century and more ago shiploads of immigrants would arrive every day. Professional conman George C. Parker had a number of close contacts among the stewards on the boats. They were not averse to earning a little on the side by informing him about passengers who were rich, but not too bright.

The stewards would direct potential victims to Brooklyn Bridge, where they would find a 'Bridge For Sale' sign along with a smooth-talking Parker lurking in the shadows. Parker would strike up a conversation with them and tell them about the fortune they could earn investing in the bridge and imposing a toll. The gullible immigrants couldn't believe their luck. America was indeed the land of unlimited opportunity! After paying anything between $200 and $1,000, the buyer would receive an authentic-looking receipt for 'One bridge, in good condition.'

The police regularly had to take steps to prevent deluded new owners from building toll booths and barriers. To combat these fraudulent practices, officials on Ellis Island, where the immigrants arrived, handed out leaflets saying 'You can't buy public buildings or streets' (Cohen, 2005).

In 1928 Parker was sentenced to life imprisonment for several cases of fraud. Two years later Hart Crane's densely worked epic poem *The Bridge* was published, featuring Roebling's masterpiece as the unifying metaphor. One wonders if Parker ever got his hands on a copy.

THE UNIQUE KÜFFNER–DÜRER DOUBLE PORTRAIT

In 1799 the city of Nuremberg made a rare exception and loaned out one of its most valued treasures, Albrecht Dürer's *Self-portrait with Fur-trimmed Robe* (1500). The lender was artist Abraham Küffner, who said he wanted to make a copy of the painting. To ensure that the original would be returned and not the copy, a seal was fixed onto its wooden backing. But Küffner knew how to get around that. He sawed the panel into two halves parallel to the plane of the picture and fixed his copy onto the original wood backing to which the seal was affixed. Six years later he sold the original front in Munich. The painting can still be admired there in the Alte Pinakothek, while Küffner's copy is in the Germanisches Nationalmuseum in Nuremberg.

THE U.S. JUDGES WHO LOCKED UP KIDS FOR CASH

This case came to public attention thanks to the creative satire of fourteen-year-old Hillary Transue and the persistence of her indignant mother, Laurene. In January 2007, Hillary built a MySpace page supposedly written by the assistant principal of her school, poking fun at the head teacher for being so strict. For those devoid of humour, Hillary clearly stated at the bottom of the page that it was intended as a joke. Despite this, she was charged with harassment and had to appear before the juvenile court in her home town of Wilkes-Barre, Pennsylvania. Both Hillary and her parents expected that she would get off with a stern lecture. In a hearing that lasted less than a minute, in which Hillary didn't even get the chance to speak, Judge Mark Arthur Ciavarella Jr sentenced this stellar student, who had never been in trouble before, to three months in juvenile detention. Her parents stood by stunned as Hillary was handcuffed and taken away.

Laurene Transue refused to let things go at that and called in the local law centre. The centre had been aware for some time that Ciavarella was a ridiculously severe magistrate. One child had been detained for stealing a $4 jar of nutmeg and another for throwing a sandal at a parent, while a fourteen-year-old was sentenced to six months in juvenile detention for slapping a friend at school.

After being alerted by Laurene Transue, officials at the law centre instigated a small inquiry. That soon turned into a big inquiry, which was ultimately completed by the Public Prosecutor. It was discovered that, in 1999, Ciavarella and fellow judge Michael T. Conahan concocted a scheme to enrich themselves. For starters, they saw to it that the funding of the county-run juvenile detention centre was severely reduced. Conahan, who was responsible for 'external contacts', got in touch with a private company called PA Child Care. The company subsequently announced plans to set up a juvenile detention centre. A sizeable government grant, awarded by the judges, made the plans possible. Soon after, Ciavarella announced that, given the abominable state of the county-run juvenile detention centre (which was true, of course, as a result of his own efforts to slash their budget), he had no choice but to send detained juveniles to the private detention centre. By some strange coincidence, Ciavarella's rate of custodial sentencing, which had been 4.5 per cent in the first two years of his term, rose sharply to 13.7 per cent in his third year, 1999, and peaked at 26 per cent by 2004.

In January 2002, when the centre was in full operation, Conahan signed a 'placement guarantee agreement' with PA Child Care, under which Ciavarella would see to it that enough children were detained to ensure that the firm would receive more than 1$ million a year in public money.

The agreement was very fruitful – except for the children who appeared before the judge – and at the end of 2004 the parties agreed a long-term deal worth $58 million for PA Child Care. For their cooperation, both judges received $2.6 million from PA Child Care. The money was channelled away through a company the duo controlled in Florida.

When the scandal came to light in 2008 it was dubbed 'kids for cash'. The consequences were enormous, and understandably so. This book contains few cases in which human values have been treated with such disdain. One of the first consequences was that the cases of up to 5,000 children placed in custody by Ciavarella between 2002 and 2008 had to be reviewed, including that of Hillary Transue. Second, the careers of the two magisterial deceivers came to an abrupt end. Ciavarella insisted that he thought he could take the money from PA Child Care legitimately as a 'finder's fee'. But it was not too long before both he and Conahan gave full confessions in exchange for a plea agreement which would enable them to avoid a criminal trial and receive shorter sentences. Each of them was given 87 months in jail. Furthermore, since they both committed a felony while in office, they lost their pensions.

In July 2009, federal judge Edwin M. Kosik declared the plea agreement void. Ciavarella and Conahan, he said, 'had failed to accept responsibility for their actions' and the 'prison sentence of more than seven years was too lenient' (Urbina, 2009). This meant that there would be a trial after all. Hillary Transue, who was ostracised for many months by neighbours and friends from school after the detention she received from Ciavarella, noted with satisfaction: 'It's nice to see him on the other side of the bench' (Pilkington, 2009). In August 2011 Ciavarella was sentenced to 28 years in prison; the following month Conahan received a seventeen-and-a-half-year sentence.

THE UNMISTAKEABLE ADOLF HILTER DIARIES, IN 60 OR 61 VOLUMES

In his youth Konrad Kujau (1938–2000) spent some time in prison for burglary and theft. Later, he opened a shop in Stuttgart specializing in military memorabilia, mainly from the Third Reich. Before long Kujau realized that he could increase his profits by reducing his acquisition costs and started forging his own Nazi memorabilia as well as drawings and paintings he sold as by the young Adolf Hitler. In the 1970s, in a room at the back of his shop, he also worked on his favourite forgery:

Hitler's diaries. He sold the first excerpt in 1978, but this was no more than an insignificant notebook compared to the real project, which would take him many years: Hitler's diaries from 1932 to 1945, in 60 volumes. Kujau knew it would be the 'find of the century', although much of the content was very banal: 'Because of the new pills I have violent flatulence, and – says Eva – bad breath' (Leidig, 2004).

To publicize the diaries Kujau worked with Gerd Heidemann, a journalist at *Stern* magazine. Heidemann was, to put it mildly, fascinated by the Third Reich and liked to invite elderly former Nazi officials to join him on his yacht *Carin II*, which used to belong to Hermann Göring. Two former SS generals were witnesses at his wedding. Heidemann spun the editors of *Stern* a tale that was partly verifiable but mostly fabricated. Nine days before he committed suicide, Adolf Hitler ordered ten aircraft carrying staff members and important cargo to fly from Berlin to Salzburg. On 21 April 1945 one of the planes crashed near Dresden. According to Heidemann the diaries were recovered from the wreck and stored in a shed, where they remained hidden almost 40 years later. Although the shed was in the German Democratic Republic, the documents could be smuggled to the West with the help of high-ranking East German army officers. Stern paid around 9 million German marks for the diaries. Even the editors did not know where exactly they had come from and who had supplied them. Heidemann said that he could not reveal their names for fear of reprisals by the East German authorities. The journalist not only deceived *Stern*, but was also not honest with Kujau. He kept back for himself several millions of the proceeds from *Stern*, much more than he had privately agreed with the magazine would be needed to pay the 'smugglers'.

In April 1983 the diaries were handed over to *Stern*. The magazine had already been busy trying to sell the text to other interested parties. The *Sunday Times* in London (in company with *Newsweek* magazine) offered around £600,000 for the serial rights and sent its own historian, Hugh Trevor-Roper, to authenticate the work. After examining the diaries under pressure of time in a badly lit bank vault, Trevor-Roper declared them authentic. On 22 April *Stern* held a press conference attended by some 200 journalists. By then, Trevor-Roper and a German colleague already seemed to have had their doubts. The British historian had heard that no conclusive link had been established between the diaries and the plane crash on 21 April

1945. But the owner of the *Sunday Times*, Rupert Murdoch, blindly pushed ahead with publication.

As soon as the first excerpt from the diaries was published, sceptical historians set about analysing the text, while *Stern* finally had the actual physical documents examined scientifically. The results left no room for doubt. The covers of the books contained polyester, which was not produced in Germany until after the Second World War. On every cover the (plastic) initials 'FH' in Gothic script had been glued (Kujau mistakenly thought the difficult Gothic letters read 'AH', hence his reason for attaching them; and at first no one so much as noticed this ignorant error). The paper, the ink and the glue under the labels on the covers all dated from after 1950. And it was difficult to believe that, in wartime, Hitler had been able to find identical notebooks to write 60 volumes over a period of thirteen years. It was also strange that no one had ever known that Hitler, who was always surrounded by his staff, had kept a diary. Hitler himself rarely ever wrote anything, even dictating personal letters to his secretary. Many graphology experts said that the handwriting did not even resemble that of the Führer. Besides, he suffered from a progressive palsy of both hands and, after 1943, wrote only in pencil. On 20 July 1944 Hitler was injured in a bomb attempt on his life and both his forearms were dressed in bandages and compresses. Yet the diary included an entry apparently written that day. The diaries were bound in imitation leather and as Nicolaus von Below, one of Hitler's adjutants, said: 'For Hitler there was real leather or nothing' (Henry, 1983). As for the content of the diaries, large sections proved to have been lifted from the book *Hitlers Reden und Proklamationen, 1932–1945*, published in 1962–3 by Nazi-era archivist Max Domarus. Even the mistakes had been duplicated.

For weeks, *Stern* was the object of derision. The *London Standard*, for instance, said that it had acquired 'exclusive right to the diaries of Genghis Khan' while the *New York Times* mused whether *Stern* had taken on Clifford Irving (Henry, 1983; and see GHOSTING AN AUTOBIOGRAPHY).

Kujau was sentenced to four and a half years in prison, and Heidemann to four years and eight months. *Stern*'s reputation was in tatters. Two editors resigned and the magazine sank into the deepest crisis it had ever experienced. Hugh Trevor-Roper's reputation as a respected historian never recovered.

After Heidemann had served his prison sentence his life went downhill. His wife left him, his son died of AIDS and his daughter made a new life for herself in Australia, far away from her scandal-racked father. By 2008 Heidemann had run up debts of €700,000. Social security was paying his rent and insurance and providing him with a benefit of €350 a month.

After his release Kujau made an honest living as a painter copying works by famous artists. These, which he signed twice – with the original painter's signature and his own, fetched between €2,000 and €5,000 and were hugely popular.

And the diaries? *Stern* sold its 60 volumes to Fritz Stiefel, a collector of Nazi memorabilia, for 200,000 German marks while the trial was still going on. After Kujau died, a 61st volume was discovered, which was sold at an auction for €6,500.

V

A VERY UNSAFE PRODUCTS TESTER: IBT LABS

In 1975 an inspector at the U.S. Food and Drug Administration accidentally got to see a report on the arthritis treatment Naprosyn, tested by Industrial Bio-Test Laboratories (IBT), a company that specialized in product safety testing. The report aroused suspicions and an inspection of the laboratory showed that it was a complete shambles. The described studies conducted by the laboratory as 'magic pencil studies', as the final reports contained analyses of tests that had never been carried out. According to data files, some laboratory rats died twice and the weights of long-deceased rats continued to be recorded. Autopsies on rats were sometimes so delayed that the animals were decomposed. An investigation showed that 100 per cent of the rat studies conducted by IBT were unreliable. When testing TCC, an antibacterial agent used in many deodorants, IBT 'forgot' to mention that the testicles of rats already atrophied at the lowest dose being given. In 1983, by which time the Environmental Protection Agency had determined that only 16 per cent of IBT's results were valid, which jeopardized the safety of many products then in use and assumed to be safe, three former managers of the company were found guilty of fraud. They received prison sentences of a maximum of one year and one day.

VICTOR LUSTIG AND HIS STOOPID SHERIFF

Victor Lustig was born into a respectable family in 1890 at Hostinne, now in the Czech Republic. His father was mayor of the town and he was educated at a boarding school in Dresden, where he was known for his quick intelligence. As well as Czech, he also quickly learned to speak German, English, French and Italian. Intelligence, a command of five languages and charisma: if he had been of good character, Lustig could have been a diplomat. But, lacking any such good virtues, he became a conman.

Lustig learned the tricks of his trade on cruise ships crossing the Atlantic. On these floating palaces, representatives of old money and the nouveau riche passed the time drinking and playing cards for enormously high stakes. Lustig, by now an accomplished bridge and poker player and cheat, not to mention one of the best billiards players in Europe, did well for himself. On one of his voyages he met a colleague, Nicky Arnstein, and the two worked together for a year. Lustig learned an important lesson from his partner: a con artist has to manipulate his victims into a position in which they actually want to give him money. To drive his point home, Arnstein openly admitted to a fellow voyager that he was a conman who played cards for money. The man, fascinated, continually challenged Arnstein to a game, but the latter refused until the night before the ship docked in New York. He then relieved his victim of $30,000.

Lustig unfailingly homed in on his potential victim's weak spot. And he always had a number of 'enterprises' in hand in case he had to save his skin, even if he had to improvise. Once, on the insistence of a banker he had tricked, he was arrested by Sheriff S. R. Richards in Ramsen County, Oklahoma. The sheriff was not quite sure how to respond to having an aristocrat in his jail and was impressed by his prisoner's good manners. They started to chat a little. The chat turned into a full-scale conversation and, in no time, the two were sitting together at the sheriff's table, sharing a bottle of confiscated illegal whisky. Lustig could have talked about art, stocks and shares or the theatre, but soon discovered the sheriff's weak spot: women. So he talked about the splendid Paris brothels he had frequented and what went on there. Richards let slip that he regularly visited Bourbon Street in frenchified New Orleans, also famed for its brothels, and that he had set up a young lady there in a love nest. A drink later and the sheriff admitted that he had financed this by dipping his hand in the state's coffers: his worrysome secret borrowing currently stood at an enormous $25,000. Lustig offered him a way out. Using a key provided by his prisoner, the Sheriff collected a package from a luggage locker. It contained a wooden box about the size of a shoebox, with impressive-looking knobs, slots and levers. Lustig told the sheriff it was a money duplicator and that he would demonstrate how it worked. He explained that it did not produce counterfeit money, but a duplicate of an existing note. He took a $100 bill from his own wallet and fed it into the machine. Twelve hours later, the machine spewed out the original note plus an identical copy, both soaking wet. In reality they were both genuine notes before Lustig had forged the serial numbers to make them identical. Seeing a solution to all his financial worries, Sheriff Richards paid Lustig's asking price for the machine: $10,000 and the chance to 'escape'. Presumably it then took the sheriff around twelve or thirteen hours to realize he had been taken for a ride. Some months later, he found Lustig in a hotel room and threatened to shoot him. The conman suggested that the sheriff had probably done something wrong while duplicating the notes and said he would be pleased to hand back the $10,000 until they found out what the problem was. He gave Richards the money and advised him to have a night out in Bourbon Street. A few days later, the sheriff was arrested in New Orleans and charged with distributing counterfeit money. He was given a prison sentence.

In May 1925 Lustig was back in Paris, together with an associate, Dapper Dan Collins (alias Monsieur Dante, real name Robert Arthur Tourbillon, nickname Ratsy). Together they performed Lustig's most famous con, a true stroke of genius. Lustig's creative capabilities started to work after he read an article in a Paris newspaper about the bad state of repair of the Eiffel Tower. The giant steel monster, built to the dismay of *tout Paris* for the World's Fair in 1889, was still there 35 years later, in a pitiful state. Posing as deputy director-general of the Ministry of Post and Telegraphs, which was responsible for the tower, Lustig invited five scrap-metal dealers to the Hôtel Crillon, under conditions of strict secrecy. The 'deputy director-general' made a sensational announcement: the French government had decided that the Eiffel Tower was not worth the costs of keeping it maintained; furthermore, as many artists had insisted, it did not fit in with the architecture of the capital. It was therefore to be demolished, which would mean 700 tons of scrap metal. Lustig asked his guests to submit offers. He was not even interested in four of the five, but only in the response of André Poisson, a 'working-class boy made good' with more money than sense. It was Poisson's offer that the self-appointed deputy director-general accepted.

Afterwards, Poisson started to get suspicious. He wondered why the negotiations took place in a hotel room and not, as would be expected, at the ministry. In the last meeting, at which Poisson paid for the right to dismantle the tower, Lustig allayed his fears. He explained that the negotiations did not take place at the ministry because government officials were accustomed to receiving a 'commission'. Not wishing to appear stupid, Poisson paid the bribe and the agreed price for the scrap metal. A few hours later, Lustig and Tourbillon were on their way to Switzerland in a car with the money. In the weeks that they were there, there was not a single word about the 'sale' of the Eiffel Tower in the newspapers. Lustig realized that Poisson wished to save himself the humiliation of reporting the scam to the police, which meant he was free to sell the tower again. He and Tourbillon returned to France, where they set up the same scenario again. This time, however, a suspicious client did go to the police and the pair had to beat a hasty retreat.

On 5 December 1935, under the name Robert Miller, Lustig was sentenced to twenty years in prison. He died of pneumonia on 11 March 1947. His death certificate was filled in by someone with a sense of humour. Under 'occupation' he was listed as 'apprentice salesman' (Johnson, 1961).

W

WERNER PURGATHOFER'S PROMISING LECTURES

Werner Purgathofer is a bona fide Austrian scientist with a strong aversion to commercially organized conferences with no substance. Visualization and Intelligent Design in Engineering and Architecture (VIDEA) is one of these annual circuses. Purgathofer learned that VIDEA '93 had been organized without a single meeting of the programme committee or a single paper being submitted to the committee, proving to him that the conference organizers were not interested in the quality of its content.

In the run-up to VIDEA '95 Purgathofer decided to conduct an experiment. He submitted to the organizers four abstracts of lectures to be held at the conference. The first addressed the issue of how to create footprints on the walls of public spaces. The text was complete nonsense, as this extract shows:

> The basic footprint function is a combination of trivial, i.e. easy to implement, parametric functions. The footprint is divided into a ball and a heel which can have independent sole textures. The sizes are chosen such that a simulation of shoe sizes 35 to 42 for women profiles and 39 to 46 for men profiles is performed. (Purgathofer, 1995)

The second abstract described the correct method for rendering interior rooms without light, which would clearly produce a completely black image. The third abstract was VIDEA's own call for papers, while the fourth was literally gobbledygook. Forty sentences were plucked at random from a dictionary of information processing terms and joined together to make an extremely technical sounding text. The dictionary was cited as the source. The abstracts were submitted in November 1994. On 14 January 1995 Purgathofer received the exciting news that all four had been 'reviewed and provisionally accepted' (Purgathofer, 1995). The letter also made it clear where the organizers' real priorities lay. Because of the large number of papers submitted, each participating institution would only be permitted to present one paper at the conference. These would be published in the proceedings – after the institution had paid its registration fee. The publishers of the proceedings, including Elsevier Science Publishers, were probably unaware that they were printing rubbish that had not been peer-reviewed.

WHAT HARRY POTTER DID NEXT

China is undoubtedly the world's most prolific producer of forgeries. Besides the more well-known genres (forged art, fake designer products), China has added a product of its own to the forger's catalogue: contemporary books. A few examples are enough by way of illustration. In China, alongside the seven novels in the Harry Potter series familiar to readers in the West, there are a number of volumes available to which author J. K. Rowling did not contribute a single word, including *Harry Potter and the Big Funnel* and *Rich Dad, Poor Dad and Harry Potter*.

Another example is a pirated version of Bill Clinton's autobiography *My Life*. Although based on the authentic text, the Chinese version displays a number of changes. It describes how young Bill and his family used to talk about the great inventions produced by Chinese culture that 'left us in the dust'. Bill also explains to his wife Hillary that his name means 'Big Watermelon', while all criticisms of restrictions on the freedom of expression in China are left out. The opening sentence of this version says it all. In the original text Clinton needed 48 words to describe his birthplace. In the Chinese version, he simply says: 'The town of Hope, where I was born, has very good feng shui' (*International Herald Tribune*, 2004).

WHEN HEMINGWAY SHOT HIMSELF – IN THE FOOT

Ernest Hemingway made his debut in 1925 with a collection of short stories, *In Our Time*, published by Boni & Liveright. In the same year F. Scott Fitzgerald's *The Great Gatsby* was published by Charles Scribner's Sons. Fitzgerald told his publisher about the promising young Hemingway and Scribner's editor Maxwell Perkins sent Hemingway a letter offering to publish his future work. As Scribner's was larger, better known and more prestigious than Boni & Liveright, Hemingway was enthusiastic about the offer. Scribner's also offered a superior financial deal. But there was one problem. Under his contract, Hemingway had to produce three books for Boni & Liveright, of which *In Our Time* was only the first. Since his debut was such a success, it was unlikely that the publishers would be prepared to cancel his contract. To evade his obligations to Boni & Liveright, Hemingway decided to write a book that was so bad that they would not want to publish it. That would constitute breach of contract, giving Hemingway the opportunity to switch publisher.

In December 1925, between writing and rewriting his masterpiece *The Sun Also Rises*, Hemingway rushed off a short book in six or seven days. He took a number of steps to ensure that this work, *The Torrents of Spring*, ludicrously subtitled *A Romantic Novel in Honor of the Passing of a Great Race*, would be refused by his publisher. First, this novella – less than 100 pages long – was a parody of *Dark*

Laughter, a recent novel by Sherwood Anderson (1876–1941). That gave Hemingway the opportunity to kill two birds with one stone. Since Boni & Liveright published Anderson, they would never accept a parody of Anderson's work. And Hemingway's offering made it abundantly clear that if Anderson had ever been his mentor, the roles would certainly now be reversed. Hemingway was now his own boss and no longer needed to listen to mentors.

Second, *The Torrents of Spring* was no ordinary novel, as a short summary shows. The main characters are Scripps O'Neill, a Harvard graduate with a few published stories to his name, and Yogi Johnson, an ex-soldier. They meet each other while working in a factory in Petoskey, Michigan. When O'Neill discovers that his wife has left him, he goes to Chicago. On the way he marries Diana, a down-at-heel British waitress in a diner. He soon leaves her for Mandy, another slightly less down-at-heel waitress in the same place. Mandy then loses out to O'Neill's dreams about a nameless Indian squaw who appears in the restaurant one night, naked except for a pair of moccasins. But it is Yogi Johnson who disappears into the night with the squaw, throwing off his clothes as he leaves. They are followed by two Native Americans who are planning to sell Johnson's clothes to the Salvation Army. Johnson is also accompanied by an Indian who has lost both arms and both legs in the First World War, but who can still play a decent game of pool, saying: 'Me not shoot so good since the war.' In the meantime, O'Neill takes mescaline and hallucinates about his life as the President of Mexico.

Besides the bizarre pseudo-plot, Hemingway succeeded in giving the book a high burlesque tint by mentioning great artists at strange moments. When, for example, the academic O'Neill applies for a job at the factory, he reflects on his situation:

> Why shouldn't he work with his hands? Rodin had done it. Cézanne had been a butcher. Renoir a carpenter. Picasso had worked in a cigarette factory in his boyhood. Gilbert Stuart, who painted those famous portraits of Washington that are reproduced all over this America of ours and hang in every schoolroom – Gilbert Stuart had been a blacksmith. Then there was Emerson. Emerson had been a hod-carrier. James Russell Lowell had been, he had heard, a telegraph operator in his youth.

Hemingway's plan worked. Boni & Liveright refused to publish the book. But at the time Hemingway was suffering from one of his addictions: women. His marriage to Hadley was as good as over and the future Mrs Hemingway, Pauline Pfeiffer, had already appeared on the scene. Pfeiffer somehow persuaded Hemingway that *The Torrents of Spring* was worth publishing and the novella thus became part of the author's negotiations with Scribner's. When it was published in 1926, many critics did not how to respond; most saw it as a faux pas, but Hemingway none the less established his name later that same year with *The Sun Also Rises*. This was followed by a series of masterpieces (and best-sellers), earning Hemingway the Nobel Prize for Literature in 1954.

WHY A LETTER SANK THE LABOUR PARTY

On 8 October 1924 Britain's first Labour government found itself facing a motion of no confidence. With elections coming later in the same month, the political tension intensified. Would the Labour Party be able to repair the damage to its reputation or would the Conservatives take power?

On 25 October, four days before the elections, the *Daily Mail* splashed the following headline across its front page: 'Civil War Plot by Socialists' Masters: Moscow Orders to Our Reds; Great Plot Disclosed' (Norton-Taylor, 1999). The paper published a letter sent to the British Foreign Office on 9 October, allegedly from Grigori Zinovjev, president of the Soviet-controlled Communist International (Comintern), and addressed to the Central Committee of the Communist Party of Great Britain (CPGB). The letter called on the CPGB to mobilize 'sympathetic forces' within the Labour Party to 'stir up the masses of the British proletariat' and to encourage 'agitation-propaganda' in the armed forces (Norton-Taylor, 1999/Cordon, 2000).

On 29 October 1924 Labour suffered a humiliating defeat in the elections. Although some historians dispute the claim that the Zinovjev letter had a significant effect on the results, it certainly played its part. It has consequently remained a source of fascination ever since, especially within the Labour Party.

The truth about the letter did not come to light until 1999 when, with Labour once again in office, the government published a report on the affair. As Labour supporters had claimed for many years, the letter was indeed a forgery. Who the forger was and who gave the order for the letter to be written remains a mystery. What is certain is that the Foreign Office had sent the document to MI6, the British Secret Intelligence Service, which had declared it genuine. The letter was then leaked to the *Daily Mail*, most probably by Major Desmond Morton, an MI6 officer and close friend of Conservative MP Sir Winston Churchill. Given that it was they who declared the letter authentic and then leaked it to the press, it is not unlikely that the origins of the forgery should also be sought in these elite Conservative circles.

WILLIAM LAUDER'S DIATRIBE AGAINST *PARADISE LOST*

Forgeries are often used to support the supposed authenticity of other forgeries (for example, a forged certificate of authenticity for a forged painting). The case of William Lauder (*c.* 1710–1771), a Scottish amateur poet, offers an interesting variation on this theme: forgeries intended to prove that an authentic work is not authentic.

When Alexander Pope made a comment that favoured fellow English poet John Milton (1608–1674) at the expense of another Scottish poet, Arthur Johnston (1587–1641), Lauder – an admirer of Johnston – decided to take revenge by showing that Milton's masterpiece *Paradise Lost* had largely been plagiarized from other works. In a series of articles in 1747, he alleged that it was based on various earlier poems, including *Sarcotis* by Jacob Masen (1606–1681), *Adamus Exul* by Hugo Grotius (1583–1645) and the *Poemata Sacra* by Andrew Ramsay (1574–1659). He supported his argument by comparing lines from *Paradise Lost* with those in the supposedly plagiarized texts.

Lauder's claim was disputed in 1750 by John Douglas in *Milton vindicated from the charge of plagiarism, brought against him by Mr Lauder, and Lauder himself convicted of several forgeries and gross impositions on the public*. Douglas showed that Lauder himself was the forger: he had inserted lines from a Latin translation of *Paradise Lost* into the sources he quoted. Lauder however stuck to his guns and in 1752–3 republished his accusations. The number of allegedly plagiarized quotations had by now increased to 97.

After more wrangling, Lauder turned his back on the world of letters and emigrated to Barbados. There he opened a bric-a-brac shop and bought a slave girl, who bore him a daughter.

THE WINNING SLIPS OF A WOULD-BE JUDGE

When a new judge is selected in Fairfax County, Virginia, lawyers who are members of the bar can choose from six candidates. When this happened in February 1996, Thomas E. Gallahue was the only one who merited the bar's 'highly recommended' designation and was tipped to win.

When the votes were counted, the electoral commission noticed that some ballot slips were of a slightly different colour and texture. The printer was called in to check and 326 of the 1,055 slips turned out to be fake. And Gallahue's name had been ticked on all of the forgeries. He was completely perplexed and, wondering what could have happened, thought of lawyer Robert W. O'Brien. The two were friends, had done a couple of cases together, and went out to dinner from time to time. When O'Brien had asked him if he could lobby on his behalf, Gallahue had given his consent.

At his interrogation, O'Brien burst into tears. He had been convinced that without his help Gallahue would never win the vote, and had resorted to illegal means to help his friend. He confirmed that Gallahue knew nothing.

Although Gallahue's name had also been ticked on most of the 729 valid ballot slips, he was passed over because of the fraud and the candidate who finished second, Lorraine Norlund, was appointed judge.

WRITING A WINNER FOR PUBLISHAMERICA

Anyone wishing to publish a book can go to a vanity press. These pseudo-publishers will publish anything, as long as the author pays. The quality of the books tends to leave much to be desired, both physically and in terms of content.[34]

PublishAmerica explicitly claims that it is not a vanity press. Strictly speaking, they are right, in that they do not make their authors pay to be published. In practice, however, it comes down to the same thing. They have no editors on their staff to check and improve manuscripts. They do not have print runs or editions in the traditional sense, but print books to order. There is almost no chance that one of their titles will ever end up in a bookshop. As they do nothing to publicize the books they publish, the only orders come from the authors themselves. What makes PublishAmerica guilty of fraud is that they claim to be a traditional publisher, one that rejects 80 per cent of authors and employs 30 full-time editors (Zeitchik, 2004).

Early in 2004 a website run by PublishAmerica carried an extremely critical report on science fiction and fantasy writers, accusing them of being 'literary parasites' (Martelle, 2005). Science fiction author Jim Macdonald was furious and decided to take revenge. He found 30 fellow writers willing to help him write the worst book they could come up with. To set the ball rolling, he gave them the basic setting:

> Bruce Lucent makes hamburgers for Penelope Urbain as Isidore arrives . . . Bruce is a 20-something software developer. Isidore has red hair and a ponytail. Penelope Urbain is really stacked. (Martelle, 2005)

The book had no plot. Each of the authors was responsible for one chapter. They did not consult and they didn't know whether they were writing chapter One, chapter Thirty or something in between. They all did their best to write the worst prose possible. This is an example of the results of their efforts:

> Yvonne poured herself a drink and melted into the chair across from Callie. She brushed a strand of moltenly hair from her eyes and proceeded to carve the ham. Callie watched intently. Juice streamed from the ham in rivulets like saliva drooling from the fierce jaws of a wild dingo poised over the dead carcass of its prey in the dingo-eat-dingo world. (Tea, 2004)

In the final manuscript chapter Twenty-one remained blank, as the author had not met his deadline, while another chapter appeared twice. The closing chapter (Thirty-four) is composed of the halves of two other chapters, which were entered into a computer program that places words and phrases in random order. Macdonald then accepted all the suggestions of his computer's spellcheck. The result was a pure delight:

> Bruce walked around any more. Some people might ought to her practiced eye, at her. I am so silky and braid shoulders.

At sixty-six, men with a few feet away form their languid gazes. (Tea, 2004)[35]

The 71,503-word manuscript was given the title *Atlanta Nights* and sent to PublishAmerica. The author's name was a phonetic joke: Travis Tea. On 7 December 2004 Travis received the following joyous message: 'PublishAmerica has decided to give "Atlanta Nights" the chance it deserves' (Martelle, 2005). To avoid possible legal problems, the hoaxers did not sign the enclosed contract. That evening, they confessed the hoax on the internet.

PublishAmerica tried to save face by sending an email stating 'Upon further review, it appears that your work is not ready to be published' (Martelle, 2005).

But PublishAmerica were wrong. Although *Atlanta Nights* could be downloaded free of charge, the hoax achieved such notoriety that its creators decided to have it published by a vanity press. All the proceeds go to the Science Fiction and Fantasy Writers of America Emergency Medical Fund.

Y

YAHYA JAMMEH'S MEDICAL AIDS

Like many of his African colleagues, such as Thabo Mbeki, President Yahya Jammeh of Gambia has his own ideas about medicine. He is himself, in his own words, a wonderful healer who works with charisma, magic, herbs and charms. He also claims he can cure AIDS. 'The cure is a day's treatment', he says, 'asthma, five minutes' (Goldacre, 2007).

Z

ZIMBABWE'S MAGIC FUEL

For many decades the Zimbabwean government led by President Robert Mugabe has been busy ruining the country's economy. One of the main problems the country faces is chronic fuel shortages.

There was a glimmer of hope for the none too bright team of ministers when, at the end of 2006, it was rumoured that 'spirit medium' Rotina Mavhunga could conjure liquid out of a rock, just like Moses in the Bible. Whereas Moses could manage only water, Mavhunga succeeded in coaxing diesel fuel from the rock. A ministerial delegation immediately set out for the scene of the miracle, the Maningwa Hills some 70 miles northwest of the capital, Harare. The delegation included State Security Minister Didymus Mutasa, Home Affairs Minister Kembo Mohadi and Defence Minister Sydney Sekeramayi. Mavhunga, however, was not prepared to display her skills without the necessary preparations. First, their excellencies had to take off their shoes, participate in a 'magic ritual' and bathe in a pool of diesel. The ministers splashed around like excited schoolboys. And then, after some mumbling and abracadabras from Mavhunga, a steady jet of diesel spouted from the rock.

This wondrous solution to Zimbabwe's fuel problems was announced with a lot of pomp and circumstance. Mavhunga was showered with land, money and – of course – cars. Within a couple of months she managed to magically accumulate the equivalent of about £600,000.

Mavhunga was exposed due to the vigilance of a few cabinet ministers who did have a minimum of knowledge of the ways of the world, including Science and Technology Minister Olivia Muchena and Minister of Mines Amos Midzi. They took a closer look at the magic mountain and discovered a concealed pipe leading to an old container full of diesel on the top of the rock. Later, it was discovered that Mavhunga had cooked up the idea after finding the container. Besides a couple of pipes, all she needed was an accomplice to open the tap when she uttered the right magic spell. As diesel for the trick was not available in Zimbabwe, she bought it in neighbouring Zambia.

Mavhunga was charged with fraud but, before she was tried, she was accused of a second offence: selling a stone weighing 18 kilograms, which she claimed was gold, for a cow. In September 2010 she was sentenced to 27 months in jail and given a nineteen-month suspended sentence for both offences. Mugabe defended his ministers by arguing that they were 'blinded by Mavhunga's beauty' (Nkatazo, 2007). That the cabinet consisted of incurable dimwits should be clear from the fact that even those who accused Mavhunga of fraud feared the consequences of her supernatural powers (*ZimDaily*, 2009).

REFERENCES *and* SOURCES

INTRODUCTION REFERENCES

1 Much has been written about the pathology of collecting ('I'm only making a list of deceivers . . .'). A personal favourite is Philipp Blom's *To Have and to Hold: An Intimate History of Collectors and Collecting.*

2 This implies that I restrict myself to human deception, in which animals play at most a supporting role (see, for example, NOT-SO-CLEVER HANS). Studying deception by animals requires expertise that I do not possess. However, one example should be sufficient to show that this is a subject worth studying. For many years, the Japanese city of Kagoshima has been plagued by crows. The birds prefer to build their nests in the electricity pylons, causing regular power cuts. So the city council established a Crow Patrol to destroy the nests. The response from the crows was amusing, to say the least: they started to build dummy nests all over the city. This had two consequences. If a real nest was destroyed, the evicted crows had a large number of dummies to choose from which they could easily upgrade. But even better is that the Crow Patrol wasted much of its time destroying crows' nests that were not really crows' nests at all. Over a three-year period, some 600 nests were destroyed, but 'the number kept increasing, as did the black-outs.' (Fackler, 2008) On the other hand, of course, the crows' resistance cost them a lot of energy, which they could not use to pass on their genetic make-up to their young. It would be reasonable to assume that these *trade-offs* are a principal factor in deception by animals.

3 The danger of such an approach is that it sees the world through an overly narrow lens, but if it is used carefully, it can produce interesting insights. See, for example, *The Encyclopædia of Stupidity* by Matthijs van Boxsel.

4 A good example comes from American senator and presidential candidate John McCain. During the election campaign in July 2008, he said one morning in Colorado: 'I want to look you in the eye: I will not raise your taxes nor support a tax increase' (Cooper, 2008). McCain appears to have been given a telling off from one of his advisors, who advised him not to take such clear standpoints. That same evening in Kansas City, his message had changed to: 'in any negotiation that I might have, when I go in my position will be that

I am opposed to raising taxes' (Cooper, 2008). The second statement gives the impression that McCain is taking a position ('I am opposed to raising taxes'), while in fact he is not taking a position at all ('Anything is possible').

5 This unambiguous statement is a position. Why politicians do not like taking positions is clear from what happened in August 1998, when Clinton was confronted with incontrovertible evidence that he definitely did have sexual contact with Lewinsky. With a clever example of reasoning, Clinton tried to reconcile his position and reality by arguing that oral sex does not fall under the definition of sexual contact.

6 For an interesting approach to this very pressing topic, see David L. Perry, '"Repugnant Philosophy": Ethics, Espionage and Covert Action'.

7 In the traditional interpretation, the serpent's intention is not animal in nature, but satanic.

8 The great economic impact of faked goods, which the European Commission and the OECD are so concerned about, is denied in an interesting article in the *British Journal of Criminology* (Wall, 2010). In a nutshell, the article claims that a distinction should be made between the faking of 'safety-critical' goods (aircraft components, medicines) and of luxury goods like watches, handbags and shoes. While the interests at stake in the first category (safety and public health) are serious, the article says that those involved in the faking of luxury goods (cheated buyers and brand or economic damage to manufacturers) are regularly overestimated. This is easy to demonstrate: anyone who buys a Louis Vuitton bag for ten euros can reasonably be expected to know that it is a fake, so they cannot consider themselves cheated. On the contrary, people like getting high-status goods for little money. Nor is there any economic loss to the manufacturer. According to Wall, it is a misconception to assume that, if the fake product were not available, the buyer would have bought the real thing. Not everyone who buys a fake Rolex for ten euros would buy a genuine one for 10,000 euros if the fake were not available. In other words: anyone wealthy enough to buy the original will not buy a fake, while anyone who buys a fake is not wealthy enough to buy the original. Wall also says that brand damage is exaggerated: every fake that goes into circulation is free advertising for the brand. He therefore advises using limited public funds to combat the faking of the first kind.

INTRODUCTION SOURCES

Ahmed, Murad, 'Swiss Army Knife Now Comes With Chips', *The Times*, 26 March 2010

Babbage, Charles, *Reflections on the Decline of Science in England, and on Some of its Causes*, London: B. Fellowes, 1830

Barboza, David, 'Tradition of Fake Goods a Real Problem in China: Cut-throat Capitalism Mars Industry', *International Herald Tribune*, 6 June 2007

Bennet, James and Jill Abramson, 'The Testing of a President: The Overview; Lawyers Say Tape of Clinton Shows Regret and Anger', *The New York Times*, 20 September 1998

Blom, Philipp, *To Have and to Hold: An Intimate History of Collectors and Collecting*, London, etc.: Penguin Books, 2003

Blume, Mary, 'It's True: These Museum Exhibits are Fake', *International Herald Tribune*, 10 February 2006

Bodoni, Stephanie, 'Counterfeiters Shift to Toothpaste from Rolex Watches', *International Herald Tribune*, 16 June 2007

Bok, Sissela, *Lying: Moral Choice in Public and Private Life*, New York: Vintage Books, 1999

Boxsel, Matthijs van, *The Encyclopædia of Stupidity*, London: Reaktion Books, 2003

Callow, James, 'Flavio Briatore Free to Make F1 Return in 2013 as FIA Lifts Life Ban', *The Guardian*, 12 April 2010

Chittenden, Maurice, 'Six Months Old and He Can Tell Good from Evil', *The Sunday Times*, 9 May 2010

Cooper, Michael, 'Once More, With (a Little Less) Feeling', The Caucus – The Politics and Government Blog of *The Times*, 30 July 2008, http://thecaucus.blogs.nytimes.com/2008/07/30/once-more-with-a-little-less-feeling, 12 August 2009

Cooperman, Alan, 'Some Say Natural Catastrophe Was "Divine Judgment": When Disaster Hits, Explanations Take On Moral Tone', *Houston Chronicle*, 3 September 2005

De Volkskrant, 2008. '*Geschorste artsen behandelen nog patiënten*', *de Volkskrant*, 21 January 2008

Elliott, Valerie, 'Fake Christmas Goods "Funding Terrorists"', *The Times*, 22 November 2003

European Commission, Communication of 11 October 2005 from the Commission to the Council, the European Parliament and the European Economic and Social Committee on a Customs Response to Latest Trends in Counterfeiting and Piracy, Com (2005) 479 final – not published in the Official Journal, 2005

Fackler, Martin, 'Japan Fights Crowds of Crows', *The New York Times*, 7 May 2008

Feldman, Robert S., Jason C. Tomasian and Erik J. Coats, 'Nonverbal Deception Abilities and Adolescents' Social Competence: Adolescents With Higher Social Skills Are Better Liars', *Journal of Nonverbal Behavior*, vol. 23, no. 3 (Autumn 1999), pp. 237–49

Foxe, Ken, 'Gardai Crack Down on Christmas Fakes; £500,000 Illegal Goods Seized', *The Daily Mirror*, 5 December 2000

Galbraith, Robert, 'Made in Italy: Counterfeits That Were Once Mere Imports', *International Herald Tribune*, 4 October 2006

Gibson, Owen and Sachin Nakrani, 'Flavio Briatore Banned for Life for Fixing Singapore Grand Prix', *The Guardian*, 21 September 2009

Gilbert, Daniel T., Douglas S. Krull and Brett W. Pelham, 'Of Thoughts Unspoken: Social Inference and the Self-Regulation of Behavior', *Journal of Personality and Social Psychology*, vol. 55, no. 5 (November 1988), pp. 685–94

Gino, Francesca, Michael I. Norton and Dan Ariely, 'The Counterfeit Self: The Deceptive Costs of Faking It', *Psychological Science*, vol. 21, no. 4 (March 2010), pp. 1–9

Gollin, Rob, '*Wathey wekte Sint Maarten tot leven*', *de Volkskrant*, 12 January 1998

Henry, Robin, 'Tourists Warned over Fake Designer Goods', *The Times*, 22 August 2009

Horizon, 'Winning Gold in 2012', BBC, broadcast 18 March 2006.

Jarvis, Alice-Azania, 'The Science of Lying: Why the Truth Really Can Hurt', *The Independent*, 5 July 2010

Jones (ed.), Mark, *Fake? The Art of Deception*, London: British Museum Publications Ltd, 1990

Kannankutty, Nirmala, 'Unemployment Rate of U.S. Scientists and Engineers Drops to Record Low 2.5% in 2006', *Science Resources Statistics*, NSF 08-305 (revised), National Science Foundation, April 2008

Koffman, Lawrence, *Crime Surveys and Victims of Crime*, Cardiff: University of Wales Press, 1996

Larson, Charles M., *Numismatic Forgery*, Irvine, CA: Zyrus Press, 2004.

Loh, Deborah, 'Fakes Multiply as Makers Diversify', *New Straits Times* (Malaysia), 25 April 2006

NRC Handelsblad, 'ClaudeWathey (1926–1998); Absoluut vorst', 12 January 1998

NRC Handelsblad, 'Corruptierel in crickettop India', 26 April 2010

NRC Handelsblad, 'Diplomaat na borrel door 't stof', 14 September 2010

NRC Handelsblad, 'FIFA onderzoekt corruptie bestuurders voetbalbond', 18 October 2010

Office of Research Integrity, *Annual Reports*, 1998–2009, Rockville, MA: ORI

Organisation for Economic Co-operation and Development, *The Economic Impact of Counterfeiting and Piracy, Executive Summary*, Paris: OECD, 2008

Perry, David L., '"Repugnant Philosophy": Ethics, Espionage and Covert Action', *The Journal of Conflict Studies*, vol. XV, no. 1 (spring 1995), pp. 92–115

Shenker, Jack, 'Egypt's "Election" was Pure Stagecraft, Directed by a Dictator', *The Guardian*, 1 December 2010

Smith, David, 'Third of Zimbabwe's Registered Voters are Dead', *The Guardian*, 21 January 2011

Stouwdam, Henk, 'Kijkje in de duistere dopingwereld', *NRC Handelsblad*, 17 December 2009

Straaten, Floris van, 'De edele sumoworstelaars werden platte geldwolven', *NRC Handelsblad*, 17 February 2011

Van Natta Jr, Don, 'A Clinton Adviser Testifies About First Days of Lewinsky Crisis', *The New York Times*, 12 August 1998

Various sources, 2009. 'Overzicht grote dopingaffaires in Tour de France', *de Volkskrant*, 26 January 2009; Alasdair Fotheringham, 'Cycling: Stage-winner Astarloza tests Positive for Epo', *The Independent*, 1 August 2009; Kevin Eason, 'Former Bath Players found Guilty of Misconduct', *The Times*, 4 August 2009; 'International Tennis Federation wants Longer Suspension for Richard Gasquet', *The Guardian*, 7 August 2009; Michael

S. Schmidt, 'In Day of Statements, United Front Behind David Ortiz Speaks Volumes', *The New York Times*, 9 August 2009; 'Internationaal gokschandaal omvat 200 duels', *de Volkskrant*, 20 November 2009

Wall, David S. and Joanna Large, 'Jailhouse Frocks: Locating the Public Interest in Policing Counterfeit Luxury Fashion Goods', *British Journal of Criminology, Delinquency and Deviant* Social *Behaviour*, vol. 50, no. 6 (1 November 2010), pp. 1094–1116.

Woolley (ed.), David, *The Correspondence of Jonathan Swift, vol. 2: Letters 1714–1726*, Frankfurt/New York: Peter Lang, 2001

A–Z REFERENCES

1 In publications Steve Shaw is usually referred to as *Banachek*, his stage name.

2 In the somewhat grey world of legal practice, Kenealy was a colourful character. He was a poet in his spare time and translated poems from Latin, Greek, German, Italian, Portuguese, Russian, Irish, Persian, Arabic, Hindustani and Bengali. He was sentenced to a month's imprisonment for 'punishing with undue severity' his illegitimate son Edward Hyde. He also pretended to be 'the twelfth messenger of God', and to be part of a line that included Adam (rather logical for a believer, I should think), Jesus Christ and Genghis Khan (Hamilton, 2004). In the trial against ARTHUR ORTON, Kenealy slandered nearly every Roman Catholic institution he could think of, intimidated witnesses and treated the judges and members of the jury with contempt.

3 During the trial, expert witness Dr Elmer Belt was asked: 'You just do not seem to think much of the instrument, do you, Doctor Belt?' 'I couldn't even use it to amuse the children,' Dr Belt replied (Smith, 1968).

4 Von Däniken is a pseudo-scientist in the literal sense. When I tried to find out more about his education, I discovered a reference to his secondary school in the extremely selective biography on his website, but only one solitary academic achievement: an honorary doctorate awarded by La Universidad Boliviana. I cannot help but feel that he is clutching at straws when I read: 'Illustration of my honorary doctorate: *front* and *rear (with confirmations)*' (Däniken, 2009). That he emphasizes the authenticity of his honorary doctorate speaks volumes about Däniken's state of mind.

5 Roughly half of the sources I used stated Malley's oeuvre as consisting of sixteen poems, while the other half spoke of seventeen. As I was unable get hold of the original publication I cannot be sure about this.

6 Potential saints did not have to do much to be canonized by John Paul II. This pope collected them like garden gnomes. During his pontificate he beatified or canonized some 1,800 people. His predecessors had taken about five centuries to reach the same tally.

7 This is incidentally hearsay. Einstein himself never put this to paper.

8 When visiting the organization's website I came across one of the strangest buttons I have ever seen on a site: *Request Prayer Online*. You can also call: 1-800-NOW-PRAY.

9 By 1945 the U.S. Army comprised 9 million men, and throughout the conflict tanks and aircraft had rolled non-stop off the production line.

10 The group had several members who would later make their mark in their own professions, including Ellsworth Kelly (1923, painter), Louis Dalton Porter (1919–2006, visual artist), Art Kane (1925–1995, photographer) and Bill Blass (1922–2002, fashion designer).

11 To achieve this the group had 100 of the largest loudspeakers in production at the time: each one took up a whole army truck.

12 As regular soldiers the men of the Ghost Army were no match for the Germans. Though they had been given basic training, with the exception of a small group, they were very inadequately armed.

13 Although there were many rumours circulating during his lifetime, it was only in the years after Hughes's death on 5 April 1976 that it became clear how much his mental illness had influenced his life. In the last ten to fifteen years of his life, the billionaire would walk around naked wearing Kleenex boxes for shoes in his hotel rooms, which were empty except for a mattress on the floor. His hair and nails were cut once a year. Hughes was so afraid of being infected that he insisted on using thick layers of tissues to pick up objects and described the procedures for doing so down to the last ridiculous detail. In April 1976 the pathologist found that Hughes only weighed 41 kg at the time of his death. Hughes was heavily addicted to opiates and x-rays revealed that his body was full of broken-off hypodermic needles.

14 The term 'pseudo-lama' is itself problematic, as it suggests that there are also real lamas. This is the same problem as with RELICS. Can a lama be real? Yes, in as much as it refers to someone who is a Buddhist teacher. No, if it refers to reaching a certain 'spiritual level' or to a person who is an incarnation of a previous lama, as in the case of the Dalai Lama.

15 Fellow forger Theo van Wijngaarden may have helped produce these works.

16 One school of Holy Lance enthusiasts claim that Hitler had the 'real' lance buried at the end of the Second World War, after which it was found by the Americans. This explains America's current status as the leading world power. Unfortunately, it does not explain why Hitler lost the war.

17 After this drama unfolded, one of the players did have a book published. Savannah Knoop's account, *Girl Boy Girl: How I Became JT LeRoy,* came out in 2008.

18 I would like to make it clear that a single illusion or hallucination is not necessarily a symptom of a sick brain. My literature study showed that of 134 Marian apparitions there were indications of psychic pathology in only four cases.

19 A sceptic might of course be justified in asking why Mary would make this now superfluous announcement fourteen years after the announcement of the dogma, rather than a century before it.

20 For the sake of completeness I would like to note that psychiatry now has a reasonable, if still hypothetical, explanation for Soubirous's hallucinations. Raised by three different mother figures, she had spent

several enjoyable years living with her godmother when, a few weeks before seeing the first apparition, she had to return to her natural parents in Lourdes, in a household ruled by drink, cold and lice where she did not know whether the next meal would appear on the table. The apparition was perhaps an idealization of her godmother, a hypothesis supported by her calling out 'Mother! Mother! How can I leave you?' during one of her last visits to the grotto before entering a convent and being forbidden to speak ever again of her experiences (Carroll, 1985).

21 Interestingly enough, this text was recently changed. Smith may well be the prophet who read the golden plates, but the current leaders obviously know better. The new text reads that the Indians have the chance to become 'a pure and a delightsome people', which sounds marginally less racist.

22 Schiaparelli (1835–1910) deserves an endnote, if only to illustrate how a small error can lead to serious nonsense. The Italian astronomer observed the planet Mars in 1877 and discovered that the surface was covered with channel-like lines. He did not know how they were caused, by erosion perhaps or meteorite impacts. In describing his findings, he used the Italian word *canali*. Although *canali* can be caused naturally, writers in English tended to translate them as 'canals', which are the product of human intervention. And so the Martians were born.

23 On 24 August 2006 the International Astronomical Union decided that Pluto was not a planet. Together with Ceres and Xena, it would be referred to as a dwarf planet. In June 2008, the IAU announced that the term 'dwarf planet' would be replaced by 'plutoid', marking the penetration of politically correct use of language into deep space.

24 Transitional fossils are of great importance in the theory of evolution. Creationists sometimes use the fact that they are seldom found to argue against the theory of evolution. The rarity of these fossils, however, is easy to explain: intermediate varieties only exist for a relatively short period of time, as they are soon supplanted by the species into which they evolve.

25 The theory of evolution has not had an easy ride. For much of the twentieth century many states had statutes prohibiting the teaching of the theory in schools. These statutes were declared illegal in 1968, after the Supreme Court case of Epperson v. Arkansas.

26 Opponents of intelligent design often do not agree with the first part of this statement, that the world is perfectly constructed. Anyone who has a house built that turns out to be of the same quality as the human body, for example, would be perfectly entitled to sue the architect and the builder for breach of contract. That our bodies are not the product of 'intelligent design' should be obvious from superfluous components like the hymen, goose pimples, the clitoris, male nipples, the vestiges of a third eyelid in the corners of our eyes and wisdom teeth.

27 The supporters of intelligent design have proved very reluctant to initiate research into the limitations of evolution. Around the turn of the century, the Templeton Institute invited them to submit research proposals and offered to fund the research. No proposals were received.

28 A good example of the erroneous use of fudge-factoring. The number 25 was actually chosen because this division resulted in an outcome close to an inch. 'Being close to' something and then seeing an intention in it is anything but scientific.

29 Dutch astronomer Cornelis de Jager made a merciless parody of this kind of pseudo-mathematics in 1990. De Jager introduced Velosofie (Cyclosophy), a mathematical system in which all physical constants could be traced back to three measurements of De Jager's bicycle, which he referred to as the '*Heilige Fietsduim*' (HFD), the 'Sacred Bicycle Unit'.

30 In 1520, for example, St Salvator's church in Utrecht was hunting for relics of St Boniface. The church's records state that it 'exchanged part of the right upper arm of St Frederick for a piece of the jaw of St Boniface' (De Kruijf, 2009). Hopefully, the church of origin also kept accurate records.

31 In the words of a 2007 United Nations report, 'Guatemala is a good place to kill' (Franklin, 2010).

32 A possible third deception by Newton was the unlikely story of how a falling apple in his parents' orchard had inspired him to formulate the theory of gravity. The credibility of his claim is cast into doubt by the fact that Newton had not visited the orchard for at least twenty years before he developed the theory. The fact that he only added this detail to the story when he was older also suggests it is a fabrication. Perhaps he was trying to antedate his discovery so as to deny the possibility of his being influenced by his contemporaries.

33 Others who sold the bridge include the Gondorf brothers, William McCloundy (aka I.O.U. O'Brien) and Reed C. Waddell.

34 Vanity press is often seen as a synonym for printing on demand. There are indeed great similarities but there is also one major difference of principle. A vanity press earns only from the sale of books to the author, while in the case of printing on demand there is, at least in theory, the possibility that others than the author will also buy the book.

35 Author Natalie Koch said of the phrase 'I am so silky and braid shoulders', 'it is of such immeasurable poetic beauty that I am going to start using the "random selection" method' (Koch, 2009).

A–Z SOURCES

ADOLF HITLER, SECRET AGENT

Sam Roberts, 'The Nation: And Maybe Stalin Was a Kulak?', *The New York Times*, 17 February 2002.

ALBERT EINSTEIN COULDN'T FIGURE IT OUT

Christoph Meier, 'Research off the rails', *ETH Life*, 29 April 2004, http://archiv.ethlife.ethz.ch/e/articles/campuslife/faelschungendiek.html, 3 October 2009.

THE ALPHA PROJECT AT THE MCLAB

William J. Broad, 'Magician's Effort to Debunk Scientists Raises Ethical Issues', *The New York Times*, 15 February 1983. *James Randi* (pseudonym of Randall James Hamilton Zwinge), 'The Project Alpha Experiment: Part 1. The First Two Years', *Skeptical Inquirer*, vol. 7, no. 5 (summer 1983), pp. 24–33. *James Randi* (pseudonym of Randall James Hamilton Zwinge), 'The Project Alpha Experiment: Part 2. Beyond the Laboratory', *Skeptical Inquirer*, vol. 8, no. 1 (autumn 1983), pp. 36–45. Michael A. Thalbourne, 'Science Versus Showmanship: A History of the Randi Hoax', *The Journal of the American Society for Psychical Research*, vol. 89 (October 1995), pp. 344–66.

ARSENIC QUEEN AUDREY HILLEY AND THE TWIN WHO NEVER WAS

'Fugitive in Poisonings May Change Personalities; Warrant Issued by FBI.', *The New York Times*, 16 October 1980. 'Murder, death plot catch up with woman', *Free Lance-Star*, 9 June 1983. 'Woman Found Guilty in Family Killing, Poisoning', *The Washington Post*, 9 June 1983. 'Husband-Killer Dies of Exposure After Escape; "Black Widow" Caught in Her Own Web', *Los Angeles Times*, 27 February 1987. David Randall, 'Faking it: How to do a Reggie and get away with it', *The Independent*, 20 July 2008.

ARTHUR ORTON, TICHBORNE CLAIMANT

Rohan McWilliam, 'Tichborne claimant (*d.* 1898)', *Oxford Dictionary of National Biography*, Oxford University Press, 2004, online edition October 2007, www.oxforddnb.com/view/article/20855, 18 June 2008. J. A. Hamilton and rev. Rohan McWilliam, 'Kenealy, Edward Vaughan Hyde (1819–1880)', *Oxford Dictionary of National Biography*, Oxford: Oxford University Press, September 2004, www.oxforddnb.com/view/article/15356, 11 April 2011.

ASHLEY TODD AND SOMETHING ODD

'On the trail', *Los Angeles Times*, 24 October 2008. 'Probation for McCain volunteer in fake PA Attack', *The Washington Post*, 22 May 2009. 'Pennsylvania: Probation for False Claim of Attack', *The New York Times*, 22 May 2009.

ASTROTURF – PLANTED OPINIONS

John Grant, *Corrupted Science*, Wisley: FF&F, 2007. Paul Krugman, 'Tea Parties Forever', *The New York Times*, 12 April 2009. George Monbiot, 'Climate denial "astroturfers" should stop hiding behind pseudonyms online', *George Monbiot's Blog*, 8 July 2009, www.guardian.co.uk/environment/georgemonbiot/2009/jul/08/climate-denial-astroturfers-pseudonyms, 9 July 2009.

BARONESS MURPHY'S CELLO SCROTUM

J. M. Murphy, 'Cello scrotum', *British Medical Journal*, vol. 2, no. 5914 (11 May 1974), p. 335. Elaine Murphy, John M. Murphy, 'Cello scrotum confession – Murphy's lore', *British Medical Journal*, vol. 338, no. 4 (27 January 2009), p. b288. Will Pavia, 'Cello scrotum? It's a load of . . . nonsense, admits Baroness Murphy', *The Times*, 28 January 2009. Jeremy Laurance, 'Exposed: the myth of cello scrotum', *The Independent*, 28 January 2009.

BECCAH BEUSHAUSEN AND HER BABY DOLL

David Usborne, 'Heroine of the anti-abortion lobby is exposed as a fantasist', *The Guardian*, 17 June 2009. Tom Leonard, 'Hoaxer apologises for "dying baby" blog', *The Independent*, 17 June 2009.

BERINGER'S TABLETS, THE LYING STONES

Melvin E. Jahn and Daniel J. Woolf (translated and annotated), *The Lying Stones of Dr. Johann Bartholomew Adam Beringer, being his Lithographiae Wirceburgensis*, Berkeley, CA: University of California Press, 1963.

BMW BIG BOY GOES BACK TO SCHOOL

Tom Jackman, '"Spielberg" Says Charges Are Untrue', *The Washington Post*, 13 January 2000. William P. Barrett, 'The Fakes', *Forbes Magazine*, 10 September 2004.

C. F. GOLDIE, TOWN PAINTER

'Art gallery proud to exhibit a fake', *The Timaru Herald*, 22 August 1997. 'Forger guest stars at exhibition', *The New Zealand Herald*, 8 September 2007.

THE CAPTAIN OF KÖPENICK

Paul Wietzorek, '100 Jahre "Hauptmann" von Köpenick – 1906-2006', *Die Heimat*, no. 77 (2006), pp. 169–71. George Malcolm Thomson, *The Twelve Days: 24 July to 4 August 1914*, London: Hutchinson & Co., 1964.

CHARLEY PARKHURST, STAGECOACH QUEEN

Ed Sams, *The Real Mountain Charley*, Ben Lomond: Yellow Tulip Press, 1995.

A CHRISTIAN MARTYR IN THE COLUMBINE MASSACRE

Werner Eeman, *Jong maar niet onschuldig: moordende tieners*, Baarn: Tirion, 2007. Greg Toppo, '10 years later, the real story behind Columbine', *USA Today*, 13 April 2009. *Cassie Bernall Website*, www.cassierenebernall.org, 25 April 2010.

CHRISTINE JOY MAGGIORE, AIDS DENIALIST

'Autopsy Report, 2005-03767, Scovill, Eliza', County of Los Angeles, Department of Coroner, 18 May 2005. John Moore and Nicoli Nattrass, 'Deadly Quackery', *The New York Times*, 4 June 2006. Anna Gorman and Alexandra Zavis, 'Christine Maggiore, vocal skeptic of aids research, dies at 52', *Los Angeles Times*, 30 December 2008. 'Editorial: Christine Maggiore and the price of skepticism', *The Los Angeles Times*, 3 January 2009. Ben Goldacre, 'Will stupid people and their pseudoscience cost more lives this year?', *The Guardian*, 3 January 2009. 'Certificate of Death Christine Joy Maggiore', County of Los Angeles, Department of Health Services, state file number 3052008227242, Los Angeles file number 3200819054037, 24 February 2009.

CLAUDIUS PTOLEMY, NOT QUITE THE RHODES SCHOLAR

Robert R. Newton, *The Crime of Claudius Ptolemy*, Baltimore, MA: The Johns Hopkins University Press, 1977.

CLIFTON JAMES, THESPIAN, AND HIS NAZI FOLLOWERS

M.E. Clifton James, *I Was Monty's Double*, London: The Popular Book Club, 1957. John Guillermin (director), *I Was Monty's Double*, Film Traders Ltd./Setfair Productions, 1958. (DVD release: 2007, Optimum Home Entertainment.) Ben Macintyre, 'Revealed: Nazi spy duped by failed actor in "Monty's Double" hoax', *The Times*, 8 March 2010.

CLUELESS KRUGEL COPS OUT

Transcription of *Carte Blanche*, episode 'Fingerprint of Fate', M-Net, broadcast on 29 July 2007. Ben Goldacre, 'After Madeleine, why not Bin Laden?', *The Guardian*, 13 October 2007.

COLLECTING REINHOLD VASTERS

John Russell, 'As Long As Men Make Art, The Artful Fake Will Be With Us', *The New York Times*, 12 February 1984. Yvonne Hackenbroch, 'Reinhold Vasters, Goldsmith', *Metropolitan Museum Journal*, vol. 19 (1984–1985), pp. 163–268. Pamela Kessler, 'Mimicking the Masters: Fabulous Frauds on View at the Walters', *The Washington Post*, 28 October 1987. Jones (ed.), Mark, *Fake? The Art of Deception*, London: British Museum Publications Ltd, 1990. William H. Honan, 'Forging Ahead in the Art World', *The New York Times*, 19 May 1996.

COMMON NAMES TO CONJURE WITH IN THE NEW CHINA

'Faking it', *The Economist*, vol. 379, no. 8478 (20 May 2006), p. 83.

COUNTERFEIT MEDICINES

Nicki Padayachee, 'Fake medicines flood local market', *The Sunday Times* (South Africa), 3 November 2002. Carey Sargent, 'Fake drugs are creating real dangers for consumers', *The International Herald Tribune*, 18 March 2006. Donald G. McNeil Jr., 'Phony life-saving drugs leaving thousands dead; Fake-medication epidemic spreading in Asia', *The International Herald Tribune*, 21 February 2007. Walt Bogdanich, 'Traffic in fake drugs takes free-trade route; Zones in Emirates help mask origin', *The International Herald Tribune*, 18 December 2007. *Fake Britain*, episode 'Fake Medicines', BBC, broadcast on 12 July 2010.

CRIMINAL MILKMEN

'Doodstraffen in schandaal babyvoeding', *NRC Handelsblad*, 22 January 2009. Oscar Garschagen, 'Onze kinderen zijn ernstig beschadigd', *NRC Handelsblad*, 10 April 2009. 'China executeert melkvervuilers', *NRC Handelsblad*, 24 November 2009. 'Opnieuw Chinese melk vergiftigd', *NRC Handelsblad*, 2 February 2010. 'Veel blijvende nierschade door gifmelk China', *NRC Handelsblad*, 23 February 2010. 'China gooit melkactivist 2,5 jaar cel in', *de Volkskrant*, 11 November 2010. 'China sluit helft van melkfabrieken', *NRC Handelsblad*, 4 April 2011.

D-DAY DECEPTION DIDN'T END BACK THEN

Richard Weir, 'Phony paratrooper to be feted by French, D-Day vet "misrepresented his service"', *Boston Herald*, 6 June 2009. 'U.S. veteran's D-Day lies exposed', *BBC News*, 8 July 2009, www.news.bbc.co.uk/go/pr/fr/-/2/hi/europe/8139909.stm,

8 July 2009. Frank Renout, 'Oorlogsveteraan verzon heldendaden', *Algemeen Dagblad*, 9 July 2009.

DANIEL GOLDREYER, ART RESTORER ON A ROLL

'Bijna twee ton voor Goldreyer', *Trouw*, Saturday 11 January 1997. 'Who's afraid of red, yellow and blue?', www.forensischinstituut.nl/NFI/nl/Mysterie+opgelost/Whos+afraid+of. htm, 5 December 2007; webpage no longer accessible.

DEREK ATKINS, THE VERY FISHY MARINER

Emma Bamford, 'Gutted! The fisherman caught faking his death', *The Independent*, 6 February 2009. '"Dead" fisherman – Derek Atkins – jailed for 30 months', *Fish update*, 12 February 2009, www.fishupdate.com, 11 March 2009. 'Thirty months for fisherman who faked death to escape £1m fines', *The Daily Mail*, 13 February 2009.

DISMEMBERING *MICHELLE REMEMBERS*

Denna Allen and Janet Midwinter, 'Michelle Remembers: The Debunking of a Myth', *The Mail on Sunday*, 30 September 1990. Frank W. Putnam, 'The Satanic Ritual Abuse Controversy', *Child Abuse & Neglect*, vol. 15, no. 3 (1991), pp. 175–9. F. Jonker, P. Jonker-Bakker, 'Experiences With Ritualist Child Sexual Abuse: A Case Study From The Netherlands', *Child Abuse & Neglect*, vol. 15, no. 3 (1991), pp. 191–6. Richard Singelenberg, 'Een therapeutische Nouvelle Cuisine', *Skepter*, vol. 5, no. 2 (June 1992), www.skepsis.nl/srm.html, 26 November 2009. Frits Abrahams, 'Oude Pekela revisited', *NRC Handelsblad*, 28 May 1994. 'Klacht na vermeend misbruik', *Trouw*, 20 May 2009. Marcel Haenen, 'Geld voor kind in affaire Bolderkar', *NRC Handelsblad*, 28 April 2010.

DOLLAR DUPLICITY, NORTH KOREAN STYLE

Christopher Drew and Stephen Engelberg, 'Super-Counterfeit $100's Baffle U.S.', *The New York Times*, 27 February 1996. 'Obituary: Yoshimi Tanaka', *The Japan Times*, 3 January 2007. David Rose, 'North Korea's Dollar Store', *Vanity Fair*, 5 August 2009, www.vanityfair.com/politics/features/2009/09/office-39-200909?currentPage=1, 18 December 2009. David Samuels, 'Counterfeiting: Notes on a scandal', *The Independent*, 24 August 2009.

DROWN! BATHTUB TIPS FOR STAYING MAGNETIC

Misbranding of Drown Radio Therapeutic Instrument. U.S. v. Ruth B. Drown (Drown Laboratories), F.D.C. No. 29440 [1951]. Ralph Lee Smith, 'The Incredible Drown Case', originally published in *Today's Health*, April 1968, www.chirobase.org/12Hx/drown.html, 2 October 2009. John Grant, *Corrupted Science*, Wisley: FF&F, 2007.

EBAY'S ALTERNATIVE REALITY

John Naughton, 'A handbag? eBay is going to have to be more earnest', *The Observer*, 6 July 2008. 'L'Oréal accuses eBay over sale of counterfeit cosmetics', *The Guardian*, 9 March 2009. Peter van Ammelrooy, 'Angst archeologen voor eBay "onterecht"', *de Volkskrant*, 10 May 2009. Rebecca Smithers, 'Paris court rules that eBay is not liable for sale of fake L'Oréal products', *The Guardian*, 13 May 2009. 'Boete eBay om valse parfums', *NRC Handelsblad*, 19 September 2009.

ELMYR DE HORY AND THE ART OF LIVING WELL

Clifford Irving, *Fake! The Story of Elmyr de Hory, the Greatest Art Forger of Our Time*, New York: McGraw-Hill, 1969. 'Fakes and forgeries: catalogue of an exhibition, the Minneapolis Institute of Arts, July 11-September 29, 1973', Minneapolis: Minneapolis Institute of Arts, 1973. Orson Welles (director), *F for Fake* (original title: *Vérités et mensonges*), Janus Film/Les Film de l'Apostrophe/ saci, 1974. 'Elmyr de Hory Is Dead at 65; Known as a Master Forger of Modern Art; A Master Imitator', *The New York Times*, 12 December 1976. 'Police Report Art Forger, Facing Extradition Order, Killed Himself on Ibiza', *The New York Times*, 13 December 1976. 'Top art forger has his own work forged', *The Straits Times* (Singapore), 31 December 2000.

EMIL ABDERHALDEN AND HIS UNREPEATABLE EXPERIMENTS

Ute Deichmann, Benno Müller-Hill, 'The Fraud of Abderhalden's enzymes', *Nature*, vol. 393, no. 6681 (14 May 1998), pp. 109–11.

ERICH VON DÄNIKEN'S ALIEN BELIEFS

Heyerdahl, Thor, *Aku-Aku*, Lochem: De Tijdstroom, [n.d.] Patrick Huyghe, 'UFO update: The rise, fall, and afterlife of Erich von Daniken's theory of extra-terrestrial gods', *Omni*, vol.18, no. 8 (May 1994), p. 77. Anthony F. Aveni, 'Solving the Mystery of the Nasca Lines', *Archaeology*, vol. 53, no. 3 (May–June 2000), pp. 26–36. Richard Owen, 'They came from outer space – and posed for portraits', *The Times*, 3 December 2002. 'Charioteer Of the Gods', *Skeptic*, vol. 10, no. 4 (January 2004), pp. 36–8. 'Insolvent Mysteries', *Archaeology*, vol. 60, no. 2 (March-April 2007), p. 14.

ERN MALLEY, AUSTRALIA'S BELOVED BOGUS POET

Robert Winder, 'Book Review: The importance of being in earnest: "The Ern Malley Affair" – Michael Heyward', *The Independent*, 13 August 1993. Peter Porter, 'Book Review: Sting in the tale of Ern: "The Ern Malley Affair" – Michael Hayward', *The Independent on Sunday*, 15 August 1993. Cassandra Atherton, '"Fuck All Editors": The Ern Malley Affair and Gwen Harwood's *Bulletin* Scandal', *Journal of Australian Studies*, vol. 26, no. 72 (2002), pp. 149–57. Website in honour of Ern Malley, www.ernmalley.com, 3 June 2009.

FAKE PILGRIMAGE

'Neppelgrims smokkelen cocaïne', *de Volkskrant*, 12 May 2010.

FATSO FARNAM, THE FARE-DODGING FOODIE FRAUDSTER

Crocker Stephenson, 'Cardiac arrest: Man faked heart attack when dinner bill arrived', *Journal Sentinel*, 4 July 2008. 'Man Fakes Heart Attack to Bail on Bill, Cab Fare', FoxNews, 4 July 2008, www.foxnews.com/story/0,2933,376621,00.html, 22 July 2010. 'Man faces another medical fakery charge', *Journal Sentinel*, 17 July 2008.

THE FILM FESTIVAL THAT NEVER WAS

'Mysterieuze muziekprijs', NRC *Handelsblad*, 18 February 2010.

FINDING THE PAST WITH HERR PROFESSOR PROTSCH

Matthias von Schulz, 'Mogelei im Knochenkeller', *Der Spiegel*, 11 October 2004. Luke Harding, 'History of modern man unravels as German scholar is exposed as fraud', *The Guardian*, 19 February 2005. 'Look Before You Date', *Archeology*, vol. 58, no. 3 (May–June 2005), pp. 15–16. 'Professor als Fälscher und Betruger angeklagt', *Frankfurter Allgemeine Zeitung*, 21 July 2006. 'Schädelfälscher zu Bewährungsstrafe verurteilt', *Der Spiegel*, 19 June 2009.

THE FIRST HUMAN CLONE

Barbara J. Culliton, 'Scientists Dispute Book's Claim That Human Clone Has Been Born', *Science*, vol. 199, no. 4335 (24 March 1978), pp. 1314–16. William J. Broad, 'Saga of Boy Clone Ruled a Hoax', *Science*, vol. 211, no. 4485 (27 February 1981), p. 902. William J. Broad, 'Publisher Settles Suit, Says Clone Book is a Fake', *Science*, vol. 216, no. 4544 (23 April 1982), p. 391.

A FISHY PRISON HOAX

Comte F. de Castelnau, 'On a New Ganoid Fish from Queensland', *Proceedings of the Linnean Society of New South Wales*, vol. 1, no. 3 (1879), pp. 164–5. Gilbert P. Whitley, 'Ompax spatuloides Castelnau, a Mythical Australian Fish', *The American Naturalist*, vol. 67, no. 713 (November–December 1933), p. 563–7. G. P. Whitley, 'Laporte, François Louis Nompar de Caumont (1810–1880)', *Australian Dictionary of Biography*, Volume 5, Melbourne: Melbourne University Press, 1974.

FORGERS DONATE WORKS TO STOCKHOLM'S MOMA

Marla Harper, 'Something Smelled', *The Washington Post*, 15 November 1993.

A FORGER OF FORGED ART

Joseph P. Fried, 'At Factory For Art, Freelancing Is Charged', *The New York Times*, 16 July 1993. Geordie Greig, 'Artist goes to court over "faked fake"', *The Sunday Times*, 15 August 1993. Joseph P. Fried, 'Salesman for Studio Is Convicted In Forging of Artist's Signature', *The New York Times*, 16 December 1993. Ruth La Ferla, 'His Mouth Runneth Over', *The New York Times*, 3 February 2002.

ST FRANCESCO FORGIONE AND HIS BOTTLED STIGMATA

Peter Popham, 'Padre Pio "faked his stigmata with acid"', *The Independent*, 25 October 2007. Cole Moreton, 'The strange case of Padre Pio is reopened, along with his tomb', *The Independent*, 9 March 2008. Peter Popham, 'Thousands queue to see corpse of Padre Pio', *The Independent*, 25 April 2008. Peter Popham, 'The Big Question: Who was Padre Pio, and why is he the cause of such controversy?', *The Independent*, 25 April 2008. Biography of Forgione on the Vatican website, www.vatican.va/roman curia/congregations/csaints/docments/rc-concsaints-doc-19990502-padre-pio-en.html, 17 June 2008. Nick Squires, 'Italy to build solar-energy-producing statue of saint', *The Telegraph*, 5 August 2009.

FRENCH: THE LINGUA FRANCA OF EVERYONE ELSE

Joseph Rosenblum, *Prince of Forgers*, New Castle: Oak Knoll Press, 1998. Ken Alder, 'History's Greatest Forger: Science, Fiction, and Fraud along the Seine', *Critical Inquiry*, vol. 30, no. 4 (summer 2004), pp. 702–16.

FRIEDERICH LICHTENBERGER AND THE MEDUSA WATER

Mark Rose, 'When Giants Roamed the Earth', *Archaeology*, vol. 58, no. 6 (November/December 2005), pp. 30–35.

FUDGE-FACTORING THE UNIVERSE

Donald Goldsmith, *Einstein's Greatest Blunder? The Cosmological Constant and Other Fudge Factors in the Physics of the Universe*, Cambridge, MA: Harvard University Press, 1997. Richard S. Westfall, 'Newton and the Fudge Factor', *Science*, vol. 179, no. 4075 (23 February 1973), pp. 751–8.

FURNITURE FAKERS GO VIRAL

Piet Swimberghe, 'Zo goed als oud', *Knack*, 31 October 2007.

GAZA CITY ZOO'S AMAZING ZEBRAS

'Gaza maakt zelf zijn eigen zebra's', NRC *Handelsblad*, 9 October 2009.

A GENUINE LETTER FROM BEYOND THE GRAVE

Amir Vehabović and Michael Leidig (trans.), 'Slight of the Living Dead', *Harper's Magazine*, October 2007.

GET BETTER PRAYERS

Mitchell W. Krucoff, MD, Suzanne W. Crater, RN, ANP-C, Cindy L. Green Phd *et al.*, 'Integrative noetic therapies as adjuncts to percutaneous intervention during unstable coronary syndromes: Monitoring and Actualization of Noetic Training (mantra) feasibility pilot', *American Heart Journal*, vol. 142, no. 5 (November 2001), pp. 760–69. 'Mantra II: measuring the unmeasurable', *Lancet*, vol. 366, no. 9481 (16 July 2005), p. 178. Mitchell W. Krucoff, Suzanne W. Crater, Dianne Gallup, *et al.*, 'Music, imagery, touch, and prayer as adjuncts to interventional cardiac care: the Monitoring and Actualisation of Noetic Trainings (mantra) II randomised study', *Lancet*, vol. 366, no. 9481 (16 July 2005), pp. 211–17. Herbert Benson, MD, Jeffery A. Dusek, Phd, Jane B. Sherwood, RN, *et al.*, 'Study of the Therapeutic Effects of Intercessory Prayer (step) in cardiac bypass patients: A multicenter randomized trial of uncertainty and certainty of receiving intercessory prayer', *American Heart Journal*, vol. 151, no. 4 (April 2006), pp. 934–42. John Grant, *Corrupted Science*, Wisley: FF&F, 2007.

GHOST ARMY: 23RD HEADQUARTERS SPECIAL TROOPS

Jack Kneece, *Ghost Army of World War II*, Gretna: Pelican Publishing Company, 2001. Joe Holley, 'Louis Dalton Porter; Used Artistic Skills to Trick German Army', *The Washington Post*, 8 July 2006.

GHOSTING AN AUTOBIOGRAPHY, CLIFFORD IRVING STYLE

Michael Drosnin, *Citizen Hughes*, London: Arrow Books Limited, 1986. Clifford Irving, *The Hoax*, New York: Hyperion, 2006. Clifford Irving, *Howard Hughes: The Autobiography*, London: John Blake, 2008. Website Clifford Irving, www.cliffordirving.com, 8 June 2008.

GRABBING BONBONS BY THE TRUCKLOAD

Angelique Chrisafis, 'Monsieur, with these Rocher you would not be spoiling us', *The Guardian*, 24 December 2008.

GREAT QUOTES FROM A PLUMBER

Agehananda Bharati, 'Fictitious Tibet: The Origin and Persistence of Rampaism', *Tibet Society Bulletin*, vol. 7 (1974), www.serendipity.li/baba/rampa.html, 22 October 2009. Rampa, Lobsang (pseudonym van Cyril Henry Hoskins), *The Third Eye*, [n.p.], [n.d.], www.lobsangrampa.org/research.html, 22 October 2009. Rampa, Lobsang (pseudonym of Cyril Henry Hoskins), *The Rampa Story*, [n.p.], 1960, www.lobsangrampa.org/research.html, 22 October 2009. Christopher Fowler, 'Forgotten Authors: No. 9: T Lobsang Rampa', *The Times*, 12 October 2008. Website *Tuesday Lobsang Rampa*, www.lobsangrampa.org/index.html, 22 October 2009. J. Randi, 'Rampa, Tuesday Lobsang', in *An Encyclopedia of Claims, Frauds, and Hoaxes of the Occult and Supernatural*, New York: St. Martin's Griffin, 1997. K. Robert Todd Carroll, 'T. Lobsang Rampa', *The Skeptic's Dictionary*, www.skepdic.com/rampa.html, 22 October 2009.

THE GULF IN THE WAR EVIDENCE

Stephen Fidler, 'U.S., British claims relied on fake documents, ElBaradei tells UN', *The Irish Times*, 8 March 2003. Dana Priest and Susan Schmidt, 'FBI Probes Fake Evidence of Iraqi Nuclear Plans', *The Washington Post*, 13 March 2003. Stephen Grey, 'MI6 duped by "childlike" forgeries', *The Sunday Times*, 16 March 2003. Declan Walsh, 'No answers to questions on blatant forgeries that helped spur Iraq war', *The Irish Times*, 5 August 2003.

GWEN HARWOOD, HOUSEWIFE AND POETESS

Cassandra Atherton, '"Fuck All Editors": The Ern Malley Affair and Gwen Harwood's *Bulletin* Scandal', *Journal of Australian Studies*, vol. 26, no. 72 (2002), pp. 149–57. 'Richard King on faking it', *Weekend Australian*, 31 March 2007.

HAMBURG'S TERRACOTTA WARRIORS

Gisela Schutte, 'Terrakotta-Krieger sind illegale Kopien', *Die Zeit*, 10 December 2007. Kate Connolly, 'Fake warriors "art crime of decade", say German critics', *The Guardian*, 13 December 2007. Gisela Schutte, 'Über den Schaden von Fälschungen im Museum', *Die Zeit*, 21 February 2008.

HAN VAN MEEGEREN, THE VERMEER FORGER WHO FOOLED THE NAZIS

Hope B. Werness, 'Han van Meegeren fecit', in Dennis Dutton (ed.), *The Forger's Art: Forgery and the Philosophy of Art*, Berkeley, CA: University of California Press, 1983. Frederik H. Kreuger, *Han van Meegeren. Meestervervalser*, Diemen: Veen Magazines, 2004. Neil Hanson, 'Painting himself into a corner', *The Sunday Times*, 27 August 2006. Edward Dolnick, *The Forger's Spell: A True Story of Vermeer, Nazis, and the Greatest Art Hoax of the Twentieth Century*, New York: Harper, 2008. Errol Morris, 'The Nazi Aesthetic' ('Bamboozling Ourselves', part 3), *The Times*, 31 May 2009.

THE HAND-CRANK BANK

'Glozel Takes a Place Among Historic Fakes', *The New York Times*, 28 October 1928.

HARVARD'S 'PRINCE OF CHARLATANS'

Edward Lurie, 'Louis Agassiz and the Races of Man', *Isis*, vol. 45, no. 3 (September 1954), pp. 227–42. Stephen Jay Gould, *The Mismeasure of Man*, revised and expanded edition, London, etc.: Penguin Books, 1996. Edward Lurie, 'Louis Agassiz', *American National Biography Online*, February 2000, www.anb.org/articles/13/13- 00016.html, 8 July 2009. Reginald Horsman, 'Nott, Josiah Clark', *American National Biography Online*, February 2000, www.anb. org/articles/12/12-00671.html, 8 July 2009. Horace Freeland Judson, *The Great Betrayal: Fraud in Science*, Orlando, etc.: Harcourt, Inc., 2004.

HEINRICH SCHLIEMANN AND THE TREASURE TROVE OF TROY

Marcel C. Lafollette, *Stealing into Print: Fraud, Plagiarism, and Misconduct in Scientific Publishing*, Berkeley, CA: University of California Press, 1992.

HELENE HEGEMANN, A REAL LITERARY MIXER-UPPER

Tony Paterson, 'Publish and be damned: Young writer's ego dramatically punctured', *The Independent*, 19 February 2010.

THE HOLY LANCE – THE ONE AND THE MANY

Laura Hibbard Loomis, 'The Holy Relics of Charlemagne and King Athelstan: The Lances of Longinus and St. Mauricius', *Speculum*, vol. 25, no. 4 (October 1950), pp. 437–56. Howard L. Adelson, 'The Holy Lance and the Hereditary German Monarchy', *The Art Bulletin*, vol. 48, no. 2 (June 1966), pp. 177–92. 'Discovery of the Holy Lance', *History Today*, vol. 48, no. 6 (June 1998), p. 38. Core Design, *Tomb Raider: Chronicles*, [n.p.], Eidos Interactive, 2000.

HONEST ABE'S FORGED SPEECHES

Andrew Ferguson, 'What Al Wishes Abe Said', *The Washington Post*, 10 June 2007.

HOW THE NUMBERS ADD UP IN HOMEOPATHY

Mark Traa, 'Homeopathie', *Trouw*, 8 January 1997. Marc Meuleman, 'Homeopathie: wetenschap of geloof?', *Eos-magazine*, no. 10 (October 1998), www.skepsis.nl/eoshomeo.html, 24 October 2009. Marcel Hulspas and Jan Willem Nienhuys, *Tussen waarheid & waanzin – een encyclopedie der pseudo-wetenschappen*, Breda: De Geus, 2002. 'Homeopathie is "uit" bij huisartsen', *de Volkskrant*, 24 October 2009.

HUBERT-JOSEPH HENRY AND THE DREYFUS AFFAIR

Rowland Strong, 'Latest Doings In Paris: Another Dreyfus Mystery', *The New York Times*, 20 March 1898. 'De Dreyfus-zaak', *Utrechtsch Nieuwsblad*, 26 May 1899. Chapman, Guy,*The Dreyfus Case, A Reassessment*, London: Rupert Hart-Davis, 1955. 'Joseph Henry (1846-1898)', *1906 Dreyfus Réhabilité*, www.dreyfus.culture.fr/fr/bio/bio-html-joseph-henry.htm, 16 April 2011.

JESUS DROPS A LINE

Walter Bauer, *Orthodoxy and Heresy in Earliest Christianity, edited and supplemented by Robert A. Kraft and Gerhard Kroedel*, Philadelphia: Fortress Press, 1971. Eusebius Caesariensis, *The ecclesiastical history, I. With an English translation by Kirsopp Lake. II. With an English translation. by J. E. L. Oulton, taken from the ed. publ. in conjunction with H. J. Lawlor*, Cambridge, MA: Cambridge University Press, 1980.

JOBSEEKING, GERT POSTEL STYLE

Harald Merkelbach, 'Een postbode wordt psychiater', *Skepter*, vol. 17, no. 3 (autumn 2004), pp. 8–12.

J. R. BRINKLEY, THE TESTICULAR QUACK

Richard Newnham, *The Guinness Book of Fakes, Frauds & Forgeries*, Enfield: Guinness Publishing, 1991. Howard Markel, 'The Billy Goat War, Morris Fishbein and the AMA's Crusade Against America's Consummate Quack, John Brinkley', *The Journal of the American Medical Association*, vol. 299, no. 18 (14 May 2008), pp. 2217–19.

JOHN ADAM, THE MODEL HOSTAGE

'So-called U.S. hostage appears to be toy', CNN, 1 February 2005, 12 January 2008; webpage no longer accessible. '"Captured GI" A Real Doll, Photo Of "Hostage" U.S. Soldier Appears To Be Toy Action Figure', *CBS News*, 2 February 2005, www.cbsnews.com/stories/2005/02/01/iraq/main670972.shtml,12 January 2008.

JOHN OLSEN, FORGETFUL FORGER

John Olsen, authentic work by Chloe Adams, 'Sellers deny "fake" claims', *Herald Sun*, 26 November 2002.

JOYCE HATTO, ARGUABLY THE WORLD'S GREATEST PIANIST

Jeremy Nicholas, 'Obituary – Joyce Hatto, Brilliant pianist whose career was cut short by cancer which struck in the 1970s', *The Guardian*, 10 July 2006. David Weininger, 'Alleged Hatto plagiarism shakes music world', *The Boston Globe*, 23 February 2007. Lee Glendinning, 'Husband doctored virtuoso's work to save her legacy', *The Guardian*, 27 February 2007. Geoff Edgers, 'Cherished music wasn't hers, Husband admits to doctoring CDs', *The Boston Globe*, 27 February 2007. Mark Lawson, 'Our ears may deceive us, Revelations that a feted pianist's recordings were heavily doctored should spur us to listen carefully', *The Guardian*, 2 March 2007.

KOUADIO KOUASSI AND HIS HOTEL BARS

Russ Buettner, 'Authorities Say Scheme to Steal Hotel Was Foiled', *The New York Times*, 30 December 2006. 'Man Pleads Guilty in SoHo Hotel Plot', *The New York Times*, 18 November 2007.

THE LAND-GRAB *DONATION* OF EMPEROR CONSTANTINE

J.A. Farrer, *Literary Forgeries*, New York: Longmans, Green, and Co., 1907. Valla, Lorenzo and Christopher B. Coleman (trans.), *Discourse on the Forgery of the Alleged Donation of Constantine, In Latin and English*, New Haven, CT: Yale University Press, 1922.

LAURA ALBERT AND HER MANY IDENTITIES

JT LeRoy (pseudonym of Laura Albert), *Sarah*, New York: Bloomsbury, 2001. Stephen Beachy, 'Who is the Real JT LeRoy?', *New York Magazine*, 10 October 2005. Warren St. John, 'TheUnmasking of JT Leroy: In Public, He's a She', *The New York Times*, 9 January 2006. Warren St. John, 'Figure in JT Leroy Case Says Partner Is Culprit', *The New York Times*, 7 February 2006. Alan Feuer, 'Going to Court Over Fiction by a Fictitious Writer', *The New York Times*, 15 June 2007. Alan Feuer, 'In Writer's Trial, Testimony of Life as Strange as Fiction', *The New York Times*, 16 June 2007. John Marshall Mantel, 'Writer Testifies About Source of Nom de Plume', *The New York Times*, 20 June 2007. Alan Feuer, 'Jury Finds "JT LeRoy" Was Fraud', *The New York Times*, 23 June 2007. Alan Feuer, 'Judge Orders Author to Pay Film Company $350,000 in Legal Fees', *The New York Times*, 1 August 2007.

LAUREL ROSE WILLSON, VICTIM OF EVERYTHING

Bob Passantino, Gretchen Passantino and Jon Trott, 'Satan's Sideshow: The True Lauren Stratford Story', *Cornerstone*, vol. 18, no. 90 (1990), pp. 23–8. Bob Passantino, Gretchen Passantino and Jon Trott, 'Lauren Stratford: From Satanic Ritual Abuse to Jewish Holocaust Survivor', *Cornerstone*, vol. 28, no. 117 (1999), pp. 12–16, 18. Stefan Maechler, 'Wilkomirski the Victim: Individual Remembering as Social Interaction and Public Event', *History & Memory*, vol. 13, no. 2 (autumn–winter 2002), pp. 59–95.

LAWSONOMY: A ZIG-ZAG THEORY OF LIFE, THE UNIVERSE AND EVERYTHING

Alfred William Lawson, *Born Again, A Novel*, New York/Philadelphia: Wox, Conrad company, 1904. 'Lawson Liner Off Today', *The New York Times*, 19 September 1919. 'Lawson's Giant Plane Crashes to Earth As It "Takes Off" for Its Maiden Voyage', *The New York Times*, 9 May 1921. Lawson, Alfred William, *Lawsonomy Volume One*, Detroit: Humanity publishing company, [n.d., probably 1935]. 'Education: Zigzag & Swirl', *Time*, 24 March 1952. Grant, John, *Discarded Science*, Wisley: FF&F, 2006.

LEE ISRAEL AND HER BUSY OLD TYPEWRITERS

'Screw Our Principles – We're Totally Reading Lee Israel's Book', *New York Magazine*, 24 July 2008. Julie Bosman, 'She Says It's True, Her Memoir of Forging', *The New York Times*, 24 July 2008. Thomas Mallon, 'Forging On', *The New York Times*, 3 August 2008.

LIFE AT THE FINAL CHECK-OUT DESK

'Women try to take body on plane', BBC *News*, 6 April 2010, www.news.bbc.co.uk/go/pr/fr/-/2/hi/uk-news/england/8604663.stm, 6 April 2010. James Meilke, 'Two women arrested after attempt to smuggle body onto plane', *The Guardian*, 6 April 2010. John Fahey, 'Women arrested "trying to smuggle dead relative out of UK"', *The Independent*, 6 April 2010.

THE LOST STONE AGE TRIBE IN THE PHILIPPINES

Jamie James Monday, 'The Tribe Out of Time', *Time*, 19 May 2003. Tim Radford, 'Too good to be true', *The Guardian*, 13 November 2003.

LOTT'S FALSE RESEARCH AND HIS SHADY STUDENT

Richard Morin, 'Scholar Invents Fan To Answer His Critics', *The Washington Post*, 1 February 2003. Donald Kennedy, 'Editorial: Research Fraud and Public Policy', *Science*, vol. 300, no. 5618 (18 April 2003), p. 393.

LOURDES' APPARITIONS AND MIRACLE CURES

Cherry Duyns (director, composition and narration), *Het genadeoord*, VPRO, 1977. Michael P. Carroll, 'The Virgin Mary at LaSalette and Lourdes: Whom Did the Children See?', *Journal for the Scientific Study of Religion*, vol. 24, no. 1 (March 1985), pp. 56–74. Herman Beukers, 'Lourdes', *Skepter*, vol. 12, no. 3 (September 1999), pp. 27–30. Benedict de Spinoza, *Theological-Political Treatise* (Jonathan Israel (ed.), Jonathan Israel and Michael Silverthorne (trans.)), Cambridge: Cambridge University Press, 2007. Timothy McGrew, 'Miracles', *Stanford Encyclopedia of Philosophy*, 2010, http://plato.stanford.edu/entries/miracles/, 17 December 2010. *Lourdes-france.org*, http://fr.lourdes-france.org/, 17 December 2010.

MARTIN LUTHER, EARTHLING

John Grant, *Discarded Science*, Wisley: FF&F, 2006.

MARY TOFT, A REAL BUNNY GIRL

S. A. Seligman, 'Mary Toft – The Rabbit Breeder', *Medical History*, vol. 5, no. 4 (October 1961), pp. 349–60. Jan Bondeson, *A Cabinet of Medical Curiosities*, London/New York: I.B. Tauris Publishers, 1997. Emma Donoghue, *The Woman Who Gave Birth to Rabbits*, London: Virago Press, 2002. Philip K. Wilson, 'Toft , Mary (*b.* 1703, *d.* 1763)', *Oxford Dictionary of National Biography*, Oxford University Press, 2004, www.oxforddnb.com/view/article/27494, 17 August 2008.

MELVIN EARL DUMMAR'S ROADSIDE BUM

David Margolick, 'Show Them the Money', *The New York Times*, 5 October 1997. Barlett, Donald L. and James B. Steele, *Howard Hughes, His Life & Madness*, London: André Deutsch, 2003. 'Utah: Suit Over Howard Hughes's Will Dismissed', *The New York Times*, 10 January 2007. 'Melvin and Howard', *The Internet Movie Database*, www.imdb.com/title/tt0081150, 18 March 2010.

MEMORANDUM 46

Zbigniew Brezinski, National Security Council Memorandum-46, 17 March 1978. Casey Lartigue Jr., Eliot Morgan, 'Talk Radio Can't Handle the Truth', *The Washington Post*, 5 August 2007.

MENDEL'S PERFECT PEAS

Víteslav Orel, *Gregor Mendel, The First Geneticist*, Oxford: Oxford University Press, 1996. [anon.], 'Peas on Earth', *Hort Science*, vol. 7 (1972), p. 5.

MESMER'S ANIMAL MAGNETISM

Roy Porter, '"Under the Influence": Mesmerism in England', *History Today*, vol. 35, no. 9 (September 1985), pp. 22–9. B.R. Hergenhahn, *An Introduction to the History of Psychology*, Belmont: Wadsworth Publishing, 1986. Michael Shermer, 'Mesmerized by Magnetism', *Scientific American*, vol. 287, no. 5 (November 2002), p. 41.

MICROPROCESSING MONEY

Robert Farish, 'Fake Microprocessors Find Home in Russia', *The Moscow Times*, 26 May 1998.

MISSING, PRESUMED TOTALLED: WILF KENDALL, AUTO PARTS DEALER

Susan Saulny, 'Relatives Recall 9/11 Victim; Prosecutors Say It's Fiction', *The New York Times*, 5 August 2003. Susan Saulny, 'Queens Man Sentenced to Prison; Claimed Fake Son Died on 9/11', *The New York Times*, 17 September 2003.

MITTERRAND'S *AFFAIRE OBSERVATOIRE*

Henry Giniger, 'Rightist Accused of Paris Bombing; Pesquet, Involved in Attack on Senator, Is Held for Assembly Explosion', *The New York Times*, 30 November 1959. Robert O. Paxton, 'The Mitterand Mystery', *The New York Times*, 28 June 1987. Ronald Tiersky, *François Mitterand: A Very French President*, Lanham: Rowman & Littlefield Publishers, 2003.

MORMON SMITH FINDS PLATES – GOES WEST – GETS ALL SHOT UP

[anon. (Smith, Joseph)], *The Book of Mormon*, Utah: The Church of Jesus Christ of Latter-day Saints, 1976. Richard L. Bushman, 'Smith, Joseph', *American National Biography Online*, February 2000, www.anb.org/articles/08/08-01413.html, 12 December 2009. Timothy Garton Ash, 'Could you vote for a man who abides by Moronish wisdom?', *The Guardian*, 27 December 2007. Dan Waddell, 'Chasing the dead: genealogy and the art of recruitment', *The Independent*, 24 August 2009. Reed Cowan and Steven Greenstreet (director and composition), *8: The Mormon Proposition*, David v. Goliath Films, 2010.

MOTHER'S BOY

'U.S. man "posed as his dead mother"', BBC *News*, 17 June 2009, www.news.bbc.co.uk/2/hi/americas/8106010.stm, 23 June 2009. Kristen Hamill, 'Prosecutors: Man impersonated dead mother, collected benefits', CNN, 18 June 2009, 23 June

2009. Sophie Tedmanson, 'Man "dressed as his dead mother" in bizarre plot for money', *The Times*, 18 June 2009.

NEW SIGNINGS – A SPORTS ROUNDUP

Robert McG. Thomas Jr., 'Sports Business', *The New York Times*, 24 April 1991. Jim Byers, 'Something phony is going on: Nostalgia is big business, but so too are forgeries and fakes', *The Toronto Star*, 29 March 1992. 'Many baseball collectibles are fakes, expert warns', *The Toronto Star*, 14 April 1997. David Greenberg, 'Pair Accused of Selling Fake Sports Memorabilia', *The Daily News* (Los Angeles), 25 June 1999. Yeoh En-Lai, 'Fakes hit sporting legends', *The Straits Times* (Singapore), 1 January 2002. Russell Gould, 'Former stars in black market', *Sunday Herald Sun*, 16 February 2003. Eric Fisher, 'One of these Wayne Gretzky autographs is authentic. The other is a fraud. Can you tell?', *The Washington Times*, 11 September 2003. 'By George, that Best signature is a fake', *The Express*, 18 November 2004. Rich Freedman, 'Benician writes story of forged autographs', *Vallejo Times Herald*, 29 September 2006.

NOT-SO-CLEVER HANS: KARL KRALL'S UNDER-PERFORMING HORSES

'Can Horses Think? Learned Commission Says "Perhaps"', *The New York Times*, 31 August 1913. 'Krall, Karl', *Deutsche Biographische Enzyklopädie*, München/Leipzig: K. G. Saur, 1995–2003. Bondeson, Jan, *The Feejee Mermaid and Other Essays in Natural and Onnatural History*, Ithaca, etc.: Cornell University Press, 1999. Robert Todd Carroll, 'Clever Hans phenomenon', *The Skeptic's Dictionary*, www.skepdic.com/cleverhans.html, 1 November 2009.

NOTHING'S SO NICE AS BASMATI RICE

Johannes van Dam, 'Bezwendeld', *Elsevier*, vol. 64, no. 9 (4 March 2008).

OMAR KHAN, THE STRAIGHT-A STUDENT WHO WORKED NIGHTS

Superior Court of California, County of Orange, Harbor Justice Center, Newport Beach Facility, *The People of the State of California* vs. *Omar Shahid Khan/Tanvir Singh*, no. 08hf1157, 17 June 2008. Chris Ayres, 'Schoolboy hacker Omar Khan who upped his grades faces 38 years in jail', *The Times*, 19 June 2008. Rebecca Cathcart, 'Hacking Case Jolts Affluent California High School', *The New York Times*, 24 June 2008. Tori Richards, 'Overachiever Gets Jail for Stealing Tests, Hacking Faculty's Computers', *Aol-News*, 22 March 2011, www.aolnews.com/2011/03/22/overachiever-omar-shaid-khan-gets-jailfor-stealing-tests-hacki, 18 April 2011.

OMID AMIDI-MAZAHERI, THE DEMON DENTIST

Sam Lister, 'Fake dentist jailed as life of luxury is opened wide', *The Times*, 4 March 2005. '600 patients of bogus dentist at risk of hiv and hepatitis', *The Guardian*, 16 September 2005. 'Mogjan Azari struck off', *British Dental Journal*, vol. 200, no. 3 (11 February 2006), p. 128.

007 IMPERSONATOR MICHAEL NEWITT

James Sturcke, 'James Bond fantasist jailed', *The Guardian*, 31 October 2008. Nico Hines, 'Two years in jail for fantasy James Bond', *The Times*, 31 October 2008. 'Fantasist fooled police into believing he was spy', *The Times*, 1 November 2008.

OPERATION ANDREAS: THE BIG MONEY GAMBLE

Adolf Burger, *The Devil's Workshop*, London: Frontline Books, 2009.

PERCIVAL LOWELL'S LIFE ON MARS

Percival Lowell, *Mars as the Abode of Life*, New York: The MacMillan Company, 1908. Lowell, Percival, *Mars and Its Canals*, New York/London: The MacMillan Company/MacMillan and Co. Ltd., 1911. Norriss S. Hetherington, 'Lowell, Percival', *American National Biography Online*, February 2000, www.anb.org/articles/13/13-01024.html, 6 November 2009. Kevein Zahnle, 'Decline and fall of the Martian empire', *Nature*, vol. 412, no. 6843 (12 July 2001), pp. 209–13. Gil Clark, 'Percival Lowell (book)', *Astronomy*, vol. 30, no. 3 (March 2002), p. 88. Robert Crossley, 'Percival Lowell and the History of Mars', *Massachusetts Review*, vol. 41, no. 3 (September 2000), pp. 297–318. 'Dolfijnen fluiten namen, Pluto is planeet af', *NRC Handelsblad*, 30 December 2006. 'Dwergplaneet heet voortaan "plutoïde"', *NRC Handelsblad*, 12 June 2008.

THE PERILS OF COOKING UP STORIES

Transcript of *BBC Newsnight*, item: 'The bogus SAS man', BBC, 14 November 2001, www.news.bbc.co.uk/2/hi/events/newsnight/1660604.stm, 9 December 2009. Toby Young, 'Who dares fibs...', *The Independent*, 18 November 2001. Audrey Gillan, 'The fantasy life and lonely death of the SAS veteran who never was', *The Guardian*, 24 January 2009.

PERU'S FAT GANGSTERS

Guy Adams, 'Peru's "human fat killers" were invented to cover up deaths', *The Independent*, 3 December 2009.

PETER CHAPPELL, THE HARMONIC HOMEOPATH

Ben Goldacre, 'Aids quackery in Africa, and nearer home', *The Guardian*, 1 December 2007. Website van Peter Chappel, www.healingdownloads.com, 18 August 2008, 25 May 2009.

PHILOSOPHY AND ETHICS REVISITED

Albin Eser, 'Misrepresentation of Data and Other Misconduct in Science, The German View and Experience', in: Cheney (ed.), Darwin, *Ethical issues in research*, Frederick, Md: Univ. Publ. Group, 1993. 'Ströker, Elisabeth', *Deutsche Biographische Enzyklopedie*, K.G. Saur Verlag, München – Leipzig, http://gso.gbv.de/db=2.176/SET=1/ttl=2/lng=du/shw?frst=2, 7 February 2008.

THE PILTDOWN TURKEY

Xing Xu, Zhonghe Zhou, Xiaolin Wang, 'The smallest known non-avian theropod dinosaur', *Nature*, vol. 408, no. 6813 (7 December 2000), pp. 705–08. Timothy Rowe, Richard A. Ketcham, Cambria Denison, *et al.*, 'The Archaeoraptor forgery',

Nature, vol. 410, no. 6828 (29 March 2001), pp. 539–40. *Horizon*, episode 'The Dinosaur That Fooled the World', BBC, broadcast on 21 February 2002. Zhonghe Zhou, Julia A. Clarke, Fucheng Zhang, 'Archaeoraptor's better half', *Nature*, vol. 420, no. 6913 (21 November 2002), p. 285. Ian Sample, 'Unearthed: the murky world of fossil collecting', *The Guardian*, 22 May 2009.

PINKHAM'S PANACEA

Sarah Stage, 'Pinkham, Lydia Estes', *American National Biography Online*, February 2000, www.anb.org/articles/12/12-00725.html, 11 February 2010. C.N.M. Renckens, 'Alternative treatments in reproductive medicine: much ado about nothing', *Human Reproduction*, vol. 17, no. 3 (1 March 2002), pp. 528–33.

POLES APART: HOW TO REACH AN INCREASINGLY ICY RELATIONSHIP

'Peary Found No Trace of Cook at Pole: Members of Crew Surprised When Informed of the Former's Claim', *The New York Times*, 8 September 1909. 'Washington Awaits Proofs: Peary's Message Strengthens Doubt of Cook's Story, Though', *The New York Times*, 9 September 1909. 'Peary Sends Report to the Government: Notifies State and Navy Department That Polar Territory Belongs to Us', *The New York Times*, 12 September 1909. 'Armstrong Pictures Cook as Romancer: He Didn't Get Half Way Up Mt. McKinley, Says Another Member of the Party', *The New York Times*, 15 October 1909. 'Naval Committee Examines Peary: Explorer Tells About North Pole Dash and Submits His Original Diary', *The New York Times*, 8 January 1911. Stafford, Marie Peary, 'Marie Peary Stafford's Journal, Voyage on the schooner "Morrissey" in June through September 1932 to Cape York on the West Coast of Greenland', www.ernestina.org/history/MPStafford_Greenland-1932.html, 6 June 2009. John Noble Wilford, 'Doubts Cast on Peary's Claim to Pole', *The New York Times*, 22 August 1988. John Noble Wilford, 'Peary Notes Said to Imply He Failed to Reach Pole', *The New York Times*, 13 October 1988. Warren E. Leary, 'Peary Made It to the Pole After All, Study Concludes', *The New York Times*, 12 December 1989. Russell W. Gibbons, 'Time Doesn't Improve Peary's North Pole Claim', *The New York Times*, 13 January 1990. Warren E. Leary, 'Who Reached the North Pole First? A Researcher Lays Claim to Solving the Mystery', *The New York Times*, 17 February 1997. Rik Nijland, 'Strijd om Noordpool werd strijd tussen vrienden', *de Volkskrant*, 6 April 2009.

PROFESSOR BEHE ON INTELLIGENT DESIGN

John E. Jones III, *In the United States District Court for the Middle District of Pennsylvania, Tammy Kitzmiller, et al., v. Dover Area School District, et al.*, case number 04cv2688, memorandum opinion, 20 December 2005. John Grant, *Discarded Science*, Wisley: FF&F, 2006. Sean B. Carrol, 'God as Genetic Engineer', *Science*, vol. 316, no. 5830 (8 June 2007), pp. 1427-8. Kenneth R. Miller, 'Falling over the edge', *Nature*, vol. 447, no. 7148 (28 June 2007), pp. 1055–6. Richard Dawkins, 'Inferior Design', *The New York Times*, 1 July 2007. '*Department Position on Evolution and "Intelligent Design"*', Bethlehem: Department of Biological Sciences, [n.d.], www.lehigh.edu/~inbios/news/evolution.htm, 28 July 2009.

PROJECT JENNIFER'S MURKY DEPTHS

Seymour Hersch, 'CIA Salvage Ship Brought Up Part of Soviet Sub Lost 1968, Failed to Raise Atom Missiles; Hughes Built Ship', *The New York Times*, 19 March 1975. 'The Great Submarine Snatch', *Time*, 31 March 1975. 'Behind the Great Submarine Snatch', *Time*, 6 December 1976. Michael G. Collins, 'The Salvage of Sunken Military Vessels. Project Jennifer: A Dangerous Precedent?', *Journal of Maritime Law and Commerce*, vol. 8 (1976–1977), pp. 433–54. Michael Drosnin, *Citizen Hughes*, London: Arrow Books Limited, 1986.

PROTOCOLS OF THE ELDERS OF ZION

Bernstein, Herman, *The History of a Lie*, New York: Ogilvie Publishing Company, 1921. Graves, Philip, *The Truth About the 'Protocols', A Literary Forgery: Taken from The Times of August 16, 17, and 18, 1921*, London: The Times Publishing Company, 1921. Marc Levin (director and composition), *Protocols of Zion*, HBO/Cinemax Documentary, 2005. Edward Rothstein, 'The Anti-Semitic Hoax That Refuses to Die', *The New York Times*, 21 April 2006. NB. The *Protocols*, with comments and related documents, can be accessed at www.ddickerson.igc.org/protocols.html.

THE PUB CURE FOR CANCER

Inspectieonderzoek naar aanleiding van klachten over de handelwijze van de orthomoleculair therapeute and de arts in het Integraal Medisch Centrum Maria Magdalena te Roosendaal,' Hertogenbosch: Inspectie voor de Gezondheidszorg, December 2007. Margreet Vermeulen, 'Kosmische energie "slaat kanker dood"', *de Volkskrant*, 21 December 2007. Noël van Bemmel, '"Internist" misleidde ernstig zieken', *de Volkskrant*, 10 January 2008. 'Geschorste artsen behandelen nog patiënten', *de Volkskrant*, 21 January 2008. 'Therapeute geroyeerd om "goddelijke genezingen"', *Trouw*, 25 March 2008.

PYRAMID SMYTH INCHES HIS WAY OUT OF THE ROYAL SOCIETY

Smyth, F.R.S.E., F.R.A.S., Piazzi, *Our Inheritance in the Great Pyramid*, London: W. Isbister & Co., 1874. Cornelis de Jager, 'Velosofie: Rekenen aan de Grote Piramide en m'n fiets', *Skepter*, vol. 3, no. 4 (December 1990), pp. 13–15. Hermann A. Brück, 'Smyth, Charles Piazzi (1819–1900)', *Oxford Dictionary of National Biography*, Oxford University Press, 2004, www.oxforddnb.com/view/article/25948, 11 December 2009.

QUESTIONABLE QUIZZING IN THE 1950S

Val Adams, '"Twenty-One" Quiz Dropped by N.B.C.; TV Show Under Scrutiny of Grand Jury Here Will Be Replaced by Sponsor', *The New York Times*, 17 October 1958. Charles Van Doren, 'All The Answers', *The New Yorker*, 28 July 2008. 'Quiz Show', *The Internet Movie Database*, www.imdb.com/title/tt0110932, 24 December 2009.

REJECTION, A TALE

Joseph Hixon, *The Patchwork Mouse*, New York: Anchor Press/Doubleday, 1976.

RELICS

Rev. E. Cobham Brewer, LL.D., *A Dictionary of Miracles*, London: Chatto & Windus, 1901. Joe Nickell, *Inquest on the Shroud of Turin*, New York: Prometheus Books, 1983. David Hugh Farmer, *The Oxford Dictionary of Saints*, Oxford: Oxford University Press, 2004. Anique C. de Kruijf, 'Terug van weggeweest: De thuiskomst van Utrechtse relieken na de Reformatie', in: Eerden, Ria van der, Roman Koot, Huib Leeuwenberg, *et al.* (ed.), *Jaarboek Oud-Utrecht 2009*, Utrecht: Vereniging Oud-Utrecht, 2009.

RENÉ-PROSPER BLONDLOT'S RADIATION WAVES

R. W. Wood, 'The n-Rays', *Nature*, vol. 70, no. 1822 (29 September 1904), pp. 530–31. Irving Langmuir, Robert N. Hall, 'Pathological Science', *Physics Today*, vol. 41, no. 10 (October 1989), pp. 36–48. Collins, Paul, *Banvard's Folly, Thirteen Tales of Renowned Obscurity, Famous Anonimity, and Rotten Luck*, New York: Picador, 2001.

RENIER CHALON AND THE FORTSAS RARE BOOKS AUCTION

Walter Klinefelter, *The Fortsas Bibliohoax, With a Reprint of The Fortsas Catalogue and Bibliographical Notes and Comment by Weber Devore*, Newark: The Carteret Book Club, 1941.

RICHARD MEINERTZHAGEN: SHAM ORNITHOLOGIST AND MAYBE MURDERER

Michael Lipske, 'Detective Rasmussen gets her owl', *International Wildlife*, vol. 29, no. 6 (November-December 1999), pp. 30–33. Rex Dalton, 'Ornithologists stunned by bird collector's deceit', *Nature*, vol. 437, no. 7057 (15 September 2005), pp. 302–03. John Seabrook, 'Ruffled Feathers', *The New Yorker*, 29 May 2006. 'Col. Richard Henry Meinertzhagen CBE DSO (I12767)', *W. H. Auden – 'Family Ghosts'*, www.auden.stanford.edu/cgi-bin/auden/individual.php?pid=I12767&ged=auden-bicknell.ged, 27 November 2010.

ROMANOVS

James Blair Lovell, *Anastasia: The Lost Princess*, New York: St. Martin's Press, 1995. Kathryn Hughes, 'Lost duchess', *The Guardian*, 10 March 2007. Fred Attewill, 'Remains of tsar's heir may have been found', *The Guardian*, 24 August 2007. Luke Harding, 'Bones found by Russian builder finally solve riddle of the missing Romanovs', *The Guardian*, 25 August 2007.

ROSEMARY BROWN, THE COMPOSERS' COMPOSER

Douglas Martin, 'Rosemary Brown, a Friend of Dead Composers, Dies at 85', *The New York Times*, 2 December 2001. Ian Parrott, 'Rosemary Brown, Musical medium claiming extrasensory contact with dead composers', *The Guardian*, 11 December 2001.

ROYAL PRETENDER, KARL WILHELM NAUNDORFF

Madol, Hans Roger, *The Shadow King*, London: George Allen & Unwin Ltd., 1930. Francq, H.G., *Louis XVII, The unsolved mystery*, Leiden: E. J. Brill,

1970. Daalen, A.P.A. van, *Het mysterie Lodewijk XVII, Koningszoon zonder troon, 1785– 1985*, Delft: Gemeentelijke Archiefdienst, 1985. Petrie, J.H., *Lodewijk xvii ~ Naundorff, Een mysterie ontrafeld*, Amsterdam: De Bataafsche Leeuw, 1995.

THE SAD TALE OF KATE HUME'S DECEIT

'The Dumfries Atrocity Hoax', *The Times*, 29 December 1914. 'The Atrocity Hoax', *The Times*, 30 December 1914.

THE SCIENTIFIC SHAMBLES OF COLD NUCLEAR FUSION

Robert Pool, 'Fusion Followup: Confusion Abounds', *Science*, vol. 244, no. 4900 (7 April 1989), pp. 27–9. Robert Pool, 'Skepticism Grows Over Cold Fusion', *Science*, vol. 244, no. 4902 (21 April 1989), pp. 284–5. William J. Broad, 'Brilliance and Recklessness Seen in Fusion Collaboration', *The New York Times*, 9 May 1989. Robert Pool, 'Cold Fusion: Bait and Switch?', *Science*, vol. 244, no. 4906 (19 May 1989), p. 774. Robert Pool, 'Cold Fusion: End of Act I, *Science*, vol. 244, no. 4908 (2 June 1989), pp. 1039–40. Robert Pool, 'Only the Grin Remains', *Science*, vol. 250, no. 4982 (9 November 1990), pp. 754–5. 'Here we go again', *The Economist*, vol. 362, no. 8263 (9 March 2002), p. 77. Ian Sample, 'Cold fusion raises its head above the parapet again', *The Guardian*, 23 March 2009.

SEEING DOUBLE IN THE AUCTION HOUSES

'NY dealer accused of art scam', *The Guardian*, 12 March 2004. 'Forged Gauguin exposes artful dodger', *The Guardian*, 15 December 2004.

SEX IN SPACE: THE EMISSION LOG

Robert A. Freitas Jr., 'Sex in Space', *Sexology Today*, no. 48 (April 1983), pp. 58–64. 'Sex In Space; Do You Want Your Tax Dollars To Support This?', *Miami Herald*, 9 July 1985. William J. Broad, 'Recipe for Love: A Boy, a Girl, A Spacecraft', *The New York Times*, 11 February 1992. James Oberg, 'Space sex hoax rises again', persbericht United Press International, 23 February 2000. Jon Henley, 'Astronauts test sex in space – but did the earth move?', *The Guardian*, 24 February 2000.

SEX TIP NO. 1: BE YOURSELF

Tomer Zarchin, 'Arab man who posed as Jew to seduce woman convicted of rape', *Haaretz*, 20 July 2010. 'An Arab man who had consensual sex with a Jewish woman in Israel has been convicted of rape in a "sex through fraud" case and sentenced to 18 months in jail', persbericht Reuters, 21 July 2010.

SHINICHI FUJIMURA BURIES THE PAST

Susie Boniface, 'Archaeologist digs himself into a hole', *The Guardian*, 6 November 2000. 'Newspaper unearths archaeologist's fake find', *The Guardian*, 6 November 2000. Kristin M. Romey, '"God's Hands" Did the Devil's Work', *Archaeology*, vol. 54, no. 1 (January–February 2001), p. 16. 'Hoax Update', *Archaeology*, vol. 55, no. 1 (January–February 2002), p. 9.

SHOOTING A SELFIE GUATEMALA STYLE

Jonathan Franklin, 'The truth about Guatemala's YouTube murder', *The Guardian*, 13 January 2010. Ezra Frieser, 'The Guatemalan Who Ordered His Own Murder', *Time*, 14 January 2010.

SINGING ALONG WITH MILLI VANILLI

'Milli Vanilli Didn't Sing Its Pop Hits', *The New York Times*, 16 November 1990. Jon Pareles, 'Wages of Silence: Milli Vanilli Loses A Grammy Award', *The New York Times*, 20 November 1990. 'Milli Vanilli Explains Its Lip-Synching', *The New York Times*, 21 November 1990. 'Judge Rejects Milli Vanilli Refund Plan', *The New York Times*, 13 August 1991. 'Small Victory for Milli Vanilli Fans', *The New York Times*, 31 August 1991. Pierre Perrone, 'Obituary: Rob Pilatus', *The Independent*, 7 April 1998. Ed Pilkington, 'Hollywood pays lip service to Milli Vanilli', *The Guardian*, 15 February 2007. Andrew Gumbel, 'Milli Vanilli: the movie – a sorry tale of music, manipulation and miming', *The Independent*, 16 February 2007.

SIR ISAAC NEWTON'S FRAUDULENT REPORT

Richard S. Westfall, 'Newton and the Fudge Factor', *Science*, vol. 179, no. 4075 (23 February 1973), pp. 751–8. Broad, William and Nicholas Wade, *Betrayers of the Truth: Fraud and Deceit in the Halls of Science*, New York: Simon & Schuster, 1982. *The Story of Science*, episode 'What is out there?', BBC, broadcast on 27 April 2010.

SOUTH AFRICAN SALAD COMBATS THE AIDS CRISIS

Ben Goldacre, 'The health minister, the African potato and a state in denial over AIDS', *The Guardian*, 26 August 2006. Ben Goldacre, 'AIDS quackery in Africa, and nearer home', *The Guardian*, 1 December 2007. 'Verantwoordelijk voor aidssterfte, Manto Tshabalala-Msimang (1940–2009), minister van Volksgezondheid', *NRC Handelsblad*, 17 December 2009. Peter Vermaas, 'Aidsremmers nekken uitvaartbranche', *NRC Handelsblad*, 24 November 2010.

STIRRING UP THE SCIENCE WARS

Alan D. Sokal, 'Transgressing the Boundaries: Towards a Transformative Hermeneutics of Quantum Gravity', *Social Text*, no. 46–7 (1996), pp. 217–52. Harald Merkelbach, 'Een postbode wordt psychiater', *Skepter*, vol. 17, no. 3 (autumn 2004), pp. 8–12.

TIP-TOP GUNS

Oscar Garschagen, 'Chinese piloten hebben "valse cv's"', *NRC Handelsblad*, 7 September 2010.'Pilots' fake records confirmed', *China Daily*, 9 September 2010.

THE TOXIC SAUSAGES OF FRÉDÉRIC PAGÈS

Doreen Carvajal, 'Philosopher Left to Muse on Ridicule Over a Hoax', *The New York Times*, 9 February 2010. John Crace, 'The greatest literary hoax ever?', *The Guardian*, 10 February 2010. 'Bernard-Henri Lévy: filosoof die niet bestaat, heeft toch Kant ontmaskerd', *NRC Handelsblad*, 10 February 2010.

'UNDER THY SHADOW BY THE PIERS I WAITED . . .': SELLING BROOKLYN BRIDGE

'Forger Gets Life Term', *The New York Times*, 18 December 1928. Gabriel Cohen, 'For You, Half Price', *The New York Times*, 27 November 2005.

THE UNIQUE KÜFFNER–DÜRER DOUBLE PORTRAIT

Frank Arnau, *3,000 years of deception in art and antiques*, London: Jonathan Cape, 1961. Dolnick, Edward, *The Forger's Spell: A True Story of Vermeer, Nazis, and the Greatest Art Hoax of the Twentieth Century*, New York: Harper, 2008.

THE U.S. JUDGES WHO LOCKED UP KIDS FOR CASH

Ian Urbina and Sean D. Hamill, 'Judges Plead Guilty in Scheme to Jail Youths for Profit', *The New York Times*, 12 February 2009. Ed Pilkington, 'Jailed for a MySpace parody, the student who exposed America's cash for kids scandal', *The Guardian*, 7 March 2009. Edwin M. Kosik, *In the United States District Court for the Middle District of Pennsylvania, United States of America v. Michael T. Conahan and Mark A. Ciavarella, JR., Memorandum and Order*, No. 3:-09-cr-28, 31 July 2000. Ian Urbina, '2 Ex-Judges May Be Tried in Sentencing of Juveniles', *The New York Times*, 24 August 2009. 'Pennsylvania: Former Judge Sentenced In Bribery Tied to Juvenile Court', *The New York Times*, 11 August 2011.

THE UNMISTAKEABLE ADOLF HILTER DIARIES, IN 60 OR 61 VOLUMES

William A. Henry, Gary Lee and Melissa Ludtke, 'Hitler's Diaries: Real or Fake?', *Time*, 9 May 1983. Anthony Lewis, 'Abroad at Home; Anything for a Story', *The New York Times*, 12 May 1983. Ed Magnuson, 'Hitler's Forged Diaries', *Time*, 16 May 1983. William Drozdiak, 'Dealer Confesses Forgery: Reporter in Hitler Hoax Arrested', *The Washington Post*, 28 May 1983. 'Forgeries may be valuable/ The "Hitler diaries"', *The Guardian*, 11 October 1984. Hannah Cleaver, 'Hitler diary forger turns his skills to old masters', *Sunday Express*, 30 April 2000. Michael Leidig, 'Hoax Hitler diaries sold for £4,000', *The Guardian*, 23 April 2004. James Fenton, 'Review: Things that have interested me: James Fenton on the art of forgery – and getting away with it', *The Guardian*, 24 November 2007. Allan Hall, 'Living in poverty, the man who "found" Hitler's diaries', *The Independent*, 24 April 2008. Brian MacArthur, 'Hitler diaries scandal: "We'd printed the scoop of the century, then it turned to dust"', *The Telegraph*, 24 April 2008. Robert Harris, *Selling Hitler: The Story of the Hitler Diaries*, London: Faber & Faber, 1986.

A VERY UNSAFE PRODUCTS TESTER: IBT LABS

William Broad and Nicholas Wade, *Betrayers of the Truth: Fraud and Deceit in the Halls of Science*, New York: Simon & Schuster, 1982. 'Federal Court Finds IBT Officials Guilty of Fraud', *Science*, vol. 222, no. 4623 (4 November 1983), p. 488.

VICTOR LUSTIG AND HIS STOOPID SHERIFF

'Pair Held in Paris Claim Link With Capone; "Who's Who" of Chicago Gangland Omits Them', *The New York Times*, 6 July 1929. 'Count Seized Here With Bogus

$51,000; Arrest of Suave Jail-Breaker, Shadowed for Seven Months, Leads to Subway Cache', *The New York Times*, 14 May 1935. '"Count" Lustig is Seized in Pittsburgh', *The New York Times*, 29 September 1935. 'Lustig Back, Gets a Cell in Tombs; "Count", Who Escaped From Federal Detention House, Is Held in $100,000 Bail', *The New York Times*, 1 October 1935. '"Count" Lustig Reveals Escape Technique, But Conceals How He Got Wire Nippers', *The New York Times*, 2 October 1935. 'Lustig Pleads Guilty As a Counterfeiter; Interrupts Trial as Former Aide Testifies – Federal Judge to Impose Sentence Today', *The New York Times*, 6 December 1935. 'Lustig Sentenced to 20-Year Term; Counterfeiter's Escape From Jail Here Adds 5 Years to 15-Year Penalty', *The New York Times*, 10 December 1935. 'Lustig, "Con Man," Dead Since 1947; Brother of "Count," Notorious Counterfeiter, Tells of Death in Jail That Went Unnoticed', *The New York Times*, 31 August 1949. Johnson, James F. and Floyd Miller, *The Man Who Sold The Eiffel Tower*, New York: Doubleday, 1961.

WERNER PURGATHOFER'S PROMISING LECTURES

Werner Purgathofer, Eduard Groeller and Martin Feda, 'Warning: Beware of VIDEA!', 23 March 1995, www.cg.tuwien.ac.at/~wp/videa-paper.html, 4 August 2009. Werner Purgathofer, email to the author, 13 April 2011.

WHAT HARRY POTTER DID NEXT

'Bootlegging Clinton in China', *The International Herald Tribune*, 25 October 2004. Howard W. French, 'An economic revival minted in counterfeit; Letter from China', *The International Herald Tribune*, 4 August 2007.

WHEN HEMINGWAY SHOT HIMSELF – IN THE FOOT

'Mr. Hemingway Writes Some High-Spirited Nonsense', *The New York Times*, 13 June 1926. Richard B. Hovey, 'The Torrents of Spring: Prefigurations in the Early Hemingway', *College English*, vol. 26, no. 6 (March 1965), pp. 460–4. Robert E. Burkhart, 'The Composition of The Torrents of Spring', *The Hemingway Review*, vol. 7 (autumn 1987) p. 64. Hemingway, Ernest, *The Torrents of Spring*, New York: Scribner, 1998. Charles Robert Baker 'Hemingway, Ernest', in: Jay Parini (ed.), *The Oxford Encyclopedia of American Literature*, The Oxford University Press, 2004/2005, www.oxford-americanliterature.com/entry?entry=t197.e0117, 6 January 2010.

WHY A LETTER SANK THE LABOUR PARTY

Richard Norton-Taylor, 'Zinovjev letter was dirty trick by MI6', *The Guardian*, 4 February 1999. Robin Cook, 'The hidden hand', *The Guardian*, 4 February 1999. Gavin Cordon, 'Documents reveal the MI6 cover-up in Zinovjev affair', *The Independent*, 23 June 2000. Francis Elliott, 'The truth about Churchill's spy chief and the Zinovjev Letter', *The Independent*, 8 October 2006.

WILLIAM LAUDER'S DIATRIBE AGAINST *PARADISE LOST*

J. A. Farrer, *Literary Forgeries*, New York: Longmans, Green, and Co., 1907. Paul Baines, 'Lauder, William (*c.* 1710–*c.* 1771)', *Oxford Dictionary of National Biography*, Oxford University Press, 2004, www.oxforddnb.com/view/article/16121, 27 January 2008.

THE WINNING SLIPS OF A WOULD-BE JUDGE

Robert W. O'Brien and Peter Baker, 'A Stuffed Ballot Box in Fairfax: Lawyer Won Bar Vote, Lost Bid for Judgeship', *The Washington Post*, 6 March 1996.

WRITING A WINNER FOR PUBLISHAMERICA

Steven Zeitchik, 'Authors Allege Publisher Deception', *Publishers Weekly*, vol. 251, no. 47 (22 November 2004), p. 13. *Tea, Travis, Atlanta Nights*, [n.p.], [no publisher], 2004, www.sff.net/people/rothman/atlantanights.htp, 19 December 2004. Scott Martelle, 'Please publish this dud', *Los Angeles Times*, 5 February 2005. Natalie Koch, email to the author, 20 December 2009.

YAHYA JAMMEH'S MEDICAL AIDS

Ben Goldacre, 'AIDS quackery in Africa, and nearer home', *The Guardian*, 1 December 2007.

ZIMBABWE'S MAGIC FUEL

Lebo Nkatazo, 'Mugabe: "Diesel mystic's beauty blinded ministers"', *New Zimbabwe*, 17 November 2007. 'Diesel N'anga fails to appear in court', *The ZimDaily*, 10 July 2009. 'Zimbabwaanse "tovenares" beduvelde Mugabe', *de Volkskrant*, 28 July 2009. 'Diesel n'anga Rotina Mavhunga sent to jail', *The Herald*, 29 September 2010.

PHOTO ACKNOWLEDGEMNTS

The publishers wish to express their thanks to the below sources of illustrative material and /or permission to reproduce it.

Dullhunk: p. 215; © Manuel González Olaechea y Franco: p. 133; Library of Congress, Washington, DC: pp. 32, 49, 69, 103, 106, 127, 137, 149, 163, 185; MWAK: p. 43; National Archives, Washington, DC: p. 174; Peary-Macmillan Arctic Museum, Bowdain College, Brunswick, Maine: p. 173; Quistnix: p. 99; Shutterstock: pp. 146 (pogonici), 191 (suronin), 217 (360b); Victoria and Albert Museum, London: p. 52.

INDEX